The Cleansing
of the Heart

The Cleansing of the Heart

The Sacraments as Instrumental Causes
in the Thomistic Tradition

REGINALD M. LYNCH, OP

The Catholic University of America Press
Washington, D.C.

Design and typesetting by Kachergis Book Design

Cataloging-in-Publication Data available
from the Library of Congress
ISBN 978-0-8132-2944-7

For my father

God's own descent
Into flesh was meant
As a demonstration
That the supreme merit
Lay in risking spirit
In substantiation.

—Robert Frost,
Kitty Hawk

Contents

Acknowledgements

This book originated in 2012 as my Licentiate thesis at the Dominican House of Studies in Washington, D.C. Thanks are due to the Pontifical Faculty, the library staff, and the Dominican community at the House of Studies for the support they offered me during this time. I am grateful to Thomas Joseph White, OP, for directing this project in its initial phase and for the guidance he offered during subsequent years as I continued to work toward its completion. I am also indebted to Andrew Hofer, OP, Cajetan Cuddy, OP, Romanus Cessario, OP, and Archbishop Augustine DiNoia, OP, each of whom assisted and encouraged me in innumerable ways during the completion of this book.

I am thankful for the support of the Friars, staff, and parishioners of St. Patrick Church in Columbus, Ohio. During my assignment there, 2012–2015, I was able to build substantially on the work done for my original thesis to create the book as it now stands. I am also grateful to the faculty and students of the Pontifical College Josephinum where I taught, 2014–15, and in a particular way to Peter Veracka and the Josephinum library staff, who aided my research during the final stage of this project.

I have benefited a great deal from the comments and suggestions of Matthew Gaetano, Sr. Mary Dominic, OP, Jörgen Vijgen, and an anonymous reviewer at the Catholic University of America Press, who read drafts of this book at various stages. Their insights have greatly improved this book, and any faults remaining are certainly of my own design.

Parts of chapters 1, 3, and 4 have appeared in articles or rely in part on previously published material. I am grateful to the editors of *Nova et Vetera, The Thomist,* and *Angelicum* for permission to republish revised portions of the following works: "The Sacraments as Causes of Sanctification," *Nova et Vetera* (English) 12, no. 3 (2014): 791–836; "Cajetan's Harp: Sacraments and the Life of Grace in Light of Perfective Instrumentality," *The Thomist* 78, no. 1 (2014): 65–106; "Domingo Bañez on Moral and Physical Causality: Christic Merit and Sacramental Realism," *Angelicum* 91 no. 1 (2014): 105–26. Most of all, I am exceedingly grateful to my parents, Daniel and Ellen, and to Dan and Maureen for their unfailing support.

Abbreviations

———— : ————

Jo. Ev. Tr.	*In Johannis evangelium tractatus*
Leonine ed.	*Opera Omnia iussu impensaque Leonis XIII P.M. edita.*
LG	*Lumen Gentium*
LS	*A New Latin Dictionary*
LSJ	*A Greek-English Lexicon*
LThK²	*Lexikon für Theologie und Kirche,* 2nd edition
LThK³	*Lexikon für Theologie und Kirche,* 3rd edition
NABRE	*The New American Bible, Revised Edition*
NCE¹	*New Catholic Encyclopedia,* 1st edition
NCE²	*New Catholic Encyclopedia,* 2nd edition
ODCC	*Oxford Dictionary of the Christian Church,* 3rd ed., revised
Op. Ox.	*Opus Oxoniense*
PA	*De Partibus Animalium*
PL	*Patrologia Latina*
Quodlib.	*Quaestiones Disputatae et Quaestiones Duodecim Quodlibetales*
Relect. de Sacram.	*Relectio de Sacramentis*
RSV	*The New Oxford Annotated Bible, Revised Standard Version*
SC	*Sources chrétiennes*
Sent.	*Sententiae in IV libris distinctae*
ST	*Summa Theologiae*
Summa Sent.	*Summa Sententiarum*
Summa Theol. (Halensis)	*Summa Theologica*
Super Ioan.	*Super Evangelium s. Ioannis lectura*
Super Sent.	*Scriptum Super Libros Sententiarum*
Wadding	*Opera Omnia (1639)*

The Cleansing of the Heart

Introduction

In Christian usage, the concept of "sacrament" came to signify a wide array of theological ideas early in the Church's history, being applied broadly to define essential traits of the Church, both ritually and doctrinally.[1] More than a reference to individual sacraments, "sacramentality" says something essential about the Christian mystery and speaks subsequently of particular ritual acts in light of this. To the degree that we are tempted to reduce the concept of sacramentality, the Second Vatican Council teaches that the Church herself is the "visible sacrament" of the unity offered to all through the sacrifice of Christ.[2] In this, Vatican II refocuses the paradigm for the theological use of the term within the patristic tradition, such that the theological naming of the ritual dimension of the Church's life links the concept of sacramentality intrinsically not only to who the Church is but what she does.[3] As the title indicates, this book is concerned with "the cleansing of the heart"[4]—a phrase borrowed from St. Augustine that describes the effects that natural elements (such as water) have on the human person when taken up by the Church as sacramental signs.

1. See Johann Auer, *A General Doctrine of the Sacraments and the Mystery of the Eucharist*, vol. 6 of *Dogmatic Theology*, ed. Johann Auer and Joseph Ratzinger (Washington, D.C.: The Catholic University of America Press), 10–11.

2. Vatican Council II, *Lumen Gentium* (LG). *November 21, 1964.* 9. All in-text English translations of Vatican II taken from Austin Flannery, ed., *Vatican Council II: The Conciliar and Post Conciliar Documents*, vol. 1, new rev. ed. (New York: Costello, 1998).

3. *Lumen Gentium* traces the concept of the Church herself as sacrament to Cyprian. Norman Tanner, ed., *Decrees of the Ecumenical Councils* (Washington, D.C.: Georgetown University Press, 1990), 2:856n1.

4. *Jo. Ev. Tr.* 80.3.

Because the Church exists for a purpose, the efficacy of the sacra-ments has been important to the Church since the beginning of her history. Because the Church is sacrament, her purpose is sacramen-tal, and those theological and ritual realities that we label sacraments must serve this ecclesial reality in order to retain their name. Sacra-mental efficacy, therefore, is in one sense a question of terminolog-ical authenticity. To say that a given theological or ritual reality is a sacrament is to say that it is intrinsically ordered to the essence and purpose of the Church's life. Because of the ecclesial nature of this question, it essentially concerns theology itself prior to hermeneuti-cal questions of method, theological school, or personal interest. For this reason the question of what the sacraments effect and how they effect it has emerged in a variety of different contexts throughout the Church's history, driven not only by pastoral or formational concerns but by the contemplative curiosity of theology itself.

This book is concerned with sacramental causality as a theologi-cal question—a terminological formulation of this same fundamen-tal question that first emerged explicitly in the early scholastic peri-od and became an essential point of theological reflection and debate for the following centuries for thinkers from across the tradition. The purpose of this volume is to explore the meaning and broader theo-logical significance of sacramental causality from a Thomistic per-spective, situating Aquinas' approach to this essential question both historically and doctrinally. For Aquinas, theology understood as *sa-cra doctrina* is essentially one science; therefore, although subjects can be studied individually, positive statements about a single sub-ject cannot be made without implicitly invoking the broader whole. Although the focus of this project will remain within sacramental theology, the broader theological connections between sacramental causality and other theological subjects will be examined. In this re-gard, we will focus in particular on the implications of a Thomistic approach to sacramental causality for other theological topics such as Christology, merit, and grace. In all this, the final aim of this book is to show both the perennial importance of sacramental causality and the contribution made by both Aquinas and the Thomistic tradition to this important theological topic.

As will be shown, Aquinas' approach to sacramental causality is notable for its use of the doctrine of instrumental causality to describe the causal link between sacramental efficacy and the instrumentality of the Incarnation itself. Christ's humanity is understood as an instrument of his divinity and the sacraments by extension as instruments of Christ that effect the purpose of his coming in the flesh in each believer who becomes a member of Christ's body, the Church. From this perspective, it is essential that the sacraments be understood not only as signs or symbols but as causes of their effects.

Vatican II implicitly calls attention to the question of sacramental efficacy by expressing its ecclesial approach to sacramentality within a similar conceptual framework. Borrowing a Thomistic phrase, Vatican II teaches that as sacrament, the Church is not only a sign of the union but an instrument of our communion with God.[5] For Vatican II the efficacious instrumentality of the Church as sacrament is incarnational: just as Christ's human nature is united to the Word and functions as an instrument at its service, so too the visible structure of the Church serves "the Spirit of Christ who vivifies it, in the building up of the body."[6] Further, Vatican II teaches that individual sacraments such as Baptism are ways in which the faithful are united to the mystery of Christ's life; in the ritual of Baptism itself this union with the death and resurrection of Christ is not only symbolized but effected.[7] Like Aquinas, Vatican II sees the efficacy of the sacraments as an extension of the instrumentality of the Incarnation. For Aquinas, the interconnected nature of *sacra doctrina* enables a nuanced consideration of the sacraments within the full theological significance of sacramentality—not as isolated causes but as Christological and ecclesial instruments. Vatican II situates this efficacious dimension of the Christian sacraments scripturally by quoting St. Paul: "For we were buried with Him by means of Baptism into His death; and if we have been united with Him in the likeness of His death we shall be

---

5. *LG* 1. In all cases cited here, the term "instrument" corresponds to the Latin *instrumentum* in the official text of the Council. As will be shown, *Lumen Gentium*'s use of "instrumentality" in the context of the sacraments not only serves as a reference to Aquinas but to many patristic authors as well.

6. *LG* 8.

7. "Quo sacro rito consociatio cum morte et resurectione Christi repraesentatur et *efficitur*." *LG* 7 (emphasis mine).

so in the likeness of His resurrection also."[8] For Vatican II, the union effected by Baptism is understood in light of Paul's theology of sonship; relying on Romans, *Lumen Gentium* describes this as a conformity of the person to the image of Christ.[9] The New Law's capacity to effect this conformity is the fulfillment of what is promised and foreshadowed in the Old.[10] This fulfillment comes with the assumption of flesh by the Son of God, who calls all persons to become members of his body.[11] Baptism is both symbolic and efficacious because of the incarnational nature of the New Law itself.

Many theologians throughout the Church's tradition have understood the efficacious quality of the New Law in sacramental terms. During the scholastic period, the distinction between the Old Law and the New was used to frame the question of sacramental efficacy. Like *Lumen Gentium*, scholastics found their source for this in a biblical understanding of the New Law, drawing heavily on Pauline texts and other New Testament sources to discuss the efficacious dimension of the New Law and its sacraments. Peter Lombard begins Book Four of the *Sentences* by asking about the nature of the distinction between the Old Law and the New.[12] Relying on Hebrews, Lombard argues that while the sacrifices of the Old Law are clearly signs, those of the New are sacraments in the full sense of the term because they have the power not only to signify justification but to cause it.[13] Because of Lombard's influence, this biblical approach to sacramental efficacy became normative during the scholastic period.

Aquinas follows this model, insisting that the sacraments of the New Law are more than simple external signs because of the nature

8. *LG* 7. Here Vatican II is quoting 1 Cor 12:13 and Rom 6:3–5.

9. *LG* 2. See Rom 8:29.

10. *LG* 2.

11. *LG* 2, 3, 7. Here *Lumen Gentium* relies on a wide array of texts such as Jn 19:34; Eph 1:4–5, 10; Col 1:15; 1 Cor 5:7, 5:17, 10:17, 12:13, and 12:27; Gal 6:15; Rom 12:5, and many others.

12. Peter Lombard, IV *Sent.* d. 1, c.1.2. As in *Sententiae in IV libris distinctae*, 3rd ed. 4 vols. (Rome: ad Claras Aquas, 1971–81).

13. IV *Sent.* d. 1, c. 4.2–4. See Heb 9:13–14: "For if the blood of goats and bulls and the sprinkling of a heifer's ashes can sanctify those who are defiled so that their flesh is cleansed, how much more will the blood of Christ, who through the eternal spirit offered himself unblemished to God, cleanse our consciences from dead works to worship the living God."

of the New Law.[14] Because this New Law differs qualitatively from the Old, it is not sufficient to think of the Church as a mere catechist, handing on the apostolic tradition through speech and writing alone. Unlike the Old Law, which only instructs, the New Law both instructs and justifies. Its teaching, therefore, has an effect. While the sacraments of the Old Law were only instructive signs, those of the New Law are both signs and causes of grace.[15] For St. Paul, the teaching of the New Law has an effect on the heart. In the context of the Gospel, words and texts are placed at the service of the living Word, and the one who receives this Word becomes himself a living letter, expressing the same Word to others.[16] This Word of the New Law is not exhausted by the symbolism of the external letter; it is life-giving in faith because it has an effect on the heart. It teaches not only through the communication of ideas and concepts but through effecting a living transformation. This living faith, however, cannot be fully understood without reference to sacramental mediation. For Aquinas and many other scholastics, the New Law differed from the Old precisely in its ability to cause this change, cleansing the heart through efficacious signs. As Paul tells us in Romans, "We were indeed buried with him through Baptism into death, so that, just as Christ was raised from the dead by the glory of the Father, we too might live in newness of life."[17] When introducing his own theory of sacramental efficacy, Aquinas cites Galatians explicitly, showing that for St. Paul Baptism was not only a sign but had the effect

14. *ST* III^a Q. 62 a. 1 co. All textual references to Aquinas' *Summa* will be taken from Thomae de Aquino, Sancti, *Summa Theologiae*, Editiones Paulinae (Torino: Comerciale Edizioni Paoline s.r.l., 1988), 2172.

15. *De veritate* Q. 27, a. 4, co.

16. "You are our letter, written on our hearts, known and read by all, shown to be a letter of Christ administered by us, written not in ink but by the Spirit of the living God, not on tablets of stone but on tablets that are hearts of flesh." 2 Cor. 3:2-3. Unless otherwise indicated, scriptural references will be taken from the New American Bible, Revised Edition (NABRE).

17. "Or are you unaware that we who were baptized into Christ Jesus were baptized into his death? We were indeed buried with him through baptism into death, so that, just as Christ was raised from the dead by the glory of the Father, we too might live in newness of life. For if we have grown into union with him through a death like his, we shall also be united with him in the resurrection. We know that our old self was crucified with him, so that our sinful body might be done away with, that we might no longer be in slavery to sin." Rom 6:3 –6.

of clothing the one baptized in Christ.[18] Baptism as a sacrament is an extension of the sacramentality of the New Law itself, where signs and words are never symbols alone but have the transformative power of Christ's Word dwelling within them as a kind of living *doctrina*.

For Aquinas, theology is an exploration of something perennial and alive, received through the mediation of the Church's life. Although he acknowledges that the language of causality may be viewed as a theological development in the historical sense, Aquinas argues that it should be understood as an expression of St. Paul's doctrine of the New Law of grace.[19] Defining the enterprise of theology as a kind of *sacra doctrina* not only means that different disciplines within theology are interconnected; they share a common apostolic point of origin. Understood in this sense, development within the theological tradition can never mean the addition of something foreign or new but comes rather as a deeper understanding of something that is at once both new and old: the living faith of the Apostles. For Lombard, Aquinas, and the Fathers of the Second Vatican Council, the newness of this apostolic teaching has proven to be a perennially fruitful source for both theological reflection and apostolic teaching on the nature and purpose of the Church's sacramental life.

This book will begin with a general historical introduction, followed by a detailed exposition of the development of Aquinas' approach to sacramental causality from his *Sentences* commentary to the *Summa theologiae*, concluding with a detailed study of moral causality, the most influential alternative to Aquinas in the period after the Council of Trent. Chapter 1 traces the history of sacramental causality as a theological topic, beginning with the influence of Augustine on the early scholastic period. Beginning with Lombard, special attention is paid in this chapter to the development of sacramental causality as a question among scholastics. Within the scholastic movement, contrasting approaches to sacramental causality emerged gradually, eventually developing into dramatically different theological perspectives. Although an in-depth textual consideration of Aquinas' posi-

---

18. "Manifestum est enim quod per sacramenta novae legis homo Christo incorporatur: sicut de baptismo dicit Apostolus, *Galat.* 3, [27]: *Quotquot in Christo baptizati estis, Christum induistis.*" *ST* III^a Q. 62 a. 1, co.

19. *Super Sent.* lib. IV dist. 1 q. 1 a. 4, qc. 1, co.

tion will wait until subsequent chapters, this first chapter will situate Aquinas' approach to the question of sacramental causality historically and give broad consideration to the reception of Aquinas' thought and to alternatives from within the Franciscan school and other early modern thinkers such as Melchior Cano. This chapter also considers the implications of the Council of Trent and engages contemporary discussions within sacramental theology. The following chapters, particularly the textual studies of Aquinas contained in chapters 2 and 3, depend on this first chapter for their historical context.

Chapter 2 begins our direct engagement with the texts of Aquinas by studying Aquinas' first description of the sacraments as causes in his *Commentary on the Sentences*. Aquinas' later approach to sacramental causality in the *Summa* is more advanced not only because his approach to instrumental causality in relation to supernatural ends is better developed but because sacramental causality is more closely integrated with other theological topics such as grace and Christology. However, many important elements of this final synthesis can be seen already in Aquinas' *Sentences* commentary, and this fact has not always been given sufficient attention. Of particular interest here is the broader metaphysical framework for instrumental causality that already exists in the *Sentences*, as well as the nascent steps already taken here by Aquinas to associate sacramental causality with Christological instrumentality.

The third chapter deals with the development of Aquinas' approach to sacramental causality after his *Sentences* commentary was written, focusing in particular on the deeper integration that progressively emerges between grace, sacramentality, merit, and Christology. Aquinas' development on the subject of sacramental causality was first noticed by commentators within the Thomistic tradition. It is hermeneutically important, therefore, to approach this textual development in dialogue with the evolving conversation among commentators from within the Thomistic tradition, whose work on this subject represents an important body of secondary literature. Our aim in this chapter is to study not only the nature of Aquinas' theory of sacramental causality but the systematic integration of this topic with other elements of Aquinas' thought, such as grace, the instrumentality of the hypostatic union, and the merits of Christ and of the just. Conceptual tools from within the Thomistic commentatorial tradition can provide insight for the study of the text itself in both respects. The multigenerational engagement of these commentators with the work of Aquinas has often yielded a reading that is at once especially precise in the textual sense and uniquely sensitive to the wider sapiential unity of Aquinas' project. By engaging with the text of Aquinas in conversation with classical Thomistic commentators and relevant contemporary scholarship, this study will approach the Thomistic tradition as a living reality whose insights enrich our present conversations and enable an increasing penetration of the meaning of the text itself.

The fourth chapter addresses developments within the modern period outside of the Thomistic school. In particular, this chapter will deal directly with the most popular alternative to Aquinas' theory of instrumental causality during the post-Tridentine period: Melchior Cano's theory of moral causality. This chapter establishes the historical context for Cano's theological hermeneutic in Renaissance humanism and critically examines the implications of this theory from a Thomistic perspective. Although no longer a household term, moral causality enjoyed a certain longevity in some theological environments from Trent until the twentieth century. Aquinas' approach to sacramental causality is intrinsically related to his approach to other theological topics. Similarly, it will be shown that a deep sympathy exists between moral causality and non-Thomistic approaches to topics such as merit and grace. The first chapter already provides a general overview of contrasting approaches to sacramental causality, all of which are worthy of independent study.[20]

Melchior Cano, however, is uniquely important for understanding sacramental theology in the modern period. Although Cano's moral causality no longer enjoys the popularity it once did, a study of this theory is valuable not only because it illumines a particular theory of sacramental causality but because it shows the way in which this approach to sacramental efficacy came to be integrated into broader

20. A study of Scotus on this subject would be of great intellectual interest and would function as an important historical study of pre-Tridentine sacramental theology. In this regard, Ueli Zahnd's work is worthy of mention: *Wirksame Zeichen?* Spätmittelalter, Humanismus, Reformation 80 (Tübingen: Mohr Siebeck, 2014), 167–91.

approaches to the sacraments and to theology itself after the Renaissance. Further, it shows the way in which larger intellectual trends shaped the way in which sacramental efficacy—and related theological issues such as merit—came to be presented in an environment that had grown increasingly deaf to core metaphysical insights of the Christian tradition. Although theological method has continued to evolve from the time of Cano, many of his ideas have had an enduring effect on theology even to the present day, and understanding Cano's approach to sacramental efficacy within the wider historical and methodological context of his work can illumine the challenges of addressing the issue of sacramental causality in a modern theological hermeneutic.

1

Historical Considerations

As a result of its enduring theological significance, the question of sacramental efficacy has arisen in diverse theological contexts in many periods of Church history. Because the Thomistic approach to this question is the focus of this book, this chapter will situate the medieval treatment of the sacraments specifically as causes of grace within the Augustinian and Victorine traditions and will explore the development and subsequent reception of this question in the early modern period. Finally, we will examine the question of sacramental causality in the twentieth century where a renewed emphasis on liturgical action and experience placed the efficacy of the sacraments in new context.

THE VICTORINE SCHOOL

Beginning in the early Middle Ages, theories concerning the causality of the sacraments were frequently proposed as interpretations of Augustine's sacramental doctrine. Although speculative models varied, ranging from various Neoplatonisms to the Aristotelianism of the emerging Dominican school, Augustine's influence remained a constant in this area until the twentieth century.[1] On this issue, the

---

1. Almost all Western theologians, including those of the Protestant tradition, have been concerned to show some form of continuity between their own thought and that

theological landscape of the Middle Ages was not defined by a split between Augustinianism and scholasticism; rather, one of the issues that drove the debates over sacramental efficacy in the emerging scholastic tradition was the proper interpretation of the Augustinian heritage. How were theologians to understand, defend, and preserve the teachings of Augustine in the context of fresh challenges?

During the Donatist controversy, Augustine produced a series of distinctions that would prove indispensable for sacramental theology. Perhaps most importantly, Augustine drew a clear distinction between a sacrament and its fruit: while Baptism itself cannot be repeated, the fruition or grace of the sacrament can be lost and subsequently regained.[2] Although Augustine's teaching on this subject is conditioned by the apologetic concerns of a particular period, the distinctions made by Augustine during the Donatist controversy were employed in a variety of subsequent historical periods although the terminology and surrounding theological context shifted perceptibly.

Much of the Augustinian doctrine inherited in the early scholastic period was strongly influenced by the Berengarian controversy, which significantly affected the interpretation of Augustine on the sacraments in subsequent theology.[3] As an outgrowth of this con-

---

of Augustine where the sacraments are concerned. It seems that this did not change until the midpoint of the twentieth century. (Thinkers of this period such as Rahner, Schillebeeckx, and Chauvet show decidedly less concern for the legacy of Augustine's sacramental doctrine). Augustine's doctrines concerning sign and sacramental reality are complex and have been subject to much scholarly debate. We have no intention of resolving these issues here. In the following pages, selections of Augustine's teaching that are of particular relevance to sacramental causality will be offered as a lens through which the debates and theories of scholastic and subsequent thinkers can be understood; an independent investigation of Augustinian doctrine must necessarily elude us here.

2. See *De Baptismo*, CSEL 51, 3.16.21.

3. Elizabeth Frances Rogers, *Peter Lombard and the Sacramental System* (New York: Columbia University, 1917), 30–38. Although Berengar's teaching on the Eucharist was condemned, many of his textual selections and interpretations from Augustine paradoxically came to be normative for later theology. The threefold division between *res tantum*, *res et sacramentum*, and *sacramentum tantum* was gradually developed in response to this problem. Nicholas M. Haring has convincingly argued that the word *sacramentum*—a polyvalent term for Augustine—underwent a transformation during the Berengarian controversy that gave rise to the later medieval understanding of *sacramentum* as outward sign alone. See Haring, "Berengar's Definitions of *Sacramentum* and Their Influence on Mediaeval Sacramentology," *Mediaeval Studies* 10 (1948): 109–47; Haring, "A

flict, Augustine's distinction between sacramental elements and interior grace was gradually transformed into the scholastic formula: *res tantum, res et sacramentum,* and *sacramentum tantum.*[4] However, Augustine's central distinction between the sacramental sign or event

---

Brief Historical Comment on St. Thomas, *Summa Theol.* III qu. 67, a. 5: *Utrum non baptizatus possit sacramentum baptismi conferre,*" *Mediaeval Studies* 14 (1952): 153–59. There are instances in which Augustine uses what appears to be the reverse of the familiar medieval formula, using the phrase *res visibiles* to refer to "things" or signs employed by the *sacramentum,* which can refer generally to the signate event and the lasting sacramental effect. See *De Baptismo* 3.10.15. CCL 3.15. However, Augustine's terminology is much broader than this. Elsewhere Augustine describes the sacraments as the visible form of invisible grace; *Epist.* 105.3.12. It seems that Berengar misappropriated the Augustinian understanding of *sacramentum* as referring only to the passing outward sign, whereas Augustine used the term to refer not only to signs but to their lasting effect as well. Lombard inherits this new post-Berengarian formulation of Augustinian sacramental doctrine. In *Sent IV,* d. 4 c. 1, Lombard teaches that infants and faithful adults receive the *sacramentum et rem,* but someone who receives the sacrament unworthily only receives the *sacramentum,* whereas an unbaptized martyr could receive the *res* alone. See Philipp W. Rosemann, *Peter Lombard* (New York: Oxford University Press, 2004), 148–49. Unfortunately, a more thorough investigation of this issue eludes us here.

4. For our purposes, this distinction between the end result of the sacraments (*res tantum*), the sacramental event (*res et sacramentum*), and the outward signs themselves (*sacramentum tantum*) is significant for sacramental causality because of the relationship that necessarily exists between the outward signs and the effects toward which they are directed. After Berengar, these Augustinian concepts are universally expressed through the lens of this new threefold distinction. For a study of the development of this terminology, see Ronald F. King, "The Origin and Evolution of a Sacramental Formula: *Sacramentum Tantum, Res et Sacramentum, Res Tantum,*" *The Thomist* 31 (1967): 21–82. The mature use of this threefold division is usually attributed to Hugh of St. Victor. In Hugh's *De Sacramentis,* a post-Berengarian understanding of Augustine's sacramental doctrine is evident in his treatment of the distinction between *res* and *sacramentum. De Sac.,* 1, 9. Text as in *Hugonis de Sancto Victore De sacramentis Christiane fidei,* in vol. 1 of Corpus Victorinum, ed. Rainer Berndt (Münster: Aschendorff, 2008), 209 ln.10–210 ln.2. See note 14 for text. This understanding was inherited from Hugh by his student Peter Lombard. "For [Hugh] the rite itself (*sacramentum tantum*) not only resembled or pointed to the inner reality (*res*) but also contained and conveyed that inner reality (*res et sacramentum*). The clarification was critical for the theology of the sacraments in general, a clarification made permanent by the increasingly widespread use of Peter's *Sentences.*" Thomas Finn, "The Sacramental World in the *Sentences* of Peter Lombard," *Theological Studies* 69 (2008): 568. Hugh of St. Cher (d. 1263), a Dominican contemporary of Aquinas, seems to have been the first to use the term *res et sacramentum* specifically to describe the conferral of the character found in Baptism, Confirmation, and Orders. Others such as Albert, Bonaventure, Alexander of Hales, and Aquinas follow this approach. See Bernard Leeming, *Principles of Sacramental Theology* (Westminster, Md.: Newman Press, 1963), 262.

and the lasting effect or fruit remained unobscured by these developments.[5]

Beyond his anti-Donatist writings, however, many other important elements of Augustinian thought came to be of central importance for subsequent discussions of sacramental cause. Although he did not speak directly of the sacraments as causes in the scholastic manner, Augustine had a strong sense of sacramental teleology; he saw sacraments as signs through which the power of God flows into the soul.[6] For Augustine, the sacraments are visible words or signs that manifest their interior reality. Because it is the power of the Word that sanctifies the soul, Augustine argues that inasmuch as this power flows through the physical things (*res*) used in the sacraments, those same things become signs of the presence of the Word.[7] Thus, Augustine taught

5. Because Augustine lacks the technical precision of later theology, at times he uses *sacramentum* to mean the lasting effect imparted by Baptism, as distinct from its fruit (baptismal grace). In this context, the word "*sacramentum*" can appear to be roughly equivalent with later notions of sacramental character. See *De Baptismo*, 1.1.2, 3.10.15, 3.14.19, 3.16.21, 4.25.32. At other times he uses *sacramentum* to refer to the baptismal formula of the rite, where the *verba Evangelics* impart the power and holiness of Christ to the recipient regardless of the holiness of the minister or the worthiness of the recipient. See *De Baptismo*, 3.10.15, 3.15.20, 3.14.19, 4.25.32. (This use of *sacramentum* in connection with outward rite is distinct from the use of *res visibiles* to indicate transient material signs. Lacking the threefold precision of later theology, it can be seen here that Augustine is forced to use the same term (*sacramentum*) for what we might now call the form of the sacrament (the *verba Evangelics* spoken by the minister) and the lasting effect or character (as distinct from grace). Both the conferral of the lasting effect and the spoken formula comprise an essential part of what is now spoken of as the *res et sacramentum*, that is, the reality and the sign or sacramental act taken as a whole. Taken in the broad sense, the medieval categories of *res et sacramentum*, *res tantum*, and *sacramentum tantum* appear not as a betrayal of Augustinianism but as a refusal of the Berengarian interpretation thereof.

6. Although the degree to which the concept of instrumentality is present in Augustine's thought is disputable, his emphasis on the finality of the sacraments is clear. Concerning the sacraments as signs, see Emmanuel J. Cutrone, "Sacraments," in Allan D. Fitzgerald, ed., *Augustine through the Ages* (Grand Rapids, Mich.: Eerdmans, 1999), 741–43. Concerning the efficacy of sacramental signs, Cutrone states, "Augustine insists sacraments have a power which remains even after the ritual has been performed. The use of material things, elevated to the level of sacrament, has the ability to work spiritual realities. But that efficacy is not something in the material things but flows from the very nature of the sacrament as a visible word. The sacrament only has an efficacy because it is Christ's word, the word of faith that is preached ... when such a sacrament functions within a believing Church, the power of the sacrament is always effective." Ibid., 745.

7. "*Iam uos mundi estis propter uerbum quod locutus sum uobis*. Quare non ait, mun-

that grace moved through outward signs, even the sacramental actions of an unworthy minister, as light through an unclean place or water through an aqueduct.[8] Augustine is ambiguous, however, concerning the causal status of these signs taken in themselves. Is it possible to attribute some power to the sacramental elements themselves, as instruments of God?[9]

Hugh of St. Victor (d. 1141) began a final synthesis of Augustinian sacramental doctrine that would become normative for many scholastic authors.[10] Hugh was very much animated by the Augustinian

---

di estis propter baptismum quo loti estis, sed ait : *propter uerbum quod locutus sum uobis, nisi quia et in aqua uerbum mundat? Detrahe uerbum, et quid est aqua nisi aqua?* Accedit uerbum ad elementum, et fit Sacramentum, etiam ipsum tamquam uisibile uerbum ... Vnde ista tanta uirtus aquae, ut corpus tangat et cor abluat, nisi faciente uerbo, non quia dicitur, sed quia creditur? Nam et in ipso uerbo, aliud est sonus transiens, aliud uirtus manens. *Hoc est uerbum fidei quod praedicamus, ait Apostolus, quia si confessus fueris in ore tuo quia Dominus est Iesus, et credideris in corde tuo quia Deus illum suscitauit a mortuis, saluus eris. Corde enim creditur ad iustitiam, ore autem confessio fit ad salutem.* Vnde in Actibus Apostolorum legitur: *Fide mundans corda eorum ...* quo sine dubio ut mundare possit, consecratur et baptismus. Christus quippe nobiscum uitis, cum Patre agricola, *dilexit ecclesiam, et seipsum tradidit pro ea.* Lege apostolum, et uide quid adiungat : *Ut eam sanctificaret, inquit, mundans eam lauacro aquae in uerbo.* Mundatio igitur nequaquam fluxo et labili tribueretur elemento, nisi adderetur : *in uerbo ...* quamuis nondum ualentem corde credere ad iustitiam, et ore confiteri ad salutem. Totum hoc fit per uerbum, de quo Dominus ait : *Iam uos mundi estis propter uerbum quod locutus sum uobis.*" *Jo. Ev. Tr.* 80.3. CCL 36.529. See also Contra Faust. 19.16. CSEL 25.512–13.

8. "qui uero fuerit superbus minister, cum zabulo computatur; sed non contaminatur donum Christi, quod per illum fluit purum, quod per illum transit liquidum uenit ad fertilem terram. puta quia ipse lapideus est, quia ex aqua fructum ferre non potest; et per lapideum canalem transit aqua, transit aqua ad areolas; in canali lapideo nihil generat, sed tamen hortis plurimum fructum affert. spiritalis enim uirtus sacramenti ita est ut lux: et ab illuminandis pura excipitur, et si per immundos transeat, non inquinatur." *Jo. Ev. Tr.* 5.15 CCL 36: 50. The example of light passing through an unclean place can also be found in *De Baptismo,* 3.10.15. William Harmless, "Baptism," in Fitzgerald, *Augustine through the Ages,* 88.

9. This issue will come to divide the Franciscan and Dominican schools on this subject for centuries. Philip Cary's recent interpretation is more compatible with the extrinsic legalism of Scotus and the nominalists than with the Thomist tradition. See Philip Cary, *Outward Signs: The Powerlessness of External Things in Augustine's Thought* (New York: Oxford University Press, 2008).

10. Rogers, *Peter Lombard and the Sacramental System,* 52. The Victorine School, established in Paris in 1108, was of a decidedly Augustinian turn. Hugh's principal work, *De Sacramentis* (with which we are primarily concerned here), "presents a synthesis of theology in the framework of an Augustinian vision of history as an account of the two works of God: the *opus conditionis* (creation) and the *opus restaurationis* (salvation). At

worldview and was in large part responsible for recalling the intellectual culture of twelfth-century Paris to the methodological perspective of Augustine's *De Doctrina Christiana*.[11] Hugh's *De Sacramentis*[12] follows the lines of creation and re-creation in a manner similar in structure to Augustine's *De Doctrina* and *De Civitate Dei*.[13] Throughout his work, Hugh employs a broad sense of sacramentality that reflects the influence of Augustine's *doctrina signorum*, in which the senses associated with the manifestation of the incarnate Word under the mode of the biblical letter are seen as a model for that same Word at work in the rites of the Church under the veil of sacred signs.[14]

some points he does draw expressly on texts from *De Trinitate, Contra Adimantum, De Bono conjugali*, and *Enchiridion*; for his eschatology (2.16–17) on *De civitate Dei* 20–22." Karlfried Froehlich, "Victorines," in Fitzgerald, *Augustine through the Ages*, 868.

11. Beryl Smalley, *The Study of the Bible in the Middle Ages*, 3rd ed. (Notre Dame, Ind.: University of Notre Dame Press, 1978), 83–106. For the structural influence of Augustine's *De Doctrina* on Hugh of St. Victor, see Ibid., 86.

12. Hugh is best known for his work *De Sacramentis*, which covers not only the sacraments but also offers a comprehensive theological worldview beginning with creation. See Boyd Taylor Coolman, *The Theology of Hugh of St. Victor: An Interpretation* (New York: Cambridge University Press, 2010). For a study of the textual history of this and other works by Hugh, see Roger Barron, "Hughes de Saint-Victor: Contribution à un Nouvel Examen de son Oeuvre," *Traditio* 15 (1959): 223–97.

13. Smalley, *Study of the Bible in the Middle Ages*, 90.

14. Although ostensibly a work dealing with biblical interpretation and the nature of Christian doctrine, Augustine's *De Doctrina* roots the signate dimension of reality in creation and the Incarnation. In a visceral sense, the created world is composed of material signs that draw us to God. The scriptural Word is understood in light of this, and in book three Augustine contextualizes the Christian sacraments in this way as well. *De Doct.*, CSEL 80, 3.9.13. When Hugh treats the sacraments explicitly, his use of the biblical letter as a means to understand sacramental signs mirrors Augustine in this regard. "Qvid sit sacramentum breui doctores descriptione signauerunt. Sacramentum est rei sacre signum. Quemadmodum enim in homine duo sunt corpus. & anima. & in una scriptura similiter duo. littera. & sensus. sic in omni sacramento aliud quod uisibiliter foris tractatur. & cernitur. Aliud quod inuisibiliter intus creditur & percipitur. quod foris est uisibile & materiale sacramentum est. quod intus est inuisibile. & spiritale. res siue uirtus sacramenti. Semper tamen sacramentum quod foris tractatur & sanctificatur. signum est spiritualis gratie que res sacramentum est. & inuisibiliter percipitur sed quia non omne signum sacre rei sacramentum est eiusdem conuenienter. dici potest. quoniam & litere sacrorum sensuum & forme siue picture. sacrarum rerum signa sunt quarum tamen sacramenta rationabiliter dici non possunt. icciro super memorata descriptio ad interpretationem siue expressionem uocis. magis quam ad diffinitionem referenda uidetur. Si quis autem plenius & perfectus quid sit sacramentum diffinire uoluerit. potest dicere quia sacramentum est corporale. uel materiale elementum. foris

Hugh famously taught that the sacraments were signs or instruments of sanctification, containing grace as medicine in a vial. The vial cannot heal in itself, of course, and in this sense the sacraments are simply containers. Like medicine, they have been prepared as a remedy and are meant to produce health in the one whose sickness gives occasion for the remedy's acceptance.[15] For Hugh the signate dimension of sacramentality is explicitly understood as instrumental (*id est sacrorum signa vel instrumenta*).[16] Hugh discusses causality to some extent, but seems to limit himself to what could be called formal or final causality, exploring God's reasons for instituting the sacraments.[17] For Hugh, the manner in which the sacramental instruments or signs are related to this finality is more ambiguous. Although Hugh's medical metaphor does not define sacramental causality with great precision, his description of grace's being communicated as if it were held in a physical container does have materialist overtones. For some, this could imply that the sacraments worked by a kind of material causality—as if grace were physically contained in material things such as water, bread, the sign of the cross, and similar elements.[18]

This interpretation raises a number of problems: if the grace of the *sacramentum* is contained in the sacramental elements materially, it is difficult to explain the relationship of this grace to the final recip-

---

sensibiliter propositum ex similitudine representans. & exstinctione significans. & ex sanctificatione continens aliquam inuisibilem & spiritalem gratiam." De sac. I, 9. Berndt, 209 ln.10–210 ln.2. This text shows not only similitude with Augustine's De doctrina but alludes to him directly in "*Sacramentum est rei sacre signum*," a common paraphrase of De civitate Dei: "Sacrificium ergo uisibile inuisibilis sacrificii sacramentum, id est sacrum signum est." De civ. Lib. 10.5, CCL 47.277. Lombard will use this same quote from Augustine and will develop his own definition of the sacraments that is clearly indebted to this text. See note 26.

15. "Si ergo uasa sunt spiritualis gratie sacramenta non ex suo sanabunt. quia uasa egrotum non curant. sed medicina. Non ergo ad hoc instituta sunt sacramenta. ut ex eis esset quod in eis est. sed periciam suam medicus ostenderet in illo remedium preparauit. a quo languidus occasionem morbi accepit." De sac. I, 9. Berndt, 216ln.19–23.

16. See note 17.

17. "Est igitur triplex causa hec institutionis sacramentorum omnium. humiliatio. eruditio. exercitatio hominis. Que cause si non essent. sacramenta omnio id est sacrorum signa uel instrumenta elementa per se esse non possent." De sac. I, 9. Berndt, 214 ln. 25-7. (A parallel text from the Victorine school can be found in the Summa Sententiarum 4.1, PL 176: 117).

18. Haring, "Berengar's Definitions of *Sacramentum*," 126–27.

ient thereof.[19] If grace is conceived of as a product held in a material container, it is difficult to simultaneously describe that same product as something that is effected as a final result in the recipient. Even within the Victorine school, some already began to express concerns: if the elements (or signs) as material causes (and not efficient instruments) are still to be considered the visible form of invisible grace, it would seem that water as a material element, for example, would necessarily be the form of the sacrament even prior to its use in Baptism.[20]

Although questions of causality became more refined in the early scholastic period, Augustine's teaching remained an enduring frame of reference. As speculative theology progressed, Augustine's teaching on the efficacy of the Word in relation to the waters of Baptism became an interpretive locus for sacramental causality. Although Hugh's metaphorical language would become outmoded, his definition of the sacraments in *De sacramentis* already contains allusions to an Augustinian text that would become a central point of reference for later scholastic discussion of the sacraments as causes.[21] In his tractates on John, Augustine taught that the water of Baptism, made a sacrament by the presence of the Word, not only touches the body

19. Ibid., 127. This objection is also raised by Bonaventure: *In IV Sent.* d. 1, p. 1, q. 3, contra 3.

20. This objection is raised by the author of the *Summa Sententiarum* (written between 1140 and 1146). *Summa Sent.* IV, 1; PL 176:117B. Haring, "Berengar's Definitions of *Sacramentum*," 127. The authorship of the *Summa Sententiarum* is disputed. Although it was thought for a long while to be the work of Hugh of St. Victor himself, the *Summa Sententiarum* is now commonly held to be the work of a different member of the Victorine School, composed prior to the *Sentences* of Peter Lombard. See King, "Origin and Evolution of a Sacramental Formula," 36–37. Many now attribute this work to Odo of Lucca. See Ferruccio Gastaldelli, "La 'Summa Sententiarum,' di Ottone da Lucca: Conclusione di un dibatto secolare," *Salesianum* 42 (1980): 537–46. However, U. Zahnd still lists *Summa Sententiarum* as 'Anonymous' in his list of sources. Ueli Zahnd, *Wirksame Zeichen? Sakramentenlehre und Semiotik in der Scholastik des ausgehenden Mittelalters* (Tübingen: Mohr Siebeck, 2014), 593. H. Weisweiler has also argued against an overly materialist approach to Hugh's teaching on sacramental efficacy. Heinrich Weisweiler, *Die Wirksamkeit der Sacramente nach Hugo von St. Viktor* (Freiburg: Herder, 1932), 11–22.

21. In *De sac.* I, 9, Hugh alludes to a passage from Augustine's tractates on John (*Jo. Ev. Tr.* 80.3.), at times quoting portions of it directly. See Berndt, 210 ln. 17–211 ln. 4. For the text of Augustine, see note 7.

but cleanses the heart as well: *corpus tangat et cor abluat.*[22] Because Augustine says unambiguously that the waters of Baptism cleanse the heart, it seems that something causal is being said of the water itself, albeit with obvious and necessary reference to the power and presence of the Word. The interpretation of this phrase, broadly circulated by Peter Lombard, occupied the best minds of the scholastic period.[23]

LOMBARD AND SCHOLASTIC CAUSALITY

More explicit discussion of the sacraments as causes of what they signify was introduced by Peter Lombard (d. 1160).[24] Lombard studied under Hugh of St. Victor and was strongly influenced by his sacra-

22. See note 7.

23. See Augustine's text from *Jo. Ev. Tr.* 80.3, cited in note 7. This passage, taken from an Augustinian sermon on John, was frequently cited during the medieval and scholastic period, largely owing to its use by Lombard as an explanation of the efficacy of Baptism. *Sent.* IV, dist. 3 c. 1. (However, an allusion to the same text also appears in the *Summa Sententiarum* of the Victorine School, which predates Lombard's *Sentences.* PL 176: 129c). This passage is of interest for at least two reasons. The combination between word and water, from which the mature understanding of sacramental form and matter developed, is present here. Concerning sacramental causality specifically, the concept of exterior washing and interior cleansing is of great importance. Many scholastic authors offered their theories of sacramental causality as interpretations of this passage. (For example: Bonaventure, *In IV Sent.*, d. 1, p. 1, art. unicus, q. 4; Richard of Middleton, *In IV Sent.*, d. 1, a. 4 q. 2; Aquinas, *In IV Sent.*, d. 1, q. 1, a. 4, qc. 2, s.c. 1 and d. 3, q. 1, a. 5, qc. 3, expos. and d. 18, q. 1, a. 3, qc. 1, arg. 3 and d. 26, q. 2, a. 3, ad. 1; *Summa theologiae (ST)* III, q. 38 a. 6, arg. 5 and q. 60 a. 6, co. and q. 62 a. 4, s.c.; *Quodlib.* 12 q. 10, co.; *Super Ioan.* c. 15, 1; *Super Tit.* c. 3, 1; Scotus, *Ox. In IV Sent.*, d. 1, q. 4. All textual references to Bonaventure and Scotus refer to the following editions (unless otherwise indicated): S. Bonaventurae, *Opera Omnia*, ed. A. C. Peltier (Paris: Vivés, 1866); Johannes Duns Scotus, *Opera Omnia*, Facimile reprint of Wadding (1639), ed. Georg Olms (Hildesheim: Verlagsbuchhandlung, 1968), and *Opera Omnia* (Civitas Vaticana: Typis Polyglottis Vaticanis, 1950–2013). References to Richard of Middleton are taken from Willibrord Lampen, ed., *De Causalitate Sacramentorum iuxta Scholam Franciscanam*, Florilegium Patristicum tam veteris quam medii aevi auctores complectens 26 (Bonn: Peter Hanstein, 1931). References to Lombard are taken from Magistri Petri Lombardi, *Sententiae in IV libris distinctae*, 3rd ed., 4 vols. (Rome: ad Claras Aquas, 1971–81).

24. *DTC* s.v. "Sacraments, Causalité," 577. It appears that Lombard is the first to use the word *causare* in conjunction with the sacraments. However, the notion that the sacraments convey a real effect in the recipient is clear from the Augustinian tradition. Lombard's immediate predecessors in the Victorine School maintained this as well. See the *Summa Sent.* tract. 4 c. 1, PL 176: 117.

mental doctrine.[25] Lombard argues that the sacraments should be understood as both signs and causes because they not only signify the invisible grace at work but sanctify the recipient as well.[26] For Lombard, it is the sanctifying effect of the sacraments that gives them their causal quality. He presents this causal understanding of sacramentality as an interpretation of the Augustinian doctrine of sign in which the sign conveys an imprint of what it signifies to the mind. Concerning the sacraments as signs, Lombard explicitly uses the language of causality to define the relationship between the sacraments and their sanctifying effect in the soul. Consequently, Lombard's phrase, *invisibilis gratiae forma* recalls the words of Augustine cited by Lombard earlier in his text: *Sacramentum est invisibilis gratiae visibilis forma.* This seems to make his causal articulation of sacramental instrumentality a conscious interpretation of Augustine.[27] Sign and lasting effect were properly distinguished by Augustine against the Donatists; by the thirteenth century, Lombard's *Sentences* were widely used in the schools, and his use of the word *"causare"* to describe the connection between these same sacramental signs and their effects was frequently commented upon.

Schooled by the Parisian Victorines, Peter Lombard greatly influenced the intellectual environment at Paris during the twelfth century as a professor at the university and later as bishop of the city itself. By the thirteenth century, widespread interest in Lombard's *Sentences* would coincide with another rising intellectual trend at Paris: Aristotelianism. For thirteenth-century scholastics, Lombard's language

25. Peter Lombard studied with Hugh of St. Victor, beginning while the latter was completing his *De Sacramentis christianae fidei*. See Rosemann, *Peter Lombard*, 27. At times Lombard literally transcribes selections from both Hugh's *De Sacramentis* and the *Summa Sententiarium*. Rogers, *Peter Lombard and the Sacramental System*, 66.

26. "Sacramentum enim proprie dicitur, quod ita signum est gratiae Dei et invisibilis gratiae forma, ut ipsius imaginem gerat et *causa exsistat*. Non igitur significandi tantum gratia sacramenta instituta sunt, sed et sanctificandi" (emphasis mine). Lombard, *IV Sent.* d. 1 c. 4.2. Ad Claras Aquas, vol. 2 (1981), 233.

27. Ibid. Augustine's original text can be found in *Epistola* CSEL 34, 105.3.12. See Wayne J. Hankey, "Reading Augustine through Dionysius," in *Aquinas the Augustinian*, ed. Michael Dauphinais, Barry David, and Matthew Levering (Washington, D.C.: The Catholic University of America Press, 2007), 250 n. 19, 254–55. Use of this Augustinian phrase in this context reflects in part the legacy of the Berengarian controversy. Haring, "Berengar's Definitions of *Sacramentum*," 109–16.

of sacramental causality would be necessarily entwined with the progressive reception of Aristotle's approach to causality.

With the rising influence of Aristotle in the early scholastic period, there was an impetus to describe this relationship between sacramental sign and effect using Aristotelian causal categories. Accompanying this trend was the risk of misapplication. William of Auxerre (d. 1232) is one of the first to use explicitly Aristotelian categories to explain the way in which the sacraments function as causes.[28] William took up Hugh's metaphorical description of the sacraments as containers of grace (as medicine in a vial) and made explicit Hugh's implicit materialism, arguing that the sacraments are causes in the material sense, rather than the efficient.[29] This teaching is echoed by Alexander of Hales (d. 1245) in his *Glossa* on the *Sentences*.[30]

During the thirteenth century, other traditions also developed

28. I. Rosier-Catach argues that causal language (in sacramental context) can be found in Stephen Langton, Pseudo-Peter of Poitiers, and Peter Comestor. Irène Rosier-Catach, *La Parole Efficace: Signe, Rituel, Sacré* (Paris: Éditions du seuil, 2004), 100.

29. "Ad hoc dicendum quod, cum dicitur: sacramenta iustificant, attribuitur continenti quod est contenti. Est enim sensus: gratia contenta in sacramentis iustificat. Unde sacramenta non iustificant tamquam causa efficiens, sed tamquam causa materialis. Quinque enim sunt que sanant corpus, ad similitudinem quorum quinque dicuntur sanare animam ... sacramenta iustificant tanquam medicinalia vasa, quia in ipsis sacramentis datur gratia." *Summa Aurea*, lib. IV, tract. 4, 49-66. Magistri Guillelmi Altissiodorensis, *Summa Aurea*, liber quartus, Spicilegium Bonaventurianum XIX, Jean Ribaillier, ed. (Roma: ad Claras Aquas, 1985), 63 lns. 49–66. Much of William's argument in this regard hinges on the issue of the matter involved in the sacrament. Partially intending to preserve the nonarbitrary quality of the material elements employed in the sacraments, William described their causality in terms of that same material. The theory of "dispositive causality," which was taken up by the early Aquinas in the *Sentences* commentary, seems to have originated here with William's theory of material causality. *DTC*, s.v. "Sacraments, Causalité," 578.

30. "Responsio est per hoc, dicitur 'causa' aequivoce hic et in sacramento. Bona enim vita est causa meritoria salutis, sive causa in subiecto disponens, secundum aliam Facultatem, et est salus praemium. Sacramenta autem non sunt causa meritoria, sed tantum est per gratiam meritum; sed sunt *causa materialis* in qua, ut vasa medicinalia, gratia ut medicina." (emphasis mine). *Glossa*, IV d. 1, 6e. Alexander of Hales, *Glossa in Quatuor Libros Sententiarum Petri Lombardi*, lib. IV, in Bibliotheca Franciscana Scholastica Medii Aevi, vol. 15 (Quaracchi, 1957), 13. Hales does refer to the sacraments as "causa efficiente," in distinction one of book four; however, he is referencing his general treatment of the sacraments in the introduction to book four of his *Glossa*, and it is not clear he means to indicate anything more here than Lombard's efficacious sign. "In hac prima parte agitur de sacramentis communiter. Dictum est de causa efficiente." *Glossa*, IV d. 1, 3.

that rejected the Aristotelian causal categories entirely. William of
Auvergne (d. 1249) would be the first in the scholastic period to offer
a decidedly deontological theory of sacramental causality as a counterpoint to these tendencies. As an early critic of certain Aristotelian
interpretations of the doctrine of creation,[31] Auvergne not only asserted the creation of the world from nothing, he advocated for an
understanding of divine freedom—*potentia absoluta*—which effectively stripped nature of causal efficacy.[32] These broader metaphysical positions had a decisive effect on Auvergne's theory of sacramental causality. Auvergne insisted that the sacraments function not by
their own power but by "divine pact"—that is, they have causal effect
because of divine commitment. While this theory clearly reflects Auvergne's broader approach to causality in the created order, in the specific case of the sacraments Auvergne does build on some elements
taken from Augustine's theory of signs. In Book Two of *De Doctrina*, Augustine argues that objects associated with superstition such as
amulets and rings can function as signs. While he acknowledges that
these superstitious signs may be the result of a pact with a demon, he
grants that these signs (and the resulting superstitions) may also be
entirely of human origin.[33]

31. Roland Teske, "William of Auvergne on the Eternity of the World," *The Mod-
ern Schoolman* 67 (1990): 187–205. Reprinted in *Studies in the Philosophy of William of
Auvergne*, Marquette Studies in Philosophy 51 (Milwaukee, Wis.: Marquette University
Press, 2006), 29–52.

32. E. Gilson says that for Auvergne, "created natures are undoubtedly such that
they can receive [God's] efficacy; a house has to have windows, if one wishes to gather
light; but who will maintain that a window has a right to light? In the universal distribution of divine efficacy, God alone is really Cause; creatures are only channels through
which it circulates.... This pulverisation of natures and their causal efficacy brings us
back into line with the thesis *de potentia absoluta* which goes from Peter Damien to
William of Ockham." Étienne Gilson, *History of Christian Philosophy in the Middle Ages*
(New York: Random House, 1955), 255. See William of Auvergne, *De Trinitate*, c. 11. As
in *De Trinitate: an Edition of the Latin Text with an Introduction*, by Bruno Switalski,
Studies and Texts series 34 (Toronto: Pontifical Institute of Mediaeval Studies, 1976),
73–77. See also Roland Teske, introduction to *William of Auvergne: The Trinity, or The
First Principle*, trans. Roland Teske and Francis Wade (Milwaukee, Wis.: Marquette Uni-
versity Press, 1989), 21–25. J. Laumakis has argued that textual evidence indicates that
Auvergne may not have been a strict voluntarist in all respects. John Laumakis, "The
Voluntarism of William of Auvergne and Some Evidence to the Contrary," *The Modern
Schoolman* 76 (1999): 303–12.

33. *De Doct.*, lib. 2 c. 20-3.

Auvergne extends this concept beyond its original context, applying it to the sacraments: just as certain natural things can signify by virtue of a pact with demons, the sacraments signify, not by any intrinsic power but by virtue of divine pact.[34] For Auvergne, the sacraments are signs alone with all causal efficacy attributed univocally to God. Auvergne claims that it is impossible for existing things to achieve such effects naturally or to acquire any accidental property which would make such an effect possible.[35] In effect, Auvergne offers the theory of divine pact as a counterpoint to the developing theories of physical causality that attributed some causal efficacy to the sacraments themselves on Aristotelian grounds.[36]

Although Auvergne's understanding of sacramental sign may be dependent on Augustine, his theory does not take account of other Augustinian texts which describe the communication of divine power through material signs, like water moving through an aqueduct.[37] This more intrinsic strand of Augustinian sacramental doctrine was communicated to the scholastics through Lombard and the Victorines.

Although not transmitted through the Victorine tradition, versions of occasionalist or *sine qua non* causality were taught by others before the thirteenth century. Bernard of Clairvaux (d. 1153) has been frequently cited by later scholastics in support of this theory.[38] Al-

---

34. "Quare declaratum est tibi figuras et charcteres hujusmodi non ex virtute sua aliqua naturali operari mirifica illa sed ex Daemonum pacto, quo cultoribus suis per hujusmodi signa se adesse polliciti sunt, sicut et signa sacra, quibus utitur Christiana religio, non ex virtute sua naturali aliqua, sed ex Dei altisimi pacto, qui cultoribus suis se adesse firmissima promissione pollicitus est operantur, eo tropo loquendi, quo signis hujusmodi operationes atribui fas est. Non enim signa deificat fides, aut religio Christiana; propter hoc dicit Sanctus ac sapiens Augustinus quia omnia haec pacta sunt Daemonum." *De Legibus*, c. 27 ed. Paris, 1674, p. 89b. Text as cited by Iréne Rosier-Catach, "Signes sacramentels et signes magiques; Guillaume d'Auvergne et la théorie du pacte," in *Autour de Guillaume d'Auvergne (1249)*, ed. Nicole Bériou and Franco Morenzoni (Turnhout: Brepols, 2005), 101n21.

35. *De Legibus*, c. 27. Rosier-Catach, "Signes sacramentels," 102.

36. Ibid.

37. *Jo. Ev. Tr.* 5.15. See note 8.

38. Bernard held that the sacraments should be properly understood as signs in the following way: a given thing, taken in itself, does not indicate anything more than what it is. When the same thing is understood in reference to something else, however, it becomes a sign of that other reality. Bernard uses the example of a ring, which

though twelfth-century monastic culture was strongly influenced by
Augustine, Bernard does not rely on him to explain the efficacy of the
sacraments.[39] One unintended consequence of this is the ease with
which Bernard's approach can be reconciled with theories of sacramental causality that do not trace their origins to the Augustinianism
of the Victorine school. Despite the fact that many scholastic authors
would quote Bernard in support of the *sine qua non* position, Bernard
himself did not share their larger metaphysical concerns, and when
read in the context of the investiture controversy, he could be seen to
attribute a certain efficacy to sacramental signs.[40]

---

alone is simply a material object. Understood in the context of its ceremonial use, however, it becomes a sign of hereditary investiture. "Sacramentum dicitur sacrum signum,
sive sacrum secretum.... Anulus absolute propter anulum, et nulla est significatio; datur
ad investiendum de hereditate aliqua, et signum est, ita ut iam dicere possit qui accip-
it: «Anulus non valet quidquam, sed hereditas est quam quaerebam.» In hunc itaque
modum, appropinquans passioni Dominus, de gratia sua investire curavit suos, ut invisibilis gratia signo aliquo visibili praestaretur. Ad hoc instituta sunt omnia sacramenta...." *In cena domini*, 2. "Sermones II," *Sancti Bernardi Opera*, vol. 5, ed. J. Leclercq and
H. Rochais (Rome: Editiones Cistercienses, 1968), 68, 11–18. Note the Augustinian language at work here: *"sacrum signum," "sacrum secretum," "invisibilis gratia signo aliquo visibili praestaretur."* As we have seen, Hugh of St. Victor and Peter Lombard used similar
terminology. Bernard offers many similar examples, such as the installation of a canon
by means of a book, an abbot by a crosier, or a bishop by a ring and crosier. "Variae sunt
investiturae secundum ea de quibus investimur,—verbi gratia, investitur canonicus per
librum, abbas per baculum, episcopus per baculum et anulum simul—, sicut, inquam,
in huiusmodi rebus est, sic et divisiones gratiarum diversis traditae sunt sacramentis." *In
cena domini*, 2. Leclercq/Rochais, vol. 5 (1968), 69, 1–5.

39. Both the monasteries of the Middle Ages and the universities of the scholastic period were greatly influenced by Augustine, albeit in different ways. The monastic
tradition was less concerned with the metaphysical and doctrinal implications of Augustinianism and tended to focus on its mystical or spiritual content, which was most
immediately useful for pursuing the monastic life. To this end, although Augustine was
one of the most influential thinkers for monastic theology, the monks tended to focus on his pastoral writings and biblical commentaries, to the exclusion of his texts on
doctrine and controversy. Jean Leclercq, *The Love of Learning and the Desire for God:
A Study in Monastic Culture*, trans. Catherine Misrahi (New York: Fordham University
Press, 1974), 123–24. Although he makes no reference to him in this immediate context,
it would be incorrect to say that Bernard was not influenced by Augustine. However, his
appropriation of Augustine was much different than that of Lombard and the Victorine
school, who relied on the distinctions of Augustine's anti-Donatist writings to formulate
many of the core principles of scholastic sacramental theology. By contrast, Bernard's
approach to the sacraments seems more metaphorical, and when compared to the scholastics of the thirteenth century, he hardly offers a causal theory at all.

40. Bernard's theory must be understood within the context of the investiture

Roland of Cremona (d. 1259) argued against both Auxerre and Auvergne, proposing instead that the sacraments operate as efficient causes.[41] Cremona explicitly ruled out an extrincisist approach, arguing that the power operative in the sacraments was not similar to the power of political or rhetorical persuasion. Rather, Cremona holds that the power at work in the sacraments is similar to the potency associated with an efficient cause. Because of its emphasis on movement toward an intended finality, the category of efficient cause would prove itself the most fitting way to speak of sacramental efficacy in the causal language of Aristotle. Both Lombard and Augustine

---

controversy in the eleventh century, in which some secular authorities claim the right not only to propose candidates for the episcopacy but to actually invest them on their own authority. W. Courtenay argues that these circumstances contextualize Bernard's use of the signs involved in episcopal investiture and suggest that he meant to imply that sacraments do confer real power, just as the material and ceremonial dimension of an abbot's investiture confers a real effect. William Courtenay, "The King and the Leaden Coin: The Economic Background of 'sine qua non' Causality," *Traditio*, 28 (1972): 207–8. See also William Courtenay, "Sacrament, Symbol and Causality in Bernard of Clairvaux," in *Bernard of Clairvaux: Studies Presented to Dom Jean Leclercq* (Kalamazoo: Cistercian Publications, 1973), 111–22. "[The term 'investiture controversy'] is often applied to the long series of disputes between popes and emperors from the time of the future Emp. [sic] Henry IV's withdrawal of obedience from Gregory VII at Worms in 1076 to the concordat of Worms in 1122.... *The issue of investiture in the strict sense concerned the king's right to confer upon bishops and abbots the ring and crosier that were their symbols of office....* Although the Papacy won a complete victory over the issue of lay investiture itself, lay rulers retained a varying degree of control over elections" (emphasis mine). ODCC, s.v. "Investiture Controversy." These contextual qualifications were lost on scholastic occasionalists, however, who frequently cited Bernard in their defense. Aquinas himself approaches Bernard in this way, although he is most likely concerned to refute those advocates of occasionalism among his contemporaries, rather than Bernard himself. Aquinas cites Bernard in *ST* IIIª Q. 62 a. 1 co. Although Bernard would be associated with the later nominalists, *sine qua non* causality was not always synonymous with deontology. Understood in the context of Bernard's religious life, the rich environment of monastic liturgy provides a hermeneutical backdrop for the occasionalistic metaphors he employed that has nothing to do with the rejection of Aristotelian causality or the doctrine of analogy. With the loss of this supporting structure, however, the rigors of scholastic theology began to expose the inherent weakness of this approach.

41. *In IV Sent.*, d. 1; fol. 79va. Roland seems to be contending with the thought of William of Auxerre (d. 1231), who argued that the sacraments were material causes, rather than efficient. Ephrem Filthaut, *Roland von Cremona, OP, und die Anfänge der Scholastic im Predigerorden: Ein Beitrag zur Geistesgeschichte der älteren Dominikaner* (Vechta i. O.: Albertus Magnus Verlag der Dominicaner, 1936), 165.

understood the power of each sacrament as working toward its final completion as an effect in the recipient. Efficient causality preserves the distinction between the end intended and the means by which it is accomplished while at once speaking of the relationship between the two: efficient causality is in motion toward a final end. For the sacraments, this means that the causality of sacred signs is conditioned and defined by their directedness toward the sanctification of the person, a sanctification quia made possible by the operative presence of the power of the Word.

Material causality, by contrast, is far less suitable. In this regard, Cremona recognized Hugh's medicinal imagery for the metaphor that it was: Cremona taught that the sacraments only "contained" grace in the sense that an effect can be contained in an efficient cause.[42] In this much, he saw himself as standing in continuity with Augustine's sacramental theology, citing the same passage from Augustine's tract on John used by Lombard and many others.[43] From this point forward, we begin to see efficient instrumental causality offered as an intrinsic interpretation of Augustinian sacramental teleology. After Cremona, efficient causality was the category of choice for those interested in applying Aristotle to the problem of sacramental causality in a manner that stood in continuity with the Augustinian tradition.[44]

As early as William of Auxerre, the category of dispositive causality was introduced to explain sacramental efficacy.[45] Drawn in part from Avicenna's metaphysics, by the time of Albert the Great this approach was used explicitly to explain the sacraments as caus-

---

42. *In IV Sent.*, d. 1; fol. 79va. Ibid., 165.

43. "Virtutem dixerim, quia augustinus vocat illud virtutem, non est enim virtus politica vel gramatica (!), sed vocatur virtus, sicut frigiditas vocatur virtus aque, aqua agit in corpus baptizati" (emphasis Filthaut). *In IV Sent.*, d. 1; fol. 8⁵ᵃ⁻ᵇ, cited in Filthaut, *Roland von Cremona*, 167.

44. Hugh of St. Cher seems to have continued this interpretive approach. Hugh was Cremona's student and succeeded him at Paris in 1230–31. Walter Principe, *Hugh of Saint-Cher's Theology of the Hypostatic Union*, vol. 3 of The Theology of the Hypostatic Union in the Early Thirteenth Century Series (Toronto: Pontifical Institute of Mediaeval Studies, 1970), 13. It seems that Hugh is dependent in part on Stephen Langton for this theory. Damien Van Den Eynde, "Stephen Langton and Hugh of St. Cher on the Causality of the Sacraments," *Franciscan Studies*, 11 (1951): 153.

45. *DTC* s. v. "Sacraments, Causalité," 578.

es.[46] Many scholastics applied this concept to the sacraments, arguing that while the sacramental action may cause a "disposition" for
grace, grace itself is caused immediately by God. The young Aquinas
advocated for a version of this theory in his *Sentences* commentary,
and widespread support for the concept continued among Dominicans until the sixteenth century. Despite waning interest in the years
following 1270, isolated Franciscan support for this theory can still be
found in the late thirteenth century. William of Ware, whose *Sentences* commentary dates from about 1294, argues for a view of sacramental causality that bears close resemblance to that of Aquinas in certain
respects.[47] Versions of this theory were popular among both Domin-

46. In *De sacramentis*, Albert is very much in dialogue with Augustine and Hugh
of St. Victor, and ultimately falls back on Hugh's explanation. *De sacram*. tr. 1, q. 2, especially obj. 5 and ad 5. Alberti Magni, *Opera Omnia*, Editio Digitalis, vol. 26. http://
www.albertus-magnus-online.de/# (accessed 11/9/15). In his *Sentences* commentary,
however, Albert seems to interpret Hugh of St. Victor's medicinal imagry in terms of
the disposition of matter to receive form. Although Albert uses the category of matter,
his theory differs from Auxerre's association of the sacraments with Aristotle's material
cause and is more dependent on hylomorphism directly (and a somewhat Platonizing
read of this concept at that). *In Sent*. IV d. 1B, a. 5, Solutio. B. Alberti Magni, *Opera Omnia*, ed. Borgnet, vol. 29 (Paris: Vivès, 1894), 17. H.-D. Dondaine, "A propos d'Avicenne
et de S. Thomas de la causalité dispositive," *Review Thomiste* 51 (1951): 441–53. C. Murray discusses Albert's sacramental theology in relation to that of Alexander of Hales and
Hugh of St. Cher. Campion Murray, "The Composition of the Sacraments According to
the 'Summa De Sacramentis' and the 'Commentarium in IV Sententiarium' of St. Albert
the Great," *Franciscan Studies* 16, no. 3 (1956): 177–201.

47. Ware studied at Oxford, and completed his commentary on the *Sentences* there in
1294. *NCE*[1] s.v. "William of Ware." Although he nowhere cites the Angelic Doctor, Ware
employs a rather well-developed argument for efficient instrumental causality which
takes into account the problem of creation and supernatural ends. Ware, *In Sent*. IV d. 1,
Respondeo. Ware knows that some have suggested that grace is created directly by God
and in a moment of seeming prescience Ware seems to anticipate later Thomistic commentators by proposing that the concept of obediential potency may be able to resolve
this issue. "Dicitur ergo, quod [illa dispositio] educitur de potentia obedientiali animae
secundo modo dicta et sic dicendo non concludit argumentum inconveniens, ad quod
deducit." Ware, *In Sent*. IV d. 1, Respondeo. Lampen, *De Causalitate Sacramentorum*, 42.
Ware also holds that this instrumental approach to sacramental causality is more in step
with the thought of Augustine and Lombard, interpreting these texts using Aristotelian
instrumental causality. Ware even makes use of an example of instrumental causality dear
to Aquinas: an instrumental cause is like a saw in the hands of a builder, who directs it
towards its final end. The power does not originate from nor remain within the saw but
flows from the principal agent to the final effect. Ware, *In Sent*. IV d. 1, Respondeo. As
so many authors of this time, Ware does not name his sources directly. Whatever their

icans and Franciscans through the 1250s. During this time-frame, dispositive causality was strongly endorsed by the Franciscan school at Paris which, after the death of Hales, worked to complete his *Summa*.[48] Although portions of the *Summa Halensis* can be attributed to Hales whole or in part, the treatise on the sacraments is almost certainly a product of the Parisian Franciscan school in the 1250s.[49] Reflecting the state of the question of sacramental causality during that period, the *Summa Halensis* presents both dispositive causality and *sine qua non* causality as legitimate explanations of sacramental cause, although it gives more attention to the former theory.[50] It is this framework that Bonaventure would inherit as a student and lecturer at Paris during this time.

THE DEVELOPMENT OF INTERPRETIVE TRADITIONS: THE FRANCISCAN SCHOOL

From the vantage point of the sixteenth century, Domingo Bañez identified a school of thought, distinct from the Thomistic one, that had its roots in the early scholastic period and approached the sacraments as causes of grace because, either through their presence or use, God is moved to confer grace.[51] In order to sift the multitude of causal models which were in use at the beginning of the scholastic

---

source, however, it seems clear that these doctrines could not have originated from an exclusive reading of the *Summa Halensis* and Bonaventure's *Sentences* commentary.

48. Ignatius Brady, "Alexander of Hales," in *The Encyclopedia of Philosophy*, ed. Paul Edwards (New York: Macmillan Publishing Co., 1972), 1:74.

49. William of Middleton was tasked with organizing the completion of the *Summa Halensis* after Hales' death, and large, heavily edited sections of his own *Quaestiones de sacramentis* (composed 1245–49) were included in the fourth book of the *Summa Halensis*. *NCE*[1] s.v. "William of Melitona (Middleton)." For analysis of the relationship between the work of Middleton and Hales in the *Summa Halensis*, see Killian Lynch, "The Quaestio de Sacramentis in Genere Attributed to Alexander of Hales," *Franciscan Studies* 11 (1951): 74–95, and "Texts Illustrating the Causality of the Sacraments from William of Melitona, *Assisi Bibl. Comm.* 182, and *Brussels Bibl. Royale* 1542," *Franciscan Studies* 17 (1957): 238–72.

50. *Summa Theol.* (Halensis) IV q. 5 a. 5, III. Lampen, *De Causalitate Sacramentorum*, 7–9.

51. Domingo Bañez, *Comentarios Ineditos a la Tercera Parte de Santo Tomas*, vol. 2, *De Sacramentis: QQ. 60–90*, ed. Vincente Beltran de Heredia, Biblioteca de Teologos Españoles, vol. 19 (Salamanca: 1953), 44.

period, however, we may distinguish between two trends—not yet schools—of interpretation.[52] The Berengarian controversy had made clear that, in the hands of the wrong interpreter, the ambiguities inherent in Augustine's sacramental theology could actually conceal very serious error. As a result, the need to articulate the way in which the sacraments effect what they signify gradually emerged in a more precise way as a theological question. As the scholastic movement developed, two distinct trends can be seen to emerge.

The first approach could be called "intrinsic," because it understands the sacraments as integrated into a causal action directed by God in which his power works specifically through the working of the sacramental sign. There were reactions against the attribution of the category of cause to the sacraments in themselves, however. Seeking to preserve the absolute sovereignty of God with respect to grace,

---

52. In this I follow John Gallagher, a student of J. H. Nicholas, OP, whose work on this subject is to be commended. Gallagher distinguishes two main patterns of thought that characterize the tradition received by St. Thomas: the first "sees real power in the sacramental rites to cause, under God. Its earliest form spoke of the sacraments as vials of grace, as in Hugh of St. Victor, Praepositinus, Alan of Lille, William of Auxerre, and others, who were taking up the thought of the Fathers that grace was contained in the sacraments. This notion developed into seeing grace really in the rite but as in its cause. At first, this meant as in its material cause, that is, grace was *in* the sacraments; then as in its efficient cause. The works attributed to Alexander, as well as Albert, Guerric of Saint Quentin and William of Meliton see that causality as effecting a disposition in the soul for grace. It is this opinion that Thomas will follow in commenting on the book of *Sentences*. Others, such as Roland of Cremona and Hugh of Saint Cher, hint at a causality of grace itself, though not clearly. This view will be developed by Thomas in his *Summa*." John Gallagher, *Significando Causant: A Study of Sacramental Efficacy*, Studia Friburgensia New Series 40 (Fribourg: The University of Fribourg Press, 1965), 80–81. The second "approach to the sacraments ... sees in them no real power to cause either grace or a disposition for grace. Rather God causes both of these directly, and alone. He does so, a) on the occasion of the sacraments' being given; or b) on the condition of their being given, as in Abelard, Bernard, William of Auvergne; or c) because of a pact, an ordination of the sacrament to grace.... We may place in this group William of Auvergne, Bonaventure, Fishacre, Hugh of Strasbourg, and Kilwardby. Later, moral causality will follow in the same path." Ibid., 81. The intrinsic/extrinsic distinction is also applied by Jean-Pierre Torrell in the context of Christ's resurrection. See J.-P. Torrell, "La causalité salvifique de la résurrection du Christ selon saint Thomas," *Revue Thomiste* 96 (1996): 179–208, as cited by Philip L. Reynolds, "Efficient Causality and Instrumentality in Thomas Aquinas's Theology of the Sacraments," in *Essays in Medieval Philosophy and Theology in Memory of Walter H. Principe, O.S.B.*, ed. James R. Ginther and Carl N. Still (Burlington, Vt.: Ashgate, 2005), 67–84.

others insisted on a more "extrinsic" approach in which the sacraments were at best causes in the accidental sense, acting only as occasions, conditions, or legal arrangements which invite the causal involvement of God in some way.[53] For the intrinsic approach, the sacraments are true causes in the proper sense; they produce real effects under the direction of God. According to the extrinsic model, comparatively little is said about the functioning of the sacraments themselves, lest the causal sovereignty of God be compromised. In the former, instrumental causality is portrayed as an analogical species of efficient causality; in the latter, causality is attributed to the sacraments in a more equivocal sense.

These new speculative precisions brought fresh challenges for sacramental theology: not all scholastic theories proved equally suited for conveying the received tradition. Early attempts at material and efficient causality were clearly problematic, and while the extrinsic position does avoid attributing a supernatural effect to a natural instrument, it is comparatively deontological, lacking the means to describe the causal dimension of the instrument's action in language other than that of a legal decree, in which something of no inherent value is declared invaluable by order of the king.

Concerning the Augustinian inheritance, one way in which the distinction between intrinsic and extrinsic interpretations of sacramental causality is manifested is in the interpretation of the *virtus aquae* de-

---

53. While we are aware that historical metanarrative can have serious limitations, the distinction offered here between intrinsic and extrinsic approaches to sacramental causality is of great utility because it provides a workable framework for understanding the main lines of doctrinal development that shaped this issue through the centuries. This distinction between intrinsic and extrinsic approaches to sacramental causality is broadly congruent with the division between the physical and moral causality that emerged in the schools during the modern period. However, it should be noted that, for Thomists, the crux of the issue is more aptly expressed in terms of act and potency. Gallagher's distinction is most useful as a point of departure for understanding sacramental causality; a well-developed understanding of the issue from a Thomistic perspective will necessarily transcend these categories. The categories of intrinsic and extrinsic also recall twentieth-century debates concerning nature and grace. In light of this, the work of Gallagher and others not only provides a useful paradigm for understanding the history of sacramental causality but also draws attention to the possibility that a truly intrinsic doctrine of grace must be accompanied and supported by an intrinsic sense of sacramental causality.

scribed by Augustine in the above-quoted passage.[54] Augustine himself makes it clear that this is not a power possessed by the water alone but is spoken of with necessary reference to the power of God. We have seen that Hugh of St. Victor interpreted this teaching using the language of instrumentality:[55] as a tool takes on instrumental power in the hand of a builder to work toward an end for which it has no native capacity, so too are the material elements of the sacraments taken up as instruments of divine power. Aquinas and the Thomistic School interpret this *virtus aquae* as a form of real instrumental efficient power, under the direction and impulse of God as principal efficient cause.[56] In this way, the material signs are made instruments of the Word in whose power they participate as instrumental causes directed toward a final end. However, because of the conceptual difficulty involved in attributing any form of causality to the sacramental elements without at the same time compromising divine sovereignty, the extrincisist approach was unable to develop a technical vocabulary for the *virtus aquae* and gravitated instead toward a view of the sacraments as conditions or occasions for the expression of divine power.

While the Dominican school began to center around Aquinas' intrinsic model of efficient instrumental causality, the emerging Franciscan school took a decidedly extrinsic approach. Bonaventure (d. 1274) was present in Paris in the 1240s and '50s, and his treatment of sacramental causality reflects this.[57] Broadly speaking, Bonaventure's engagement with Aristotle is reflective of the state of Parisian Aristotelianism during his time as a student of arts in the 1240s. To this end, Van Steenberghen argues that Bonaventure's work during this earlier

---

54. "Unde ista tanta virtus aquae, ut corpus tangat et cor abluat, nisi faciente verbo: non quia dicitur, sed quia creditur?" *Jo. Ev. Tr.*, 80.3. See the full text cited in note 7.

55. *De Sac.* I, 9, 4. See note 17.

56. See *Super Sent.* lib. 4, d. 1, q. 1, solutio I; *ST* III, q. 62 a. 1.

57. Bonaventure began lecturing on the Bible in 1248 but most likely studied arts at Paris beginning in 1243. During this period, Bonaventure studied under John of La Rochelle and Alexander of Hales, both of whom died in 1245. By 1250 Bonaventure was lecturing on the *Sentences*; he held the Franciscan chair in theology until his election as Minister General in 1257. Fernand Van Steenberghen, *Aristotle in the West: The Origins of Latin Aristotelianism*, 2nd ed., trans. Leonard Johnston (Louvain: Nauwelaerts, 1970), 147. The dating of Bonaventure during this period is somewhat disputed. See Jay Hammond, "Dating Bonaventure's Inception as Regent Master," *Franciscan Studies* 67 (2009): 179–226.

period displays a rather broad awareness of Aristotle and other philosophers, including Averroes.[58] After 1257, Bonaventure would become more openly critical of Aristotle.[59] In his *Hexaemeron*, which represents a series of conferences given in 1273, Bonaventure's frustration with Averroism reached its peak: alluding to the excesses of the 1260s, he strongly cautions against an interpretation of Aristotle that would set itself against divine revelation. For Bonaventure, this had direct implications for God's relationship to the world as exemplar cause.[60]

58. He notes, however, that Bonaventure himself is aware that his conceptual grasp of Aristotelian principles is not deep and that he hesitates to resolve Aristotelian disputes and "*often shows a certain reserve in his comments on opinions attributed to the philosophers.*" Van Steenberghen, *Aristotle in the West*, 150–51. In this Van Steenberghen is opposed to Gilson, who argues that Bonaventure's grasp of Aristotle was more mature. Étienne Gilson, *The Christian Philosophy of St. Bonaventure*, trans. Illtyd Trethowan and Frank Sheed (St. Anthony Guild Press, 1965). Copleston concurs with Van Steenberghen to a certain extent but criticizes his characterization of Bonaventure's philosophy as a form of eclectic and underdeveloped Aristotelianism, emphasizing instead Bonaventure's continuity with the Platonic tradition. Frederick Copleston, *A History of Medieval Philosophy* (New York: Harper & Row, 1972), 167–68. G. LaNave gives an informative account of the role of Aristotle in Bonaventure's theology in his, "Bonaventure's Theological Method," in *A Companion to Bonaventure*, ed. Jay Hammond and Wayne Hellmann (Leiden: Brill, 2014), 81–120.

59. "In the first period of Bonaventure's scientific activity, which lasted until 1257, there are over four-hundred citations in which Aristotle is treated expressly in a friendly manner; and we have found no text which would indicate the opposite. During this period, Aristotle is the Philosopher for Bonaventure just as he would always be for Thomas." Joseph Ratzinger, *The Theology of History in St. Bonaventure*, trans. Zachary Hayes (Chicago, Ill.: Franciscan Herald Press, 1989), 120. Ratzinger follows Vinca and Van Steenberghen on this point, citing Angelo da Vinca, *L'Aspetto filosofico dell'aristotelismo di S. Bonaventura*, in: *Coll Franc* XIX (1949), 41. A. Forest, F. Van Steenberghen and M. de Gandillac, *Le mouvement doctrinal du IXe au XIVe siécle* (Paris: 1951), 60. See also Van Steenberghen, *Aristotle in the West*, 150. See also Marianne Schlosser, "Bonaventure: Life and Works," in *A Companion to Bonaventure*, ed. Jay Hammond and Wayne Hellmann (Leiden: Brill, 2014), 51. Although he stresses the need to balance the Augustinian and Aristotelian influence in Bonaventure, Christopher Cullen seems to be largely in agreement with Ratzinger on this point. Christopher Cullen, *Bonaventure* (New York: Oxford University Press, 2006), 20–22, 22n78, and "Bonaventure's Philosophical Method," in *A Companion to Bonaventure*, 126–27, 157–61. In this later source, Cullen engages the long-running debate between Van Steenburgen and Gilson concerning Bonaventure's attitude toward philosophy. Although he does not dispute Van Steenburgen's claim that the later Bonaventure was reacting in large part against the Averroism of the 1260s, he is critical of Van Steenburgen's reduction of Bonaventure's philosophy to the level of eclecticism. Ibid., 127, 143, 153–54.

60. *Hexaemeron*, 6.1-6 (5, 360-61) Schlosser, "Bonaventure: Life and Works," 51–53.

Already in 1250, however, Bonaventure's *Sentences* commentary reflects a lack of comfort with an Aristotelian approach to sacramental causality. In his treatment of sacramental cause in book four of the *Sentences*, Bonaventure first proposes a version of dispositive causality current in many of the schools: while the sacramental character may be the result of efficient causality, grace itself is caused only dispositionally—that is, the sacraments create the necessary condition in the soul for the reception of grace. Concerning the final end of the sacraments, however, they are causes *sine qua non*—causes without which the final effect is not possible.[61] Bonaventure nods with deference to this position, but in the end he tentatively proposes a more radical solution: he suggests that, beyond causing a disposition in the person which is necessary for the conferral of grace, the sacraments may be only occasions for the giving of grace.

Bonaventure does acknowledge the Augustinian teaching received through the Victorines: the sacraments are comprised of both the power of the Word and material elements. However, he is concerned with the manner in which the spiritual power of the Word comes to interact with the material substrate of the elements, and he is unable to supply a fitting explanation for the way in which the natural potency or causal power of the elements (or signs) can be used in tandem with the causal power of the Word which works its effect in the recipient.[62] Following the *Summa Halensis*, Bonaventure finds each of the four Aristotelian causes lacking in this regard,[63] and his resulting emphasis on divine potency alone foreshadows the causal univocity of the nominalists. While Aquinas will resolve this difficulty using efficient instrumentality, Bonaventure seems to prefer a more idealistic solution to this problem. In an effort to explain the interrelation between the material sacramental elements and the spiritual effect for which God

---

61. *In IV Sent.*, d. 1, p. 1, q. 4, *respond.*

62. "Sed difficile videtur mihi intelligere, virtutem illam simul esse verbo et elemento collatam, quantum ad essentiam et naturam, quantum ad eius existentiam, quantum ad durationis mensuram et etiam quantum ad operationis efficaciam ; quae omnia necesse est ponere et explicare circa virtutem illam, si quis dicat, quod aliqua qualitas detur verbo et elemento, per quam agat et influat in ipsam animam." Bonaventure, *In III Sent.*, d. 40, dub. III. S. Bonaventurae, *Opera Omnia*, vol. 3 (Rome: ad Claras Aquas, 1887), 894.

63. Ibid. See *Summa Theol.* (Halensis) IV q. 5 a. 5, III.

alone is principally responsible, Bonaventure defends the legitimacy of *sine qua non* or occasionalist causality, in which the sacraments are conditions or occasions without which grace is not given; the causal necessity here stems not from anything intrinsic to the function of the sacramental elements themselves but from the authority of God who has decreed that they be used for this purpose.

In many ways, Bonaventure's approach to sacramental causality in his *Sentences* commentary reflects the influence of the *Summa Halensis*. Bonaventure studied under Hales and was present in Paris during the editing of the *Summa Halensis*, and his presentation of dispositive causality reflects this. In his treatment of sacramental occasionalism, however, Bonaventure begins to distance himself slightly from the *Summa Halensis*. Although *sine qua non* causality was also mentioned as a viable option by the editors of Alexander's *Summa*, Bonaventure gives it far more attention.[64] To illustrate this form of causality, Bonaventure uses the example of a promissory note sealed by the king—the note in itself is completely dependent on the king's power and authority, having no intrinsic power of its own and loses what power it has upon the death of the king.[65] As a result, Bonaventure will say that if the sacramental elements themselves are to be considered causes, it must be only in an extended sense.[66] Bonaventure em-

---

64. *Summa Theol.* (*Halensis*), Pars IV, q. 5, a. 5. Lampen, *De Causalitate Sacramentorum*, 6–17. *DTC*, s.v. "Sacraments, Causalité," 579–80. Versions of occasionalist or *sine qua non* causality were taught by others before him, but Bonaventure's specific use of this approach ushers in a more idealistic approach to the sacraments which comes to be adopted by the nominalists. Bernard of Clairvaux (d. 1153) proposes an early form of this view, although his work predates the question of causality that arose in the scholastic period after Lombard. See *In cena domini*, 2. See note 38.

65. "Sicut igitur litterae regiae anulo regis sigillatae magnae·sunt dignitatis et virtutis et valoris et magna dicuntur et posse et facere, tamen in eis nulla virtus est absoluta, sed sola ordinatio per assistentiam virtutis regiae—quod patet, quia, mortuo rege, non plus curator de litteris suis quam de aliis, tamen nihil absolutum amiserunt." *In IV Sent.*, d. 1, p. 1, a. 1 q. 4, *Resp.* S. Bonaventurae, *Opera Omnia*, vol. 4 (Rome: ad Claras Aquas, 1889), 24. ed. Ad Claras Aquas (1887). Lampen, *De Causalitate Sacramentorum*, 26. See also Johann Auer, *A General Doctrine of the Sacraments and the Mystery of the Eucharist*, ed. Hugh M. Riley, trans. Erasmo Leiva-Merikakis, vol. 6 of *Dogmatic Theology*, ed. Johann Auer and Joseph Ratzinger (Washington, D.C.: The Catholic University of America Press, 1995), 80.

66. "Et si tu quaeras, utrum habeant virtutem aliquam creatam super increatam; respondent, quod praeter virtutem increatam est dicere aliquam virtutem habere Sacra-

phasizes the principal causality of God, while acknowledging that the sacraments can dispose us to receive grace through upbuilding faith and devotion by this same divine power.[67] Because Bonaventure is unable to articulate analogically the relationship between secondary instrumental causes and the principal causality of God, he shifts the focus of the conversation away from the instruments and toward the causality of the principal agent, resulting in a picture of the principal agent as cause in an all but univocal sense, the instruments being comparatively equivocal.

As these respective schools continue to develop, the contrast between the Thomist and Franciscan positions on the doctrine of analogy will mark their differing approaches to sacramental causality, the intrinsic approach expressing itself in the analogical language of the Thomist school and the extrinsic in the comparative univocity of the Franciscan.[68] Although Bonaventure's sacramental theology retains a

---

mentum, sed extenso nomine virtutis. Si enim virtus dicat aliquam qualitatem vel naturam sive essentiam advenientem Sacramento, sicut proprie dicitur, sic secundum eos non est dicendum, quod habeat virtutem; sed extenditur nomen virtutis ad aliquam ordinationem, ut quando aliquid habet efficacem ordinationem ad aliquid, dicitur habere virtutem respectu illius.—Et ponunt hoc exemplum: rex statuit, ut qui habent tale signum, habeant centum libras. Post istam institutionem signum illud non habet aliquam proprietatem absolutam, quam non haberet prius; ad aliquid tamen est ordinatum, ad quod non erat prius. Et quia habet efficacem ordinationem, dicitur habere virtutem, ut faciat aliquem habere centum marcas; et dicitur illud signum valere centum marcas, et tamen nihil plus habet de bonitate nunc quam prius." Bonaventure, *In IV Sent.*, d. I p. I, a. 1 q. 4, *Resp. Opera Omnia*, vol. 4 (Rome: ad Claras Aquas, 1889), 23.

67. "Sacramento enim dicunt assistere divinam virtutem, quae est causa gratiae, et fidem et devotionem suscipientis, quae disponit ad gratiam." Bonaventure, *In IV Sent.*, d. I p. I, a. 1 q. 4, *Resp.* 2.4. *Opera Omnia*, vol. 4 (Rome: Ad Claras Aquas, 1887), 23.

68. In the mid 1200s, there were no clearly defined Dominican and Franciscan schools on this subject. The Dominican Richard Fishacre argued for versions of *sine qua non* causality, and Robert Kilwardby, also a Dominican, argued for a similar position using the category of formal causality: "Sic igitur sacramenta, quia assimilant hominem divinae voluntati, iustificant, sed non ut causa eficiens sed ut formalis. Deus enim est principalis causa et ipse est efficiens respectu utriusque, quia fidem agit intra per se ipsum, sacramentum extra per ministrum. Sed fides et sacramentum sunt unus habitus formalis integer denominans iustificatum, et ita sacramenta iustificant per modum causae formalis, et hoc ratione exterioris hominis, ut dictum est." *In IV Sent.* Q. 39. Robert Kilwardby, *Questiones in Librum Quartum Sententiarum*, ed. Richard Schenk, vol. 17, Bayerische Akademie der Wissenschaften (Munich: C. H. Beck, 1993), 206, lines 208–13. As is clear from the *Summa Halensis*, at the mid-point of the thirteenth century, as

diversity of influences from Augustinianism and medieval sources that give his thought a metaphysically robust appearance when compared to that of later Franciscans, on the subject of sacramental causality Bonaventure does represent a transition towards these later modes of thought, and it would play a decisive role in the development of the later Franciscan tradition that developed after 1277.[69]

Duns Scotus (d. 1308) inherits the concept of sacramental occasionalism from Bonaventure.[70] Unlike Bonaventure, however, Scotus makes no provision for the possibility of dispositive causality and shifts the Franciscan school definitively away from the category of efficient causality as a viable explanation for sacramental efficacy. Although Scotus allows for instrumentality under certain conditions, he denies that the agency of the sacraments can be directly compared to the working of an artist's tool.[71] Sacramental causes are not like natural efficient or instrumental causes.[72] Recalling Auvergne's approach, Scotus argues that it is through a divine pact with the Church

---

many Franciscans held versions of efficient dispositive causality as held to *sine qua non* occasionalism. These traditions become distinct, however, in the years immediately preceding the condemnations of 1277. For more on the development of these and other issues after 1277 see Maarten Hoenen, "Being and Thinking in the 'Correctium fratris Thomae' and the 'Correctorium corruptorii Quare:' Schools of Thought and Philosophical Methodology," in *Nach der Verurteilung von 1277: Philosophie und Theologie an der Universität von Paris im letzten Viertel des 13. Jahrhunderts*, Miscellanea Mediaevalia 28 (New York: De Gruyter, 2001), 417–35.

69. Christopher Cullen argues that Bonaventure escapes the charge of occasionalism in the strict sense because of his robust doctrine of sacramental signification. See Cullen, *Bonaventure*, 170. However, Cullen himself is clear that Bonaventure attributes the causing of grace in the soul to God alone.

70. Richard Cross, *Duns Scotus* (New York: Oxford University Press, 1999), 136.

71. Marilyn McCord Adams, "Powerless Causes: The Case of Sacramental Causality," in *Thinking about Causes: From Greek Philosophy to Modern Physics*, ed. Peter Machamer and Gereon Wolters (Pittsburgh: University of Pittsburgh Press, 2007), 60–62.

72. Duns Scotus, *Op.Ox.* IV.1.4–5.5–6; in Johannes Duns Scotus, *Opera Omnia*, vol. 8, Facimile reprint of Wadding (1639), 82–83. See also Marilyn McCord Adams, "Essential Orders and Sacramental Causality," in *Proceedings of the Quadruple Congress on John Duns Scotus*, part I, ed. Mary Beth Ingham and Oleg Bychov (St. Bonaventure, N.Y.: Franciscan Institute Publications, 2010), 191–203. For more on Scotus' approach to causality, see Eike-Henner Kluge, "Scotus on Accidental and Essential Causes," *Franciscan Studies* 66 (2008): 233–46. Richard Cross, *Duns Scotus on God* (Burlington, Vt.: Ashgate, 2005), 17–28; *The Physics of Duns Scotus: The Scientific Context of a Theological Vision* (Oxford: Clarendon Press, 1998), and Michael Sylwanowicz, *Contingent Causality and the Foundations of Duns Scotus' Metaphysics* (New York: Brill, 1996).

that God establishes the efficacy of the sacraments.[73] For Scotus, the sacraments cannot be causes in the proper sense but are conditions which convey a certain necessity. A sacrament has no causal power in relation to God's action; according to Richard Cross, for Scotus a sacrament is a "noncausal necessitating condition for a divine action."[74] Because of a previously established pact with the Church, God always rewards the recipient of a sacrament with the promised grace. As such Scotus' approach to sacramental causality is radically different from that of Aquinas: while Aquinas will describe the efficacy of the sacraments as working through the natural motion of the instrument (the water washing), for Scotus the effect of the sacraments is not intrinsically related to the natural action of the instrument in any way. Although in one sense this reduces the sacraments to mere signs of a divine effect, for Scotus even the signate dimension of the sacraments (the cleansing properties of water) in relation to their supernatural end is univocally dependent on divine decree.[75] Despite the earlier Franciscan tradition, Scotus' approach was broadly accepted by William of Ockham and the nominalist tradition.[76]

AQUINAS AND THE THOMIST TRADITION

Working within the received tradition, Aquinas describes sacramental causality intrinsically using the category of efficient causality. Like Roland of Cremona, Aquinas chooses to use the categories of po-

---

73. "Ad questionem secundam patet per idem quòd nec manifestè possibile, nec necessarium est ponere illam virtutem, quae sit forma realis in Sacramento.... Nec per illam si poneretur, aliquid causaretur in anima, nec causaretur ipsa regulariter, nisi ex pactione divina cum Ecclesia: & sic sine tot superfluis in aqua, & anima intermediis, potest saluari quòd pactio diuina sit immediata , respectu effectus conferendi, & recipienti Sacramenta." *Op.Ox.* IV.1.4-5.16. Wadding (*Opera Omnia 1639*), 8.105, as in Hildesheim, vol. 8 (1968), 105. Richard Fishacre holds a similar position. *In IV Sent.*, d. 1.

74. Cross, *Duns Scotus*, 137. See also McCord Adams, "Essential Orders and Sacramental Causality," 203.

75. Lauge Olaf Nielsen, "Signification, Likeness and Causality: The Sacraments as Signs by Divine Imposition in John Duns Scotus, Durand of St. Pourcain, and Peter Auriol," in *Vestigia, Imagines, Verba: Semiotics and Logic in Medieval Theological Texts (XIIth-XIVth Century)*, ed. Constantino Marmo (Turnhout: Brepols, 1997), 223-32.

76. Marilyn McCord Adams notes important differences between Scotus and Ockham on sacramental causality in "Essential Orders and Sacramental Causality," 203-4.

tency and motion to describe the way in which the sacraments contain the grace they confer. The sacraments contain grace as an instrument contains the final effect intended by an artist. To this end, he understands instrumental efficiency as a participation in the power of the principal agent, as color which moves through the air to be received by the eye, containing the form of the final cause as something as yet incomplete, as light still *in potentia* to be received by the eye. In this way, the sacraments (and all instrumental causes) are causal not equivocally (as in Bonaventure's "extended sense" of causality) but rather analogically with necessary reference to the potency of the principal agent. Divine sovereignty is not compromised, and yet the sacraments can be considered causes in a real (unequivocal) sense. This teaching also fits well with the inherited Augustinian tradition. Aquinas describes this instrumental efficiency as the power and intent of the principal agent flowing (*fluere*) through the instrument to reach its point of actualization in the intended recipient, working through the medium of motion to reach its end.[77] Thus Aquinas' description of instrumental efficient causality as light passing through air to be actuated in its reception by the eye strongly resembles Au-

---

77. "Ista dicuntur agentia univoca, sicut calor est in igne calefaciente. In quibusdam vero est idem secundum proportionem sive analogiam, sicut cum sol calefacit.... Ex quo patet quod illud quod est in effectu ut forma dans esse, est in agente, inquantum hujusmodi, ut virtus activa. Et ideo sicut se habet agens ad virtutem activam, ita se habet ad continendam formam effectus. Et quia agens instrumentale non habet virtutem agendi ut aliquod ens completum, sed per modum intentionis, ut dictum est; et forma introducta continetur in eo per modum intentionis: sicut sunt species colorum in aere, a quibus aer non denominatur coloratus. Et hoc modo gratia est in sacramentis sicut in instrumento, non complete, sed incomplete ... per modum intentionis fluentis duplici fluxu: quorum unus est de potentia in actum: sicut etiam in mobili est forma quae est terminus motus, dum movetur ut fluens de potentia in actum; et inter haec cadit medium motus cujus virtute instrumentum agit; alius de agente in patiens, inter quae cadit medium instrumentum, prout unum est movens et alterum motum." *Super Sent.* lib. 4, d. 1, q. 1, a. 4, qc. 4, Solutio. Mandonnet/Moos, vol. 4 (1947), 37. Textual citations for Aquinas' *Sentences* commentary (books 1–3 and book 4, dist. 1–22) are taken from Sancti Thomae Aquinatis, *Scriptum Super Libros Sententiarum Magistri Petri Lombardi Episcopi Parisiensis*, Mandonnet and Moos, eds., 4 vols. (Paris: Letheilleux, 1929–47). Because book four of the Mandonnet/Moos is incomplete, citations from dist. 23–50 are taken from the Parma edition. Sancti Thomae Aquinatis *Opera Omnia*, vol. 7, secundum impressionem Petri Fiaccadori Parmae 1852–73, photolithographice reimpressa, cum nova introductione generalli anglice scripta a Vernon Bourke (New York: Mesurgia Publishers, 1948).

gustine's description of the sacramental relationship of effect and sign as water passing through an aqueduct to reach its intended recipient.

In an effort to resolve the problem of a natural instrument producing a supernatural effect, in his *Sentences* commentary Aquinas bifurcates efficient instrumental causality between dispositive and perfective instrumental causality, arguing that with respect to the finality of grace, the sacraments are dispositive efficient instrumental causes.[78] In both cases, instrumental efficient causes are always distinct from the principal efficient causality that is attributable to God alone.[79] Aquinas distinguishes between those instrumental efficient causes which touch the finality intended by the principal agent (perfective) and those which do not themselves touch this finality (dispositive) but are part of a chain of efficiency which is working toward the intended finality under the aegis of the principal agent—in this sense, these instrumental efficient causes can be said to dispose for the final end.

Unlike Bonaventure (for whom dispositive causality is not a species of instrumental efficient causality), this provides Aquinas with a working model for speaking of the sacraments as real efficient causes without compromising the principal agency of God. The precise nature of Aquinas' mature teaching on this matter has been the subject of prolonged debate, however. Although most Thomists of the modern period came to see a development in Aquinas' teaching on sacramental causality between the *Sentences* and the *Summa*, Aquinas' early doctrine of

78. "Ad cujus evidentiam sciendum est quod causa efficiens dupliciter potest dividi. Uno modo ex parte effectus: scilicet in disponentem, quae causat dispositionem ad formam ultimam, et perficientem quae inducit ultimam perfectionem. Alio modo ex parte ipsius causae in agens principale, et instrumentale.... Hujusmodi autem materialibus instrumentis competit aliqua actio ex natura propria, sicut aquae abluere et oleo facere nitidum corpus; sed ulterius, inquantum sunt instrumenta divinae misericordiae justificantis, pertingunt instrumentaliter ad aliquem effectum in ipsa anima, quod primo correspondet sacramentis, sicut est character vel aliquid hujusmodi. Ad ultimum autem effectum quod est gratia, non pertingunt etiam instrumentaliter, nisi dispositive, inquantum hoc ad quod instrumentaliter effective pertingunt, est dispositio, quae est necessitas, quantum in se est, ad gratiae susceptionem." *Super Sent.* lib. 4, d. 1, q. 1, a. 4, Solutio I. Mandonnet/Moos, vol. 4 (1947), 32. Aquinas understands instrumental efficient causality (both dispositive and perfective) as distinct from the principal efficient causality attributable to God alone. See *Super Sent.* lib 2, d. 1, q. 1, a. 1–2.

79. See *Super Sent.* lib. 2 dist. 1 q. 1 a. 1–2.

dispositive cause remained the predominant position of the Thomistic commentatorial tradition for centuries.[80] Because commentary on the *Sentences* of Peter Lombard persisted as the standard for theological method and instruction through the fifteenth century, Thomist theological methodology largely conformed itself to this text.[81]

Early Thomistic commentators interacted with Thomas primarily through the framework that was in place in the wider university and employed by their intellectual peers. Because of its dominance in the academy, the *Sentences* formed the common intellectual medium for different theological schools, each of which continued to express its respective position by commenting on this common text.[82] In this

80. In his recent study, U. Zahnd notes some elements of this development but minimizes its consequences. Zahnd, *Wirksame Zeichen?*, 165–66.

81. It was not until the sixteenth century that St. Thomas' *Summa theologiae* replaced Lombard's *Sentences* as the standard textbook for western theology. Rosemann, *Peter Lombard*, 3. Unsurprisingly, it seems that the *Summa* first gained this prominence in Dominican schools, where this transition began as early as 1480–83. Gallagher, *Significando Causant*, 137. However, Dominican commentators such as John Capreolus (d. 1444) continued to use the *Sentences* as a medium for debating the nominalists at Paris in the early fifteenth century. By this time the content of these "commentaries on the *Sentences*" often had less to do with Lombard directly; written soon after the Dominican Order's return to the University of Paris in 1407 (after a long controversy surrounding the condemnations of the previous century), Capreolus' writings are proposed as a defense of Thomist teaching against the criticisms of the nominalists rather than a commentary on the thought of Peter Lombard. See Philipp W. Rosemann, "The Story of a Great Medieval Book: Peter Lombard's Sentences," in *Rethinking the Middle Ages*, vol. 2, ed. Paul Edward Dutton and John Shinners (Ontario: Broadview Press, 2007), 139–48. However, there is evidence that earlier Thomists were aware of the suggestion that Aquinas' doctrine of sacramental causality develops in the *Summa*. Although Capreolus is opposed to this claim, his argument shows that he is aware of this possibility. *Defensiones Theol.*, lib. 4 d. 1, 2, 3, q. 1 a. 1 concl. 3, (vol. 6, 4). Textual citations for Capreolus are taken from *Defensiones Theologiae Divi Thomae Aquinatis*, ed. Ceslai Paban and Thomae Pègues (Turin: Alfred Cattier, 1906).

82. By the middle of the thirteenth century, "the *Sentences* commentary [had come] into its own as a preferred medium of scholastic theological (and philosophical) discourse, certainly rivaling, and often outshining, other vehicles of theological expression (e.g. Quodlibital questions, *Summae*, Biblical commentaries). During the period of 1250–1320 it became increasingly common for theologians to produce several *Sentences* commentaries (or several variations of their one *Sentences* commentary), having either lectured on the *Sentences* several times or having taken several opportunities to rework the material used in their lectures.... Parallel with the development of the *Sentences* commentary into a major bearer of theological ideas, the very structure of the commentaries themselves changed a great deal, and certainly the thought expressed in

way, both intrinsic and extrinsic approaches to sacramental causality continued to be expressed through the medium of the *Sentences*. Conversely, Thomists since the early modern period have understood the *Summa theologiae* to be their primary window into the thought of St. Thomas—as a result Aquinas' earlier works have come to be viewed through the doctrinal lens of the *Summa*. There are good reasons to favor the later works of an author over his earliest; however, because of the lasting influence of Peter Lombard, early Thomism took Aquinas' *Commentary on the Sentences* as its point of departure, reading works such as the *Summa theologiae* only later and most likely with reference to the *Sentences*.

In this way, the textual hermeneutic of many early Thomists was vastly different than that of later Thomistic commentators and present students of Aquinas.[83] Most other theologians during this period expressed their mature thought in *Sentences* commentaries, and one might easily assume that Aquinas was no different in this respect. Further, the practical need to shape theological discourse around the medium of the *Sentences* was an unavoidable reality for the first generations of Thomists. It is helpful to recall that during this period Thomism was far from dominant, and the need to respond to—and defend Aquinas from—the rise of late scholastic nominalist interpretations was very real. As in our own times, to do this effectively meant entering into discourse within commonly accepted theological mediums.[84]

----

them saw a great deal of development.... There arose shared theological tendencies, best described as traditions: a Franciscan theological tradition and a Dominican one." G. R. Evans, ed., *Mediaeval Commentaries on the Sentences of Peter Lombard: Current Research*, vol. 1 (Boston: Brill, 2002), 42.

83. Capreolus seems to be an exception to this. In a number of passages he argues that the *Summa* should be used to correct Aquinas' earlier work where discrepancies occur. *Defensiones Theol.*, lib. 1 d. 1, q. 3, a. 1, concl. 1, (Pègues vol. 3, 87); d. 13, q. 1, a. 3, (vol. 4, 38); lib 4, d. 22, q. 2, a. 3, (vol. 6, 452). In one instance, he compares the *Summa's* function in this regard to Augustine's *Retractiones*. Lib 2, d. 17, q. 1, a. 3, (vol. 4, 123). See also lib. 2 d. 28, q. 1, a. 3, ad 3, (Pègues vol. 4, 308); q. 1, ad 3, (Pègues vol. 4, 311). On the subject of sacramental causality, however, Capreolus seems to read the *Summa* through the lens of the *Sentences*, arguing that the text of *ST* III^a Q. 62, a. 1 is doctrinally congruent with Aquinas' arguments for dispositive causality in the *Sentences*. *Defensiones Theol.*, lib. 4 d. 1, 2, 3, q. 1 a. 1 concl. 3, (vol. 6, 4). It seems that Peter of Palude (d. 1342) held a similar view. (4 *Sent.* dist. 1, q. 1; dist. 2, q. 3). See Michael Gierens, "Zur Lehre des hl. Thomas uber die Kausalitat der Sacramente," *Scholastik*, 9 (1934): 321–22.

84. In addition to textual commentary and interpretation, for Capreolus the *Sen-*

An internal factor which extended the life of Aquinas' early thought on sacramental causality was the muted quality of his shift on this subject in the *Summa*. While the explicit language of dispositive sacramental causality is not employed in the *Summa*, it is also not explicitly repudiated. As a result, almost all early Thomistic commentators believed that the sacraments were dispositive causes of grace, following Aquinas' explicit teaching in the *Sentences*. This position was also held by the young Cajetan (d. 1534) in his own *Sentences* commentary, which he produced around the year 1493.[85] Later, however, Cajetan would revise this position in his commentary on Aquinas' *Summa theologiae*. Although Aquinas makes no mention of the distinction between dispositive and perfective instrumental causality in the *Summa*, he speaks of sacramental causality in a way that for some indicates that they are perfective instruments (in the manner described in his *Sentences* commentary).[86]

Cajetan's position was controversial at the time, and one of the chief objectors was Sylvester de Ferrara (d. 1528). However, it would subsequently become the standard explanation of sacramental cause among Thomists, upheld by Domingo Bañez (d. 1604), John of St. Thomas (d. 1644) and many others.[87] One of the central issues for

---

tences provided the ground on which he could effectively engage the threat of nominalism. See note 81. See also *Jean Capreolus en son temps (1380–1444)*, Mémoire Dominicaine, numéro spécial, 1, ed. Guy Bedouelle, Romanus Cessario and Kevin White (Paris: Les Éditions du Cerf, 1997) and John Capreolus, *On the Virtues*, translated with introduction and notes by Romanus Cessario and Kevin White (Washington, D.C.: The Catholic University of America Press, 2001).

85. Cajetan's *Sentences* commentary was not edited as a published final product but consists rather of notes from students or perhaps his own lecture notes. (The argument in favor of dispositive causality can be found in his commentary on the fourth book of Lombard's *Sentences*: Cajetan, *In IV Sent.*, q. 1, a. 1). See also Bernhard Alfred R. Felmberg, *Die Ablaßtheologie Kardinal Cajetans (1469–1534)* (Leiden: Brill, 1998), 179.

86. "Causa vero instrumentalis non agit per virtutem suae formae, sed solum per motum quo movetur a principali agente. Unde effectus non assimilatur instrumento, sed principali agenti: sicut lectus non assimilatur securi, sed arti quae est in mente artificis." *ST* III, q. 62, a. 1, co.

87. Cajetan was the first Thomistic commentator to interpret Aquinas after the *Summa* was adopted as the standard text in Dominican schools and noted the implicit difference between the *Sentences* commentary and the *Summa theologiae* on the subject of sacramental cause. His position was not accepted by some older Thomist contemporaries, such as Sylvester de Ferrara, who maintained in his commentary on the *Summa contra gentiles* that Aquinas never abandoned dispositive causality. Both Cajetan's

these commentators is the definition of grace in relation to sacramental instrumentality.[88]

During the modern period and beyond, the position of Cajetan and later Thomists on the subject of sacramental causality was frequently referred to as "perfective physical causality." Although this terminology is not used by Aquinas in the *Summa*, it is intended to clearly distinguish Cajetan's teaching from that of both the earlier Thomists and those who favored an extrinsic approach. The word "perfective" is not used by Aquinas in his mature writings; however, its reference to the distinction between dispositive and perfective efficient instrumental causes in his *Sentences* commentary serves to rule out the option of a dispositive interpretation.[89] The word "physical"

---

commentary on the *Summa theologiae* and de Ferrara's commentary on the *Summa contra gentiles* have been standard companions for generations of Thomists. Both appear in the Leonine edition of Aquinas's *Operae*. For an example of this, see *In contra gentiles* IV, c. 57, *Opera Omnia S. Thomae*, ed. iussu Leonis XIII, vol. 15, p. 192. De Ferrara argues that the sacraments are dispositive causes of grace, whose instrumental efficiency extends only to the sacramental character in the strict sense; the character then disposes the soul for the reception of grace. Here De Ferrara is interpreting the text of *ST* III, q. 62. He says that some have claimed that this text teaches that grace is caused instrumentally by the sacraments in an absolute sense. Regarding this interpretation of *ST* III, q. 62, De Ferrara has this to say: "Sed hoc ad mentem S. Thomae esse non puto." See Gallagher, *Significando Causant*, 137–41. De Ferrara refutes this claim using texts from the *De potentia* and the *Sentences*. In this de Ferrara stood in line with the older commentatorial tradition claiming that Thomism in its purity is found in the *Sentences* and that later works such as the *De veritate* and *De potentia* support this teaching. The absence of an explicit retraction of his earlier position in the *Summa* only further confirms this for de Ferrara. See Reginald Lynch, "Cajetan's Harp: Sacraments and the Life of Grace in Light of Perfective Instrumentality," *The Thomist* 78 (2014): 66–71.

88. The crux of the issue here is the status of grace as either created or uncreated. Because an instrument can have no role in the creative process, de Ferrara holds that the instrumentality of the sacraments cannot extend to grace *per se* but must be limited simply to the disposition for its reception. Gallagher, *Significando Causant*, 137–41. Unfortunately, we cannot offer a thorough treatment of the subject of created and uncreated grace here. For a balanced treatment of this matter, see Réginald Garrigou-Lagrange, *Grace: Commentary on the Summa Theologica of St. Thomas, Ia IIae, Q. 109–114*, trans. Dominican Nuns of Corpus Christi Monastery, Menlo Park, California (St. Louis: Herder, 1952), 110–15. Garrigou-Lagrange makes a crucial distinction between grace as the eternal love of God and grace as a potency produced in the human person, by which we participate in his divinity. Simply put, grace is a divinizing and participatory reality, bifurcated analogically along the lines of the relationship already established between creature and creator, albeit in an elevated and entirely supernatural sense.

89. Gallagher, *Significando Causant*, 190–91. Marylin McCord Adams does not

indicates the motive potency of an instrumental efficient cause in the Aristotelian sense and eliminates those theories that rely on external forms of legal pact or moral coercion.

MORAL CAUSALITY

Around the time of the Council of Trent, what came to be called "moral causality" arose as a new development within the extrinsicist tradition. Advocates of this position argue that the sacraments do not cause grace after the manner of a physical motive cause in the Aristotelian sense but are causes after the manner of moral or legal compulsion: God establishes the sacramental economy and binds himself to respond to the sacraments with the gift of grace.[90] Although Melchior Cano (d. 1560) was the first to argue for moral causality explicitly,[91] some have claimed

mention the development in Aquinas' thought on this subject or the secondary literature surrounding it. In her critique of Aquinas' position, she describes Aquinas' theory of sacramental causality as dispositive, relying solely on the text of his *Sentences* commentary. See "Powerless Causes: The Case of Sacramental Causality," 55–58, and *Some Later Medieval Theories of the Eucharist: Thomas Aquinas, Giles of Rome, Duns Scotus and William of Ockham* (Oxford: Oxford University Press, 2010), 58.

90. This explanation of sacramental causality was extremely popular from the sixteenth century to the early twentieth. Many claim that there are strong nominalist tendencies in this school of thought. See Bañez, *Comentarios Ineditos a la Tercera Parte de Santo Tomas*, vol. 2, *De Sacramentis: QQ. 60–90*, ed. Vincente Beltran de Heredia, Biblioteca de Teologos Españoles 19 (Salamanca: 1953), 47–48. See also Aloisius M. Ciappi, *De Sacramentis in Communi: Commentarius in Tertiam Partem S. Thomae (qq.)*, Pontificum Institutum Internationale Angelicum (Torino: R. Berruti, 1957), 70–71. Gallagher, *Significando Causant*, 158.

91. Melchior Cano (d. 1560) studied under Vitoria at Salamanca, and later succeeded him as chair in 1546. He was deeply involved in the debates surrounding the sacraments at the Council of Trent, particularly those concerning the Eucharist and Penance. His most influential work is *De Locis Theologicis* (Salamanca, 1563), which proposes a new method for theology in relation to its sources. *ODCC* s.v. "Cano, Melchior." For more on the nature and influence of Cano's *De Locis*, see A. Lang, *Die Loci Theologici des Melchior Cano und die Methode des Dogmatischen Beweises: Ein Beitrag zur theologischen Methodologie und ihrer Geschichte*, Münchener Studien zur Historischen Theologie 6 (Munich: Kösel & Pustet, 1925). Cano's restructuring of theology in relation to its sources in *De Locis* had wide-ranging effects on ecclesiology in the modern period. The manner in which theologians conceived of conciliar and papal magisterial authority was deeply affected by his use of ecclesial authority. See Ulrich Horst, *Unfehlbarkeit und Geschichte: Studien zur Unfehlbarkeitsdiskussion von Melchior Cano bis zum I. Vatikanischen Konzil* (Mainz: Matthias-Grünewald-Verlag, 1982). Further, many of the manuals of the

that it was Francisco de Vitoria (d. 1546), his mentor and immediate predecessor at the University of Salamanca, who first proposed an early version of this theory.[92] Dominic de Soto (d. 1560), also a student

---

nineteenth and twentieth century are more indebted on a hermeneutical and methodological level to Cano's *De Locis* than they are to Aquinas' *Summa*. Jared Wicks, "A Note on "Neo-Scholastic" Manuals of Theological Instruction, 1900–1960," *Josephinum* 18 n. 1 (2011): 242. Cano was also deeply involved in ecclesial politics. He served as provincial of Castile and opposed the Jesuits on a number of issues, theological and otherwise. *ODCC*, s.v. "Cano, Melchior." Cano remained a controversial figure at the University of Salamanca for several centuries. During the reform of the curriculum, which began in 1771, attempts were made to replace the *Summa theologiae* with Cano's *De Locis*, whole or in part. This curriculum controversy followed Salamancan disputes of the previous century concerning Jesuits, Dominicans, grace, Jansenism, and the Chinese rites. See George M. Addy, *The Enlightenment in the University of Salamanca* (Durham, N.C.: Duke University Press, 1966), 116–17, 189–202. Some see a connection between the Molinist controversy concerning the nature of grace and the sacramental systems connected with the conferral thereof. Some see an intellectual lineage connecting the Franciscan theological positions on the sacramental conferral of grace with the later Jesuit position on grace and the development of moral theology under Melchior Cano. Subsequent thinkers who held that the sacraments were moral causes of grace were likewise involved in arguing for the Molinist position. See Auer, *A General Doctrine of the Sacraments*, 79. Dominic de Soto (d. 1560), also a student of Vitoria, initially supported a position substantially similar to Cano's moral causality. See Ciappi, *De Sacramentis in Communi*, 72n8. See also Bañez, *Comentarios Ineditos a la Tercera Parte de Santo Tomas*, vol. 2, *De Sacramentis: QQ. 60–90*, 45. For a study of Soto on this subject, see Alfonso F. Feliziani, "La Causalità dei Sacramenti in Domenico Soto," *Angelicum* 16 (1939): 148–94. The University of Salamanca provided a meeting place for a wide variety of ideas and intellectual trends in the sixteenth century. Paradoxically, the move toward a renewal in the humanities and classics within the arts faculty that preceded the Thomistic revival (roughly coterminous with Vitoria's tenure) did not transition directly into the enlightenment along with the rest of the continent but existed in a comparatively harmonious relationship with scholastic theology and other traditional disciplines for some time. See Crisogono de Jesus, *The Life of St. John of the Cross*, trans. Kathleen Pond (New York: Harper & Brothers, 1958). See also Addy, *The Enlightenment*.

92. See Ciappi, *De Sacramentis in Communi*, 71n7. This position may reflect Vitoria's exposure to nominalism while studying theology in Paris. *Sacrae Theologiae Summa*, vol. 4, *De Sacramentis, De Novissimis*, 3rd ed., (Madrid: Biblioteca de Autores Cristianos, 1956), 73n9. Francisico de Vitoria (d. 1546) assumed his chair in sacred theology at the University of Salamanca in 1526. At this time, the *Summa theologiae* was already in use as a textbook for theology at the University. It was de Vitoria who began the Thomistic revival at Salamanca that would eventually produce the Carmelite Thomistic commentatorial school known as the *Salamanticenses*. It is of anecdotal interest that, during the early stages of this revival, the Carmelite masters at Salamanca would influence a young clerical student who would come to be known as St. John of the Cross. See Crisogono de Jesus, *The Life of St. John of the Cross*, 33.

of Vitoria, initially supported a position substantially similar to Cano's moral causality.[93]

Although there are certain differences between moral causality and occasionalism or *sine qua non* causality, many theologians see a strong continuity between the theory of moral causality proposed in the early modern period and the thought of some early Franciscan thinkers, including Bonaventure.[94] We know that Bonaventure saw the sacraments as "occasions" for the reception of grace. The sacraments were causes of grace *sine qua non*: necessary conditions for the reception of grace established by divine decree.[95] Duns Scotus expands upon this by speaking of the relationship between merit and reward as a kind of contractual divine promise. Scotus argued that the sacraments conferred grace not because of any intrinsic power or form contained within them but because God has promised to give graces to those who receive the sacraments.[96] In this, Scotus' position

93. See Ciappi, *De Sacramentis in Communi*, 72 n8. See also Bañez, *Comentarios Ineditos a la Tercera Parte de Santo Tomas*, vol. 2 of *De Sacramentis: QQ. 60–90*, 45. For a study of Soto on this subject, see Feliziani, "La Causalita Dei Sacramenti in Domenico Soto," 148–94.

94. "We can see [moral causality's] roots in Scotus, Bonaventure and other Franciscans ... the chain of thought is clear, even if the diverse expressions of it do not state it in the same way, or leave implicit what is explicit in another form." Gallagher, *Significando Causant*, 158. Representatives of the Jesuit theological tradition in twentieth-century Spain include Ockham (*In* 4, d. 1, q. 1, 2) and Biel (*In* 4, d. 1, q. 1, a. 2, concl. 7) in this lineage as well. See Josepho A. de Aldama, Francisco a P. Sola and Josepho F. Sagüès, *De Sacramentis: De novissimis*, in vol. 4 of *Sacrae Theologiae Summa*, ed. Miguel Nicolau, Biblioteca De Autores Cristianos (Matriti: Editorial Católica, 1953), 65 n4. (This series was produced by the Spanish Jesuits in the mid-twentieth century). A clear lineage exists linking the early Franciscan tradition, the nominalists, and later proponents of moral causality within the Jesuit tradition. This opinion is shared by twentieth-century Dominicans as well, such as Aloisius Ciappi. Ciappi, *De Sacramentis in Communi*, 70–71. Ciappi is not alone in this regard but rather stands in continuity with the classical Thomist commentatorial tradition: Bañez argues that, in various ways, Alexander of Hales, Bonaventure, Ockham, Richard Fishacre, Scotus, Durandus, and Gabriel Biel all hold that the sacraments are causes of grace because, either through their presence or use, God is moved to confer grace. Bañez, *Comentarios Ineditos a la Tercera Parte de Santo Tomas*, vol. 2, *De Sacramentis: QQ. 60–90*, 44.

95. For Bonaventure, only the sacramental character or *ornatus* can be attributed to efficient causality. Concerning grace, the sacraments function as "occasions" or "dispositions" for grace. Bonaventure, *In IV Sent.*, d. 1, p. 1, a. 1, q. 4, resp., s.c 4. Lampen, *De Causalitate Sacramentorum*, 22–23.

96. "Merita sunt causa instrumentalis respectu praemii, & quòd per merita acquiri-

can be seen as a mature manifestation of something already proposed by Bonaventure.[97] By describing the instrumentality of the sacraments solely in terms of merit and reward, Scotus' position stands as a deeper expression of the extrinsic tradition. Although Bonaventure proposed sacramental occasionalism as a means of preserving God's causal role in the sacraments, in committing to this model, however preliminarily, he starts down a path which will close in behind the Franciscan thinkers who follow him, making it impossible to retreat to the place from whence they had come. Unlike their Thomist contemporaries, Scotus and later nominalists saw no analogical resolution to the problem of instrumental efficient causality.

Melchior Cano's theory of moral causality, which will be dealt with in a subsequent chapter, is based on a similar system of promise, merit, and reward.[98] Cano argues that there is a distinction between natural (or physical) causes, which involve physical motion, and moral causes, which involve the exercise of free will. Cano maintains that physical causes cannot reach the essence of the sacramental action, while moral causes can.[99] Cano is clear that a moral cause does not cause a physical change of any sort but functions in the order of merit.[100] Cano's theory of moral causality was the favored position of many theologians during the modern period, including Jesuits involved in the Molinist controversy such as Vázquez (d. 1604) and de Lugo (d. 1660); moral causality was also favored by many of their nineteenth-century descendants such as Franzelin (d. 1886).[101]

---

tur praemium: & tamen meritum non causat actiuè praemium in se, nec aliquam dispositionem mediam, sed solummodò ipsummet est dispositio praeuia ad praemium: non tamen sicut ratio receptiui." *Op.Ox.* IV.1.4–5.12. Wadding, 8.94, as in Hildesheim, vol. 8 (1968), 94. See also Auer, *A General Doctrine of the Sacraments*, 79–80.

97. While Bonaventure and Scotus differ in many ways, in the case of sacramental cause later Thomists saw a deep continuity between the two. See Bañez, *Comentarios Ineditos a la Tercera Parte de Santo Tomas*, vol. 2 of *De Sacramentis: QQ. 60–90*, 44; Ciappi, *De Sacramentis in Communi*, 71; and Gallagher, *Significando Causant*, 152.

98. Cano uses the idea of a note as an example of a moral cause: "Consequentia videtur esse nota, quoniam id vocamus causam, qua applicata sequitur effectus." *Relectio de Sacramentis*, pars IV, in Melchior Cano, *Opera* (Padua: Typis Seminarii, 1734) (facsimile reprint of the Hyacinth Serry edition, Kila, Mont.: Kessinger, 2011), 483.

99. *Relect. de Sacram.*, Pars IV, concl. 6, in Cano, *Opera*, 488.

100. Ibid.

101. Auer argues that the history of Cano's theory begins with Bonaventure and can be traced through the Scotists to the Jesuits of the modern period who held the

Subsequent Thomists such as Domingo Bañez who were prominent figures in the *de Auxiliis* controversy would respond with strong criticism to Cano's theory, re-articulating the position of Cajetan in the face of these new challenges.[102] Bañez reminds his reader that Aquinas himself acknowledges a category of meritorious causality present in the redemptive power of Christ's passion; however, this teaching is already couched within the framework of instrumental efficient causality, the humanity functioning as conjoined, and the sacraments as separated, instruments effecting grace in the soul. Bañez argues that although the redemptive merits of the passion can be partially described by Cano's moral causality, the actual functioning of the sacraments themselves cannot. Recall that Augustine taught that the elements, taken up in union with the Word, became sacraments, working toward the sanctification of human persons by the power of God. Later thinkers such as Hugh of St. Victor use the category of "instrumentality" to describe the way in which the sacraments effect what they signify. Is it sufficient to view the sacraments as rites ordained by God for our use, the successful completion of which God subsequently rewards? More fundamentally, should the action of sacraments themselves be understood as something we do or something God does? In response to Cano, Bañez describes sacramental instrumentality by giving the example of a pencil worked by the hand of an artist to effect an image on a sheet of paper—so too are the sacraments moved by the action of the Holy Spirit as physical causes to effect grace in the human soul.[103] Bañez highlights the importance of

---

Molinist position (e.g., Vásquez, de Lugo, and Franzelin). Auer, *A General Doctrine of the Sacraments*, 79. The connection intimated here by Auer between sacramental causality and the *de Auxiliis* controversy further highlights the importance of the definition of grace in this debate and its governing role as final cause in sacramental motion.

102. See Bañez, *Comentarios Ineditos a la Tercera Parte de Santo Tomas*, vol. 2, *De Sacramentis: QQ. 60–90*, 43–51. Bañez argues that, while Christ's passion is certainly the meritorious cause of our redemption, this assertion does not substitute for a discussion of the role of the sacramental signs themselves as physical instruments in the conferral of grace. Bañez points out that the leaden coin found in nominalist explanations of sacramental causality and the redemptive merit of Cano's moral causality both need some form of physical instrumentality to explain the actual accomplishment of the sacramental action itself. See Bañez, *Comentarios Ineditos a la Tercera Parte de Santo Tomas*, vol. 2, *De Sacramentis: QQ. 60–90*, 47–48.

103. "Sicut revera penicillus attingit ad productionem imaginis quatenus movetur

the Thomistic doctrine referred to as "physical perfective causality," in which the sacraments are understood as instrumental or analogical extensions of divine potency, functioning according to God's wisdom.

Interestingly, Francisco Suárez (d. 1617), who reacted in part against the nominalist tradition and rejected Cano's theory of moral causality,[104] argued for a version of physical causality, claiming to affirm the teaching of Cajetan in this regard. However, the differences between these two thinkers concerning the concept of physical premotion (which had such wide-ranging implications for the doctrine of grace) affect their respective understandings of sacramental instrumentality as well.[105]

---

ab artifice, ita sacramenta attingant ad productionem gratiae quatenus sunt instrumenta et movetur a Spiritu Sancto." Bañez, *Comentarios Ineditos a la Tercera Parte de Santo Tomas*, vol. 2 of *De Sacramentis: QQ. 60–90*, 47–48. Bañez is commenting on *ST* III, q. 62 a. 1.

104. *In ST* III, q. 62 a. 4, disp. 9 sec. II n. 10, 18–23.

105. Suárez affirms Cajetan's use of obediential potency in the context of sacramental causality seemingly without qualification. *In* 3, q. 62 a. 4, disp. 9 sec. II n. 13. However, Thomists are quick to point out that Suárez's failure to accept the Thomist doctrine of "physical promotion" compromises his understanding of obediential potency. For Suárez this is an active potency rather than a passive one. See Ciappi, *De Sacramentis in Communi*, 73n10. Suárez presents his teaching on active obediential potency in the context of the sacraments as an interpretation of a familiar Augustinian phrase: "Quaenam sit illa virtus, per quam possunt instrumenta Dei concurrere, quando elevantur. Diximus enim non esse rem aliquam superadditam, sed esse ipsamet entitatem rei, quae hoc ipso, quod creata est, et subordinata primo agenti, est in *potentia obedientiali active*.... Haec enim ratio obedientialis potentiae communis est sacramentis, quorum elevatio divina solum in hoc consistit, quod Deus altiori modo concurrit dando auxilium sufficiens, ut res operetur secundum hanc potentiam. Necque ad hoc refert, quod sacramenta sint imperfecta in sua entitate. Quia hic concursus non fundatur in naturali eorum perfectione, sed in praedicta infinita virtute obedientiali et in infinita Dei virtute, cui omnia subordinantur.... Quanquam fortasse non efficiant solum per ipsum motum, qui est ens imperfectum, seu modus entis, et significatur nomine ablutionis vel unctionis, sed per ipsasmet res quae moventur, vel applicantur, dum sacramenta fiunt, vel accipiuntur, ut per oleum, aquam, species panis, etc.; *sic enim dixit Augustinus aquam esse, quae corpus tangit et cor abluit*." *In* 3, q. 62 a. 4, disp. 9 sec. I n. 21 (emphasis mine). Francisci Suarez, *Opera Omnia*, tom. 20, *Commentaria ac Disputationes in Tertiam Partem D. Thomae, de Sacramentis in Genere, de Baptismo, de Confirmatione, de Eucharistia usque ad Quaestionem LXXIV* (Paris: Vivés, 1877), 147. Suárez considers this active form of obediential potency more thoroughly in his commentary on the Prima Pars: disp. 31 sect. 5 and disp. 36 sect. 6. Further divisions between Suárez and Cajetan emerge regarding the issue of natural form and potency in the context of instrumental causality. Where

THE TRIDENTINE REFORM

The Council of Trent (1545–63) proved to be a major watershed for sacramental theology. Called principally to respond to the crisis of the Protestant Reformation, the Council clearly teaches that the sacraments both contain (*continere*) grace and confer (*conferre*) or give (*dare*) it to their recipients and that their use (or a desire thereof) is necessary for salvation.[106] The Council's description of the sacraments as containing and conferring grace is reminiscent of Victorine Augustinianism and clearly rules out those most radical forms of occasionalism which had taken root in the doctrines of the Protestant reformers. However, this acknowledgement does little to resolve the longstanding conflict between the intrinsic and extrinsic approach-

---

Cajetan says that the natural form of the instrument is taken up in the potency of the principal agent, Suárez seems to imply that it remains, to be assisted by divine power in the attainment of its supernatural end. Aquinas' own teaching on this subject in the *Summa* directly denies this in *ST* III, q. 62 a. 1, co.; Cajetan's commentary on this same text reinforces this teaching. Elsewhere Cajetan returns to this concept, using the example of a musician and his instrument to demonstrate the relationship that exists between a principal agent, the instrumental causes he employs, and the final effects that only he can intend: "Exemplum utriusque motus perspice in cithara: cuius fides si moveantur a non-musico, sonabunt tantum; si vero moveantur a musico, efficient non solum sonum, sed sonum musicum, qui est effectus proprius artis musicae." Cajetan, *Commentary on ST* III, q. 62 a. 4, n. IV. Other non-Thomist theologians of the modern period argued for so-called "physical perfective causality" as well: Bellarmine (*De sacramentis in genere*, 2.11), Valentia (*Commentaria theologica*, 4 disp. 3, q. 3, p. 1), Ripalda (*De ente supernaturali*, disp. 40 s. 3 n. 13). See *Sacrae Theologiae Summa*, vol. 4, *De Sacramentis, De Novissimis*, 71n3. Even here, however, in a manual sympathetic to the Suárezian approach, the Thomist and Suárezian traditions are explicitly contrasted as intrinsic and extrinsic approaches, respectively, to efficient causality in the sacraments. Ibid., 71.

106. "Si quis dixerit, sacramenta novae legis non continere gratiam, quam significant, aut gratiam ipsam non ponentibus obicam non conferre, quasi signa tantum externa sint acceptae per fidem gratiae vel iustitiae, et notae quaedam christianae professionis, quibus apud homines, discernuntur fideles ab infidelibus: a.s." Conc. Trid. Sess. 7 decl. 1 c. 6. "Si quis dixerit, non dari gratiam per huiusmodi sacramenta semper et omnibus, quantum est ex parte Dei, etiam si rite ea suscipiant, sed aliquando et aliquibus: a.s." Conc. Trid. Sess. 7 decl. 1 c. 7. "Si quis dixerit, per ipsa novae legis sacramenta ex opere operato non conferri gratiam, sed solam fidem divinae promissionis ad gratiam consequendam sufficere: a.s." Conc. Trid. Sess. 7 decl. 1 c. 8. "Si quis dixerit, sacramenta novae legis non esse ad salutem necessaria, sed superflua, et sine eis aut eorum voto per solam fidem homines a Deo gratiam iustificationis adipisci, licet omnia singulis necessaria non sint: a.s." Conc. Trid. Sess. 7 decl. 1 c. 4.

es to sacramental causality that developed after the time of the Victorines.

Of the theological advisors present at the Council, many favored a more extrincisist approach to sacramental causality. Although not present for the session on sacramental efficacy in 1547, Cano was deeply involved in drafting some of the later Council documents on the sacraments.[107] Some have argued that the ambiguity present in the final draft of the Council document reveals that the Council Fathers sought to focus solely on the Protestant error, avoiding the condemnation of existing Catholic positions.[108] Others have argued that the use of the word *conferre* in the Council documents is an intentional attempt to avoid the use of the word *causare*.[109] This is not to say that the Council Fathers did not believe that the sacraments were causes. Rather, it seems that it was deemed most useful to avoid an official teaching that would favor one school's interpretation of the word *causare* over another's. In the climate of the Protestant Reformation, further division within the Church over sacramental theology was extremely undesirable; instead, universally acceptable language was actively sought so as to present a unified stance against Protestant doctrine. This is not to say, however, that all causal theories are

---

107. Cano was the theologian for Philip II at the Council of Trent. He was particularly involved in framing the Council's teaching on the Eucharist and Penance. *ODCC*, s.v. "Cano, Melchior." Leeming, *Principles of Sacramental Theology*, 297.

108. While the explicit definition of the sacraments as instruments was proposed in a plenary session, it was rejected in the final draft in favor of the more minimalist phrase *ex opere operato*. Leeming, *Principles of Sacramental Theology*, 10. H. Lennerz states: "In canone praeparato concilii Tridentini legabatur: 'per ipsa sacramentorum opera'; haec paucis placebant, quia erant verba Lutheri; sed pluribus displicebant, qui proposuerunt vel 'per ipsa sacramenta,' vel 'per ipsa sacramenta tamquam instrumenta,' vel 'per sacramenta ex opere operato,' 'per usum sacramentorum,' 'per opus operatum sacramentorum,' 'ex vi, virtute ipsorum sacramentorum.' Electa et approbata deinde est forma 'per ipsa sacramenta ex opere operato.' Dicit ergo concilium, per ipsum ritum sacramentalem valide positum dari gratiam; hoc definitur contra Protestantes; hinc proxime et directe in oppositione ad opus operantis ipsius subiecti, sed ex sensu quem terminus eo tempore universim habebat opponitur etiam operi operantis ministri." From this much, we can see that the Council actively sought language that would target the Protestants without causing further internal division. H. Lennerz, *De Sacramentis Novae Legis in Genere*, editio secunda (Rome: Typis Pontificiae Universitatis Gregorianae, 1939), 220. See also *Sacrae Theologiae Summa*, vol. 4, *De Sacramentis, De Novissimis*, 66.

109. Leeming, *Principles of Sacramental Theology*, 10–12.

equally in accord with the Council. Although Trent did not advocate for a specific causal model, the council does clearly teach against radical forms of occasional causality, building on the *Decree for the Armenians* from the Council of Florence (1439), which also insists that the sacraments "contain" and "confer" the grace they cause.[110] While scholastics disagreed amongst themselves about how best to describe the causality of the sacraments, reference to Hugh of St. Victor was taken for granted. This became less common in the later nominalist tradition, and the Council of Florence implicitly reasserts elements from the Victorine approach as a common framework for theological discussion of the sacraments, excluding in the broad sense those extrinsicist theories in which the sacraments "contained" nothing but functioned only as occasions for the exercise of divine power.

While the sacramental doctrine of the Protestants was radically occasionalist and extrinsicist, other ostensibly Catholic theories that we have already examined share some of these tendencies. Recall that Bonaventure, Scotus, and the nominalists favored an occasionalism which emphasized divine causality and saw little causal role for the sacraments themselves beyond disposing the recipient in faith and devotion to receive the grace which God alone confers.

Trent clearly ruled out, among other things, theories which reduced the sacraments to mere external signs.[111] Aquinas' original objection to the extrinsicist approach was that it reduced the causality operative in the sacraments of the New Law to the accidental status of a sign, no different from the sacraments of the Old Law.[112] In this way, Trent's determination to avoid sacramental models which reduce the sacraments to mere outward signs broadly reflects Aquinas' original concerns.

---

110. DS 1310–11, *Decr. Pro Armeniis*. See P. Pourrat, *Theology of the Sacraments: A Study in Positive Theology*, authorized translation from the French edition, 4th ed., (St. Louis: Herder, 1930), 182–83.

111. Conc. Trid. Sess. 7 decl. 1 c. 6. See note 106 for text.

112. "Sed si quis recte consideret, itse modus non transcendit rationem signi. Nam denarius plumbeus non est nisi quoddam signum regiae ordinationis de hoc quod pecunia recipiatur ab isto." *ST* III, q. 62 a. 1, co. The position described by Thomas here using the example of a leaden coin was held by Fishacre (*In IV Sent.*, d. 1), Kilwardby (*In IV Sent.*, d. 1) and Bonaventure (*In IV Sent.*, d. 1, a. unic., qu. 1); cited in *Summa Theologiae*, Editiones Paulinae (Turin: Comerciale Edizioni Paoline s.r.l., 1988), 2172n3. See also *ST* III, q. 62, a. 6.

After Trent, theologians tended to avoid the most radical positions of pre-Tridentine nominalism because it too closely resembled
the teachings condemned by the Council.[113] This aversion to radical
occasionalism did not lead to widespread acceptance of the Thomistic
position, however. Aside from ruling out the extremes of occasional
causality, many theologians after Trent remained very willing to consider theories of causality which were less than Aristotelian in their
structural underpinnings. It was generally held that physical causality,
taught by the Thomists, and moral causality, held by (post-Tridentine)
Scotists and many Jesuits, were both equally compatible with the letter of Trent.[114] Generally speaking, the positions established in the
theological schools during the Tridentine period regarding sacramental cause persisted without significant change until the nineteenth and
twentieth centuries. Although Cajetan's position came to be accepted
by the majority of Thomists, it was widely misunderstood and rejected
by many other theologians during the modern period.

However, Trent did affirm that the sacraments function *ex opere
operato*, rather than *ex opere operantis*.[115] This distinction—between
the working of the sacraments themselves (*opere operato*) and our use
of them (*opere operantis*)—was developed during the Middle Ages as
a means of preserving an Augustinian distinction with which we are
already familiar, forged during the Donatist controversy: the actions
of an unworthy minister are distinct from the action and effect of the
rite itself.[116] Aquinas himself insisted that this distinction differenti-
ated between the sacraments of the Old Law and the New: while the
sacraments of the Old Law function as signs which do not in themselves confer grace, the sacraments of the New Law work *ex opere operato*, conferring grace in an intrinsic manner consonant with the Augustinian approach, functioning as instrumental causes participant in
divine power.[117] Subsequent Thomists saw the working of the sacra-

---

113. A strict *sine qua non* occasionalism was almost universally recognized as unacceptable after Trent. Pourrat, *Theology of the Sacraments*, 185.

114. See Ludwig Ott, *Fundamentals of Catholic Dogma*, ed. James Canon Bastible,
trans. Patrick Lynch (Cork, Ireland: Mercier Press, 1958), 330.

115. Conc. Trid. Sess. 7 decl. 1 c. 8. See note 106 for text.

116. Pourrat, *Theology of the Sacraments*, 162–65.

117. *Super Sent.* lib 4, d. 1 q. 1 a. 5. *ST* III, q. 62 a. 6, co.

ments *ex opere operato* as an essential means of defending an intrinsic conception of the sacraments as "physical" or efficient instrumental causes.[118]

Trent clearly teaches that the sacraments are effective because of a power intrinsic to their operation; as such, a view of the sacraments as fundamentally human actions that God subsequently rewards is radically inadequate. As we have said previously, one of the questions raised by moral causality and other extrinsicist systems is this: should the sacraments be understood fundamentally as something we do or as something God does? There is no question that for Cano and the extrinsicist tradition that went before him God—and not human agents—is responsible for causing grace. But what about the sacraments themselves? Many occasionalist theories used the example of a leaden coin, made valuable only by decree of the king. Applied to the sacraments, the coin frequently represents human sacramental action—that is, a sign we invoke or participate in, such as water being used to wash. Later Protestant sacramental theories would exhibit highly exaggerated forms of occasionalism, which Trent clearly condemns. But Trent's insistence that the sacraments function *ex opere operato* also militates against an understanding of the sacraments as ritual human actions which God rewards and seems to speak in favor of an intrinsic causal approach. It is the working of the sacraments themselves—*ex opere operato*—which sanctifies the human person.

Despite this Tridentine teaching, however, many theologians in the modern period and into the first half of the twentieth century found Cano's moral causality to be an attractive alternative to an unmodified occasionalism. It shared many of the basic characteristics which made occasionalism appealing in the first place. However, moral causality had the added benefit of appearing less extrinsicist and tenuous because of Cano's added emphasis on the presence of the blood of Christ in the sacraments themselves. Although emphasizing this Pauline concept does not resolve the important questions raised in the scholastic debates over sacramental cause,[119] it does reinforce the sense that there is some saving reality contained in and

118. Ciappi, *De Sacramentis in Communi*, 69–70.
119. *Relect. de Sacram.*, Pars IV, concl. 6, in Melchior Cano, *Opera*, 488.

conferred by the sacraments themselves, even if this explanation is lacking on speculative grounds and the extrinsic legalism of the nominalist approach is not avoided.[120] (These issues and others will be dealt with in the fourth chapter, which critically examines the historical context of moral causality and its theological viability.)

CONTEMPORARY IMPLICATIONS

At the beginning of the twentieth century, interest in sacramental causality among theologians remained widespread. During this time, Louis Billot proposed a then-popular theory of sacramental causality called "intentional causality," which emphasized the identity of the sacraments as signs which expressed the intention of the agent. Although their material elements did not contain a spiritual force as such, their sign function was similar to that of a will that conveys real property to an heir.[121] When compared with the instrumental physical motion of Aquinas' causal system, the difference between this theory and moral causality seems minimal. Billot sees a kind of physical effect in the character, but the disposition to receive grace itself is a kind of moral cause.[122] Billot's emphasis on sign indicates a broader shift in sensibilities that would manifest itself elsewhere in theological circles. This is due in part to the liturgical movement; equally significant was the rise in existentialist alternatives to classical metaphysics. By this point, however, the sacramental systems inspired by moral causality, and their overtones of legalism, seemed less appealing to some. As a result, many sought completely new alternatives.

Influenced in part by Rahner and Chauvet, in the mid-twentieth

---

120. Despite its deep continuity with the nominalist tradition, many authors see moral causality as somewhat distinctive because of its heavy focus on merit and the notion that the sacraments "contain" the blood of Christ, the price of our redemption. It is this language of containing that makes moral causality appeal as a post-Tridentine model. These issues will be discussed further in chapter 4. See Leeming, *Principles of Sacramental Theology*, 299.

121. Billot's theory can be found in his work *De Ecclesiae Sacramentis*, t. I in III S. theol. q. 62.3. See A. H. Maltha, "De Causalitate intentionali Sacramentorum animadversiones quaedam," *Angelicum* 15 (1938): 337n1.

122. A. H. Maltha provides a useful description of Billot's theory in comparison with the works of Aquinas (both his early and his mature writings). Maltha, "De Causalitate intentionali Sacramentorum animadversiones quaedam," 337–66.

century widespread interest arose in the use of categories such as symbolism and experiential participation as modes of expressing sacramental efficacy.[123] This interest in experience and liturgy-as-event has its roots in the mystery theology of Odo Casel and to some extent

123. The alternative sacramental systems that emerged in the middle and later twentieth century had their roots in these historical developments. If time and space permitted us to do so, a study of Karl Rahner's symbolic approach to the sacraments would be of great interest. For a treatment of this subject generally sympathetic to Rahner, see Daniel A. Tappeiner, "Sacramental Causality in Aquinas and Rahner: Some Critical Thoughts," *Scottish Journal of Theology* 28 (1975): 243–57. Louis-Marie Chauvet has also provided an influential account of sacramentality, using the concept of symbol. See Louis-Marie Chauvet, *Symbol and Sacrament: A Sacramental Reinterpretation of Christian Existence* (Collegeville, Minn.: Liturgical Press, 1995), 46–83. Where Aquinas' sacramental theology is concerned, Chauvet is wary of the perceived implications of the concept of causality. For our purposes, Chauvet's position vis-à-vis Aquinas depends primarily on two factors: Heidegger's critique of ontotheology and Chauvet's own interpretation of Aquinas' development from dispositive to perfective sacramental causality in light of this. The first of these, although it has generated no small amount of controversy, lies outside the scope of this book; the second, however, does not. A significant amount of space in the following pages is dedicated to charting the nature of this development both historically and systematically, without the burden of predetermined ontotheological assumptions. What this analysis shows is that when Aquinas is taken on his own terms—textually, historically, and systematically—his approach offers a vibrant description of sacramental efficacy that is deeply integrated within other areas of philosophy and theology. Although this present work cannot engage all of Chauvet's concerns directly, I have addressed some of Chauvet's arguments in "Cajetan's Harp," 100–104. Others have provided more detailed analysis from a Thomistic perspective: Dominic Holtz, *Sacraments,* in *The Oxford Handbook of Aquinas,* eds. Brian Davies and Eleonore Stump (Oxford: Oxford University Press, 2012), 452–56. Bernhard Blankenhorn, "The Instrumental Causality of the Sacraments: Thomas Aquinas and Louis-Marie Chauvet," *Nova et Vetera* (English) 4 (2006): 255–94; idem., *The Place of Romans 6 in Aquinas' Doctrine of Sacramental Causality: a Balance of History and Metaphysics,* in *Resourcement Thomism: Sacred Doctrine, the Sacraments, and the Moral Life,* eds. Reinhard Hütter and Matthew Levering (Washington, D.C.: The Catholic University of America Press, 2010), 136–49. Jason A. Fugikawa, "Sacramental Causality—The Approaches of St. Thomas Aquinas, Karl Rahner, and Louis-Marie Chauvet," (PhD diss. Ave Maria University, 2011). L. Walsh has begun to address some of the important metaphysical and hermeneutical concerns that Chauvet's arguments raise. Liam Walsh, "The Divine and the Human in St. Thomas' Theology of the Sacraments," in *Ordo sapientiae et amoris: Image et message de Saint Thomas D'Aquin à travers les récentes études historiques, herméneutiques et doctrinales: Hommage au Professeur Jean-Pierre Torrell OP. à l'occasion de son 65e anniversaire,* ed. Carlos Josaphat Pinto de Oliveira (Fribourg: Éditions Universitaires, 1993), 321–52. H. Broadbent has criticized Chauvet's theological appropriation of Heidegger. Hal St. John Broadbent, *The Call of the Holy: Heidegger—Chauvet—Benedict XVI,* T&T Clark Studies in Fundamental Liturgy (New York: Bloomsbury T&T Clark, 2012).

the liturgical movement begun by Romano Guardini and others.[124] When moral causality rose to prominence in the early modern period, it represented a shift from one form of efficient cause to another. Originally, moral causality was proposed as a (non-Aristotelian) form of efficient instrumental causality. However, Casel seems to express the general sentiments of the liturgical movement in shifting the conversation away from speculative arguments about efficient causality entirely and focusing instead on the experience of entering into the mystery of the liturgy.[125] Casel frequently interprets the institution of the Eucharist in light of texts such as I Corinthians (11:26).[126] He portrays the Eucharist as a representation of—and a participation in— the passion, death, and resurrection of Jesus Christ under the veil of mystery.[127] This approach begins with liturgical experience and speaks of the gift of grace in light of our participation in the mystery of Christ. Under this approach, no kind of efficient cause is explicitly proposed as an explanation of sacramental efficacy. Rather, it is understood that, through our participation in the represented mysteries of Christ, the sacraments have their effect.

Although Casel is not particularly interested in traditional speculative categories, his emphasis on mystery can be understood as part of a larger trend in theology during the modern period. Much of

124. The liturgical movement served as a context for the work of both Casel and Schillebeeckx. See Erik Borgman, *Edward Schillebeeckx: A Theologian in His History*, vol. 1 of *A Catholic Theology of Culture (1914–1965)*, trans. John Bowden (New York: Continuum, 2003), 199–207.

125. See Odo Casel, *The Mystery of Christian Worship and Other Writings*, ed. Burkhard Neunheuser (Westminster, Md.: Newman Press, 1962), 58–60.

126. "For as often as you eat this bread and drink the cup, you proclaim the Lord's death until he comes" (1 Cor. 11:26, RSV). See Odo Casel, *Die Liturgie als Mysterienfeier*, vol. 9, *Ecclesia Orans: Zur Einführung in den Geist der Liturgie* (Freiburg im Breisgau: Herder, 1923), 63.

127. Referencing the institution of the Eucharist, Casel says: "Deshalb sagt auch Paulus (I Kor. 11, 26) 'So oft ihr dieses Brot esset und den Kelch trinket, verkündet ihr den Tod des Herrn, bis zu kommt.'... Dieser Tod aber war unsere Erlösung; er findet seinen krönenden Abschluß in der glorreichen Auferstehung, wie ja auch der nunmehr in der Eucharistie Gegenwärtige der Auferstandene und Verklärte ist. So wird die Eucharistiefeier zum Gedächtnis des gesamten Erlösungswerks; die Menschwerdung, das Leiden, die Auferstehung, die Glorie des Gottmenschen ist Gegenstand der Gedenkfeier. Vielmehr ist der Herr, wenn auch mystisch verhüllt, selbst unter seiner Gemeinde zugegen; er vollzeiht immer wieder unter ihnen sein Opfer." Ibid., 63–64.

the disinterest in traditional causal language during this period was driven by a desire to escape the empty legalism which had marked those sacramental systems influenced by the nominalist tradition;[128] it would thus be extremely unfortunate if, in some way, these same tendencies were not definitively banished but merely cloaked in mystery. Some scholars see the emphasis on mystery that appears during the modern period as an extension of the nominalist emphasis on the radical omnipotence and freedom of God and its accompanying reticence regarding causal connections. Where causal explanation fails, the rhetoric of mystery can appear as a supplement for metaphysical explanation.[129]

In the first half of the twentieth century, the shift away from the traditional language of causality was welcomed by many theologians who wanted a renewed focus on the sacraments as signs rather than continued debate over the nature of the sacraments as causes.[130] It seems that, for many, the interminable debates waged over ossified school positions had lost their savor. More to the point, the significance of the question of causality was no longer of central concern.

Scholastic explanations of efficient causality tend to begin and end with divine intentionality. For Thomists, whether one holds to perfective or dispositive physical causality, the sacraments function as instrumental efficient causes operating under the agency of God, whose motive power is extended analogically through the instrument as a *vis fluens*.[131] While other traditions from the scholastic period such as nominalism may have lacked the analogical subtlety to speak clearly about instrumentality, they certainly did not underemphasize divine volition. Moral causality, although distinct from the scholastic tradition, also focuses somewhat univocally on divine agency and

128. Joseph Martos, *Doors to the Sacred: A Historical Introduction to the Sacraments in the Catholic Church* (New York: Doubleday, 1982), 92–96, 134–37.

129. *LThK2* s.v. "Voluntarismus," 871–72.

130. For evidence of this, see either of the following: Leeming, "Recent Trends in Sacramental Theology," 204–9, or Colman O'Neill, "The Role of the Recipient and Sacramental Signification," 2 parts, *Thomist* 21 (1958): 257–301, 508–41. Many other examples of this can be found during this period. Of particular interest is the work of Rahner and Schillebeeckx.

131. Aquinas defines the actuation of potency through efficient motion as power flowing toward an end. See note 77.

identifies the value of the blood of Christ alone as a form of efficient cause. Thus, most of the standing theological positions found in seminary manuals at the beginning of the twentieth century expressed various models of efficient causality, all with reference to divine agency. In Casel and his confreres, however, we see a strong focus on the liturgical subject in history as the recipient of the fruit of a mystery in which he participates through experience. The ideas of Casel and his contemporaries reflect the turn toward the subject that is characteristic of post-Kantian thought. Casel's mystery theology can offer many insights about the nature of Christian participation in liturgical action, and its popularity might also partially explain the disinclination of many post-*Ressourcement* theologians to appropriate sacramental models that emphasize with stronger language the category of efficient cause. For some scholars, however, the ambiguities of Casel's theory only further beg the question of sacramental cause: if the sacraments are fundamentally encounters with mystery, precisely how do they cause what we say they effect?[132] Casel's disengagement from this question is a result of his own methodological choices. However, some scholars have asserted that Casel's position seems to be essentially a form of moral causality.[133] Although Casel's supporters might bristle at this, the suggestion seems plausible. At the very least, the absence of any discernible form of physical instrumentality in his system could point to a minimalist approach to efficacy.

Although not everyone in the twentieth century was convinced by the arguments of Casel, there was a decided shift toward liturgy-as-event using the category of symbol or sign, even among those of Thomist sympathies. Technically speaking, the focus here can be described in terms of the familiar threefold division of sacramental reality: *sacramentum tantum*, *res et sacramentum*, and *res tantum*. When this sequence was first formed, discussions of efficient causality in the sacraments frequently centered on the production of grace. For Aquinas, physical efficiency is tied to the final cause, which in this case is the perfection of the subject in grace. This is also called the *res tantum*. (This is especially true when Thomists speak of sacramental effi-

---

132. See Philip McShane, "On the Causality of the Sacraments," *Theological Studies* 24 (1963): 433–34.
133. See Leeming, *Principles of Sacramental Theology*, 288.

cacy in the perfective sense, as opposed to the dispositive). For some, a perceived focus on the causality of the *res tantum* alone seemed to preclude serious consideration of the sacraments as signs (*sacramentum tantum*). Because of the turn to the subject, there was an increasing tendency to view the sacraments through the lens of experience, which produced a much different perspective. If we view the categories of *sacramentum tantum*, *res et sacramentum*, and *res tantum* according to the chronology of human experience, we see that the *res et sacramentum*, as both sign and thing effected, represents the liturgical event. Because of this, the *res et sacramentum* becomes the locus for (at least) three kinds of theological concern: ecclesiology, liturgical experience (or active participation), and symbolism.

In the twentieth century, widespread theological interest in viewing the efficacy of the sacraments through the lens of either liturgical event, symbolism, or ecclesiology gave renewed focus to the *res et sacramentum* among some Thomists interested in sacramental causality. Because dispositive causality focuses on the natural scope of action proper to the instrument rather than its participation in the potency of the principal agent, the *res et sacramentum* enjoys a special focus under this theory.[134] However, this interest was not always fueled by a close study of the primary texts of Aquinas but rather by other extra-textual concerns.

From the time of Trent until the middle of the twentieth century, the early Thomistic theory of dispositive physical causality was all but abandoned.[135] Most Thomists followed Cajetan, arguing instead for physical perfective causality. For those twentieth-century dogmatic theologians still concerned to argue for some form of physical causality, however, describing the sacraments as dispositive causes came to have its advantages: dispositive causality effects the *res et sacramentum* directly, while only disposing for the finality of grace (*res tantum*). By shifting the causal focus in this way, it becomes possible to

---

134. Cajetan notices that one of the principal differences between the *Sentences* and the *Summa* in this regard is that in the *Summa* the natural form of the instrument is taken up in the potency of the principal agent. By contrast, dispositive efficient causality concerns those efficient causes whose natural form cannot "touch" the final cause. See *Super Sent.* lib. 4, d. 1, q. 1, a. 4, solutio I; *ST* III, q. 62 a. 4, co.; Cajetan, *Commentary on ST* III, q. 62 a. 4, n. IV.

135. Leeming, *Principles of Sacramental Theology*, 348.

emphasize the causality of the sign action itself as part of the liturgical event of the *res et sacramentum* using traditional speculative categories.[136]

Writing in the 1950s, Bernard Lemming argues in favor of dispositive physical causality and claims that it is preferable to perfective physical causality because the line of causality passes directly through the sign. It is the symbolic reality that causes—that is, the *res et sacramentum*.[137] This is appealing to Leeming because it focuses attention on the causality present in the sacramental event; it also allows for the articulation of a kind of sacramental cause that operates distinctly through the mystical body of Christ—that is, the Church gathered in liturgical prayer.[138] Whether or not this is faithful to the original

---

136. Although he does not share many of the sensibilities of twentieth-century theologians, Capreolus teaches that dispositive causality, as proposed by Aquinas in the *Sentences*, is focused in a certain sense on the *res et sacramentum*. Because the instrumentality of the sacraments only reaches (*pertingere*) the *res et sacramentum* (which is the sacramental character or its equivalent), there is a sense in which the efficacy of the sacraments is focused there. Speaking of material elements as sacramental instruments, he says: "Inquantum sunt instrumenta divinae misericordiae justificantis, pertingunt instrumentaliter ad aliquem effectum in ipsa anima, qui primo correspondet sacramentis, sicut est character, vel aliquid hujusmodi. Ad ultimum autem effectum, qui est gratia, non pertingunt etiam instrumentaliter, nisi dispositive, inquantum hoc ad quod instrumentaliter effective pertingunt, est dispositio, quae est necessitas, quantum in se est, ad gratiae susceptionem." Capreolus, lib. 4 d. 1, 2, 3, q. 1 a. 1 concl. 3. See Johannis Capreoli, *Defensiones Theologiae Divi Thomae Aquinatis*, vol. 6, 3–4.

137. "The earliest and most authoritative commentators on St. Thomas not only accepted the symbolic reality but judged it to be the immediate cause of grace: Hervé de Nédellec (Natalis)(d. 1323), Paludanus (d. 1342), Capreolus (d. 1444), Sylvester of Ferrara (d. 1528) and Cajetan in his *Commentary on the Sentences*, written about 1493. These theologians developed the system of "dispositive" causality, which explained that the rite causes the symbolic reality and this in turn, unless there be an impediment, causes grace. Later theologians, however, felt that this concept of sacramental causality was not acceptable and in consequence paid less attention to the *res et sacramentum*, although they all held it. Thus Cajetan in his *Commentary on the Summa*, and Dominic de Soto, d. 1560, reject the symbolic reality as an explanation of the validity of sacraments and of the 'reviviscence.'" Leeming, *Principles of Sacramental Theology*, 264. That is, the *res et sacramentum* remains the seat of sacramental character for Cajetan and de Soto (indicated here by the term "reviviscence") but not the final cause that directs the motion of the efficient cause. Leeming correctly notes that later Thomists shift the emphasis of efficient instrumental causality in the sacraments away from the *res et sacramentum*, where it has only a dispositive relationship with grace, and toward the *res tantum*, where efficient causality truly works toward the perfection of the final cause as a *vis fluens* that touches the final cause.

138. See Leeming, *Principles of Sacramental Theology*, 346–55.

thought of Aquinas, this model was appealing to some because of its causal emphasis on sacramental character, which unites us to Christ and imparts a capacity for the reception of sacramental grace through the liturgical action of the Church. Taken in this way, the sacraments themselves cause our union with Christ in the Church, through which we then receive the gift of grace. Leeming believed that this new articulation of dispositive physical causality could serve the wider interests of the Church by responding to the ecclesiological and liturgical trends of the early to mid-twentieth century.[139] However, the way in which the Church then imparts this grace, which our membership in the ecclesial body disposes us to receive, remains an open question.

Other Thomists in the twentieth century also felt that the *res et sacramentum* had ecclesiological significance.[140] Among these must

139. In 1956, B. Leeming observed that current trends in sacramental theology displayed "an inclusive tendency, greater emphasis upon the mystery of the sacraments, clearer recognition of the permanent efficacy of sacraments and stronger insistence upon the connection between sacraments and the Church as the Mystical Body of Christ." Leeming, "Recent Trends in Sacramental Theology," 204. For Leeming, these trends are "manifest first in an outlook, which tries rather to reconcile opposing views than to stress their differences; for instance on the question of sacramental causality the intransigent disputes about "moral," "physical" and "intentional" causality have far less prominence and the effort is rather to incorporate into synthesis the differing elements stressed by different theologians ... the trend is genial, but sometimes results in a lack of clearness and blunt facing of the problems." Leeming lists the following authors as exhibiting these sentiments: Scheeben, Billot, Gonthier, Vonier, de Lubac (specifically referencing *Catholicism* and *Corpus Mysticum*), Mersch, N. M. Haring, Landgraf, Weisweiler, Danielou, H. Rahner, Graber, Roguet, Haynal, Marin-Sola, Boüessé, A. M. Henry, L. Richard, M. M. Philipon, Taymans d'Eypernon, and A. Piolanti. "Recent Trends," 204n1.

140. For an example of this tendency, see Toshiyuki Miyakawa, "The Ecclesial Meaning of the *Res et Sacramentum*: the Sevenfold Cultic Status in the Visible Church as the Effect of the Sacraments," *The Thomist* 31 (1967): 381–444. J. M. Donahue states that "The special sacrament-community orientation of Vatican II theology invites renewed attention to the doctrine of the sacramental character. For in the traditional sacramental synthesis this instrumental participation in Christ's priestly power and mission is vitally involved in both the existential liturgical action and in its continuing influence on the Christian soul. The character is essential to every phase of the Church's sacramentality." John M. Donahue, "Sacramental Character: The State of the Question," *The Thomist* 31 (1967): 445. For a recent attempt to adapt Thomistic sacramental doctrine in light of the teaching of *Lumen Gentium*, see Benoît-Dominique de la Soujeole, "The Economy of Salvation: Entitative Sacramentality and Operative Sacramentality," *The Thomist* 75 (2011): 537–53.

be counted the young Edward Schillebeeckx, who argued that the Church is the fundamental locus for sacramental activity. According to Schillebeeckx, sacraments can be viewed from the perspective of the recipient community or from the perspective of God. Either way, the medium through which the sacraments work is the ecclesial symbolism of the Church. This is a sign of the Church's symbolic action and a "personal symbolic act of Christ through the institutional medium of the Church."[141] This ecclesial focus within the category of sacramental sign or symbolism is, broadly speaking, congruent with other trends in the twentieth century that desired to speak of the sacraments less as causes than as ecclesial events. This focus on ecclesiology in the context of the sacraments reflects a more anthropological—and less metaphysical—understanding of the sacraments as causes. It goes without saying that Schillebeeckx exerted an incredible degree of influence in many areas of theology throughout the second half of the twentieth century; sacramental theology was no different in this respect.[142]

Although perhaps not readily apparent, Schillebeeckx and Casel are more intimately related than one might suppose: both Schillebeeckx and Casel developed their respective theories within the context of the liturgical movement as responses to the isolated individualism of modern times and the equally isolated speculations of dogmatic theology. Both can be understood as Catholic theologies of culture that use the liturgy to express the corporate identity of the Church in society in different ways.[143] In fact, E. Borgman argues that

141. Edward Schillebeeckx, *Christ the Sacrament of the Encounter with God*, trans. Paul Barrett (Franklin, Wis.: Sheed and Ward, 1999), 74.

142. From within the Thomistic commentatorial tradition, a constructive response to these trends was offered by Colman O'Neill in the late 1950s. See Coleman O'Neill, "The Instrumentality of the Sacramental Character: An Interpretation of *Summa Theologiae*, III, q. 63, a. 2," *Irish Theological Quarterly* 25 (1958): 262–68; O'Neill, "The Role of the Recipient and Sacramental Signification," 2 parts, 257–301, 508–41.

143. "Casel's theology was not only, or even primarily, an interpretation of the Catholic liturgy, though his work was usually read in this way. Casel himself was primarily interested in a theology of culture—but not in the same way as Schillebeeckx." "In Casel's view the liturgy, in the midst of a modernity which had been stripped of any sense of mystery, was the only place where God's holiness was still experienced and venerated ... in Schillebeeckx's view the liturgical celebration of the sacraments was ultimately a concentration of the human quest for God.... Like Casel's work ... *De sacramentele heilseconomie* (Schillebeeckx's thesis) in fact contained a theological view of human nature,

Schillebeeckx's doctoral thesis can be understood as a systematic interpretation of Casel's mystery theology in light of his own Thomistic training.[144] Here an ecclesiological response to questions of cultural identity again reflects the generally anthropological focus of this new theological hermeneutic.

For many twentieth-century theologians, the impulses of both Schillebeeckx and Casel were extremely influential. However, to say that grace is mediated through the sacramental mystery of the Church does not in and of itself provide a specific account of the way in which this effect is reached. Writing in 1971, Johann Auer proposed an explanation of sacramental causality influenced by both Schillebeeckx and Casel. (This theory appears in a series of textbooks on dogma that he co-edited with Joseph Ratzinger).[145] Although in dialogue with modern trends, Auer retains several traditional causal categories from the broader tradition. He proposes that while sacramental character is "ontically real," the subsequent causation of grace is not physical but moral. Auer emphasizes that sacraments have objective efficacy as signs within the mystery of the Church. In this he seeks to follow Schillebeeckx and, implicitly, Casel.[146] Auer does not specify

---

modern culture and the significance of the Christian tradition." Borgman argues that there are important differences between Casel and Schillebeeckx, but their fundamental point of departure is very similar. Borgman, *Edward Schillebeeckx*, 201, 206.

144. "Schillebeeckx's major study on the sacramental economy of salvation [Borgman refers to his dissertation, *De sacramentele heilseconomie*] ... began especially with the so-called 'mystery theology' of the German Benedictine Odo Casel.... In a sense, *De sacramentele heilseconomie* is to be regarded as a critically modified development of Casel's theology of the mysteries." Ibid., 201. To support this, Borgman cites *LThK* (1961), s.v. "Mysterientheologie," 724–27.

145. The series *Dogmatic Theology*, edited by Johann Auer and Joseph Ratzinger, has appeared in English translation from the Catholic University of America Press. The volume in question here, *A General Doctrine of the Sacraments and the Eucharist*, vol. 6, is authored by Johann Auer. (The German original, *Allgemeine Sakramentenlehre und Das Mysterium der Eucharistie*, was first published in 1971 by Friedrich Pustet Verlag, Regensburg).

146. See Auer, *A General Doctrine of the Sacraments*, 67–82. Auer defines the sacramental character as "ontically real," and as "dispositive for grace, not in the physical but in the moral sense." Ibid., 73. He further claims that "the decisive consideration for the understanding of sacrament and its objective efficacy is that it is not regarded as a thing or object but rather as a sign and a *function within the mystery of God, Christ, and the Church*, as an organ for humans of their encounter with God (Schillebeeckx), as an answer to fundamental questions of human existence (Smulders), and as a 'sign' in the

the mode of causality involved in producing the sacramental character. However, his phrase "ontically real" leaves open the possibility that some form of physical instrumentality could be involved, albeit of the dispositive kind.[147] Even if there is dispositive physical causality involved here, however, it is clear that all physical instrumentality is ruled out with respect to the finality of grace. Here Auer seems to make explicit what Casel and Schillebeeckx only implied: while sacramental character may be effected physically or "ontologically," sacramental grace is given through the mystery of the Church's liturgy via moral causality.[148]

The Second Vatican Council ushered in a new era of reflection on the ecclesiological dimension of sacramentality which has borne much fruit in recent years. However, as the example of Auer shows, an ecclesiological approach to sacramentality does not of itself guarantee an intrinsic causal approach to the sacraments. Duns Scotus taught that the sacraments were effective because a pact had been established between God and the Church, ensuring that God would give grace when the sacraments were correctly performed.[149] Melchior Cano's system of moral causality is an adaptation of this model. Although modern ecclesio-sacramental systems ostensibly reject the legalism of previous thinkers and offer a more explicitly communal anthropology, the degree to which these new systems are truly distinct from classical moral causality is not always clear. In the case of Auer, however, it would seem that the affinity between the new and the old is greater than one might wish. The age-old question of the way in which the sacraments confer what they signify reasserts itself: the issue here remains the role of instrumental causality in the context of the relationship that exists between God and the recipient of grace, whether this recipient is conceived of in individual or ecclesiological terms.

---

comprehensive sphere of the Christian *mysterium.*" (The parenthetical references here are Auer's.) Ibid., 77.

147. Any efficient instrumentality operative here must be dispositive because its action clearly does not touch the finality of grace.

148. This is reminiscent of the dispositive model inherited by Bonaventure from Alexander of Hales and others, in which the character is the product of efficient causality, but grace itself is given *sine qua non*.

149. See note 73.

In many ways, the theological paradigm set by persons such as Casel and Schillebeeckx has dominated the discussion of liturgical theology in our time. At the risk of oversimplification, one might say that theological discussion of the sacraments in the mid- to late twentieth century has been centered on liturgical praxis or experience within the context of the Church, rather than on the nature of instrumental causality. Although some like Auer and Leeming have retained a vestige of the classical vocabulary of causality, they are clearly in the minority. For many students of sacramental theology and liturgical studies, the question of causality is not even a consideration. Be that as it may, even those who would reject the classical causal theories must turn to other conceptual models to explain the teachings of Trent and the lived experience of the Church, both of which confirm that that the operation of the sacraments themselves (*ex opere operato*) confers the grace signified. Our attempts to understand the sacramental reality of grace at work in the Church must necessarily raise the question of the way in which the sacraments have this effect. Regardless of theological vocabulary, the unavoidable question at play here is that of causality. Because the sacraments effect the sanctification of the human person, any functional theological hermeneutic must necessarily have something to say about this saving reality. Whether one chooses to embrace a classical approach or not, the question of sacramental causality will be theologically relevant so long as the sanctifying effects of the sacraments themselves remain so. This is a question that, in the end, is not always served well by ambiguity. In response to the emphasis on mystery and liturgical experience found in Casel and many authors in our own day, Bernard Lonergan warns against confusing speculative theology with the warmth of religious feeling:

Just as the equations of thermodynamics make no one feel warmer or cooler ... so also speculative theology is not immediately relevant to the stimulation of religious feeling. But unless this fact is acknowledged explicitly and systematically, there arises a constant pressure in favor of theological tendencies that mistakenly reinforce the light of faith and intelligence with the warmth of less austere modes of thought.[150]

---

150. Bernard Lonergan, "Theology and Understanding," *Gregorianum* 35 (1954): 643. As cited by McShane, "On the Cauality of the Sacraments," 434.

Although twentieth-century theologians such as Rahner and Chauvet prefer the ambiguity of symbolic language to the tight precision of scholastic vocabulary, twentieth-century Thomist Colman O'Neill, OP, reminds us that Aquinas' choice of the category of cause represents an intentional decision to describe the sacraments as something more than symbols. The causal language of creation itself can be extended to describe Christ's saving interaction with the symbolic reality of the sacraments.

The medievals, had they wanted to say of the sacraments "they cause because, and to the degree that, they are symbols," had sufficient command of Latin to say it clearly, and clarity was a tool of their trade. In fact, they used the word "cause" in their sacramentology because that was the term they used to speak of God's creating the world ... St. Thomas used it because he considered that it could be extended to signify as well the active intervention of Christ in the symbolic act of the sacrament; and he went to the trouble of explaining that he was choosing this word so as to make it clear that an exclusively symbolic account of the sacraments does not measure up to the tradition of the Fathers.[151]

Unlike its medieval, modern and contemporary alternatives, the Thomistic approach to sacramental causality offers an integration between cause and effect, sign and sacred reality, that relates intrinsically to the human person in the order of grace; this is accomplished in no small part by addressing the subject of causality—the way in which the sacraments confer what they signify—with a degree of clarity and theological precision that is not often found in contemporary sacramentology.

151. Colman E. O'Neill, *Sacramental Realism: A General Theory of the Sacraments* (Chicago: Midwest Theological Forum, 1998), p. 127. (The essay was originally published in 1983 by Michael Glazier.)

2

Creation, Artistry, and Dispositive Instrumental Causality in Aquinas' *Commentary on the Sentences*

This chapter will examine the theory of dispositive instrumental causality as it is proposed by St. Thomas in his *Commentary on the Sentences*. Although this chapter is principally concerned with the sacraments as dispositive instrumental causes, we will begin with a seeming turn away from this topic. Before treating the sacraments themselves, we will first examine Aquinas' understanding of God and creation as it appears in the *Sentences*. Here we will pay particular attention to the notion of God as first principle in relation to created efficient causality and instrumentality. This study will prove valuable because it will grant us an understanding of the broader context in which Thomas' sense of instrumental efficient causality occurs. Furthermore, an understanding of the concept of creation in relation to instrumentality will be necessary to grasp the controverted issues that surround grace as the final end of sacramental causality. Of special interest will be the image of the artist—a natural metaphor that is used by Aquinas to describe God as creator in the strict sense without instrumentality—and as governor of that which he creates through the use of instruments.

A thorough treatment of these larger metaphysical themes here in the *Sentences* will preclude the necessity of doing so in our treatment of Aquinas' subsequent works. While a study of the development of Aquinas' thought on God and creation would no doubt be fascinating in its own right, our purpose here is to chart the development of instrumental causality in the sacraments. From this perspective, the relevant features of Thomas' theory of creation remain unaltered, and so for our purposes it will not be necessary to reiterate them when dealing with Aquinas' mature works.

Following this broader treatment of God and creation, we will examine Aquinas' doctrine on sacramental cause specifically outlining his understanding of the sacraments as dispositive instrumental causes of grace. Finally, we will explore Aquinas' teaching in light of some elements of the received tradition concerning sacramental cause. In this section we will focus especially on the Augustinian dimension of Aquinas' sacramental theology as a way of contextualizing his theory of instrumentality within the outlines of the broader theological traditions of the Western Church.

GOD AND CREATION

The connection between created reality and God as creator is very strong in St. Thomas' *Sentences*. While at this stage he generally follows the order of inquiry laid out by Peter Lombard, the focus of Aquinas' commentary is markedly centered on God who creates from nothing and subsequently draws all of reality back to himself. From the outset, the role of God as first principle is assumed, and Aquinas considers everything else as gathered around him, either as coming from him as their first cause or returning to him as their final end.[1]

When Aquinas uses the term "instrumental cause," he is referring to a species of efficient causality. In the *Commentary on the Sentences* Aquinas proposes a version of Aristotle' fourfold causality, structured around the division between God as creative first principle and the contingency of the created order. Understood in this way, the

---

1. Jean-Pierre Torrell, *Saint Thomas Aquinas: The Person and His Work*, vol. 1, trans. Robert Royal (Washington, D.C.: The Catholic University of America Press, 1996), 43. Timothy Noone provides some helpful historical context for Aquinas' approach to creation. See Timothy Noone, "The Originality of St. Thomas's Position on the Philosophers and Creation," *The Thomist*, vol. 60, no. 2 (1996): 275–300.

very notion of cause is a reference to the fact of creation. God himself is uncaused, and so to speak of cause at all is to make reference to those contingent realities which proceed from him. As a result, the full meaning of the word "cause" can never be contained at the level of creaturely contingency. While physical motion and other causes may seem self-explanatory from a natural perspective, the created order is not self-caused, and this very fact must refer us back to God in the end through the teleology of the causal process itself. Even natural causes are only fully explained in light of God as first cause. Because of this, Aquinas will speak in different ways of all four Aristotelian causes in reference to the distinction between God and the world. Ours is not to examine all four of these causes here, however. Efficient causality must remain our primary concern.

Within efficient causality, Aquinas will distinguish between efficiency in the created order and that primary efficiency which can be attributed to God alone. Although in the secondary sense one may attribute an action causally to a variety of sources, in the end there can only be one principal efficient cause for being and motion in the created world.[2] The significance of Aquinas' teaching on first principles shows itself primarily in two ways: matter and form are not independent first principles but are related causally to God as first principle. Therefore, the efficient causality implied in motion, change, and generation is understood in light of God as principal efficient cause. Further, the act of creation emerges as a mode of efficient causality distinct from any kind of created motion or creaturely artistry. These distinctions help Aquinas to characterize all causal activity in the world as in some sense instrumental, functioning under the ultimate agency of God.[3]

To highlight the importance of this point, Aquinas builds on

2. For Aquinas, the existence of only one first principle is both a revealed fact and a truth of reason. Concerning the testimony of Scripture, see *Super Sent.* lib. 2, prolog. Concerning the testimony of reason, Aquinas will provide a well-developed argument from reason against the existence of several first principles and for the necessity of one first principle at the beginning of the first distinction of book 2. See *Super Sent.* lib. 2, dist. 1, q. 1, aa. 1–2.

3. Daria Spezzano shows the way in which this sense of instrumentality functions in relation to causality and participation. Spezzano, *The Glory of God's Grace: Deification according to St. Thomas Aquinas* (Ave Maria, Fla.: Sapientia Press, 2015), 105–6.

Lombard's first distinction of book two of the *Sentences*, where Lombard cites the counterexample of Plato's *Timaeus*, arguing that for Plato there are in fact three first principles: God (or the demiurge), exemplarity (or forms), and matter. Plato's model is problematic because while God is uncreated, form and matter also appear as independent, uncaused first principles.[4] Aquinas concurs, saying that Plato erred in placing the formal exemplars outside of the divine intellect as separate, *per se* subsistences. For this reason, Plato's model is unacceptable because neither the formal exemplars nor matter itself have its being from God.[5] Lombard argues that this reduces God to a kind of creaturely artist rather than being a creator in the proper sense, and Aquinas echoes this teaching.[6] In this sense, creaturely artistry manipulates existing matter to conform to an exemplar external to the artist; the artist is causally responsible only for the work of art and not for the matter or the exemplar used. God's act of creation must be distinct from this kind of creaturely artistry. However, although a creaturely artist cannot create, Lombard argues that God is not prevented from acting as a creaturely artist, continuing to work with ex-

---

4. "Plato namque tria initia existimavit, Deum scilicet, et exemplar, et materiam; et ipsa increata, sine principio, et Deum quasi artificem, non creatorem." Lombard, *II Sent.*, dist. 1, c. 1.2. Ad Claras Aquas, vol. 1 part 2 (1971), 330. Aquinas comments on this portion of Lombard's prologue in the *divisio textus*: *Super Sent.* lib. 2, dist. 1, q. 1, pr. See also *Super Sent.* lib. 2, dist. 1, q. 1, a. 1, solutio. We can see this clearly illustrated in the *Timaeus*, where Plato asserts that the demiurge or craftsman created the visible world from matter, basing it on eternal and unchanging realities. For example: "We must begin by making the following distinction: What is *that which always is* and has no becoming, and what is *that which becomes* but never is.... Now everything that comes to be must of necessity come to be by the agency of some cause, for it is impossible for anything to come to be without a cause. So whenever the craftsman [demiurge] looks at what is always changeless and, using a thing of that kind as his model, reproduces its form and character, then, of necessity, all that he so completes is beautiful." *Timaeus*, 28a–b. *Plato: Complete Works*, ed. John M. Cooper and D. S. Hutchinson, *Timaeus*, trans. Donald J. Zeyl, (Indianapolis: Hackett, 1997), 1234–35. This is an example taken from the beginning of the *Timaeus* that reflects the cosmology alluded to by Lombard. Lombard correctly observes that this theory does not resolve itself in one eternal first principle but rather necessitates three: artist, matter, and exemplar.

5. "Plato namque tria initia existimavit. Sciendum, quod in hoc Plato erravit, quia posuit formas exemplares per se subsistentes extra intellectum divinum, et neque ipsas neque materiam a Deo esse habere." *Super Sent.* lib. 2, dist. 1, q. 1, exp. text. Mandonnet/Moos, vol. 2 (1929), 43.

6. *II Sent.* dist. 1, Prolog. *Super Sent.* lib. 2, dist. 1, a. 2, solutio.

isting matter (which he has already created) to achieve specific ends.[7]

There is a way, however, in which the image of artistry can be used to describe God's act of creation without recourse to multiple first principles. As we have seen, this must be clearly distinguished from that of creaturely artistry because creation *ex nihilo* is an act attributable only to a single first principle and further implies the direct creation of the material used by the artist. Unlike the demiurge, the forms God uses in creation exist within the simplicity of his intellect, and so God does not rely on forms outside of himself when he creates but uses his own goodness as an exemplar.[8] Although this exemplarity would generally be counted as a kind of formal cause, there is a way in which God is causally responsible in an efficient (or productive) sense for things in the world as formal exemplar.

When considering created things *ad habentem tantum*—that is, according only to what they have—they exist in a causal relationship with God that Aquinas describes as *per modum communem efficientis exemplaris*. Causality considered under this aspect constitutes the *ratio quae* of a certain thing—that which explains who or what it is under a given aspect, attributed analogically to the divine attributes themselves.[9] In another way, created things, inasmuch as they are re-

---

7. "Creator enim est, qui de nihilo aliqua facit, et creare proprie est de nihilo aliquid facere; facere vero, non modo de nihilo aliquid operari, sed etiam de materia. Unde et homo vel angelus dicitur aliqua facere sed non creare; vocaturque factor sive artifex, sed non creator. Hoc enim nomen soli Deo proprie congruit, qui et de nihilo quaedam, et de aliquo aliqua facit. Ipse est ergo creator et opifex et factor. Sed creationis nomen sibi proprie retinuit, alia vero etiam creaturis communicavit. In Scriptura tamen saepe creator accipitur tanquam factor et creare sicut facere, sine distinctione significationis." Lombard, *II Sent.* d. 1, c. 2. Ad Claras Aquas, vol. 1, part 2 (1971), 330. Aquinas' approach to these issues is conceptually parallel in many respects. "In manu siquidem ejus (Deo) erant omnes fines terrae, quia ab aeterno non nisi in ejus potestate erant.... Sed ex parte actus tangit etiam duo, scilicet ornatum et obstetricationis officium. Ornatus pertinet ad dispositionem rerum, quia eas varia pulchritudine decoravit ... obstetricatio pertinet ad providentiae gubernationem, qua creaturas per se subsistere non valentes, ad modum obstetricis in esse conservat, necessaria in finem ministrat, et impedimenta repellit, etiam mala in bonum ordinando." *Super Sent.* lib. 2, prolog. Mandonnet/Moos, vol. 2 (1929), 2. See also *Super Sent.* lib. 2, dist. 1, q. 1, a. 4, solutio.

8. For a useful introduction to the causal nature of divine formal exemplarity, see Gregory T. Doolan, *Aquinas on the Divine Ideas as Exemplar Causes* (Washington, D.C.: The Catholic University of America Press, 2008), 1–43, 156–90.

9. "Respondeo dicendum, quod loquendo de attributis divinis, attendenda est attributorum ratio quae, quia diversa est diversorum, ideo aliquid attribuitur uni quod

lated to God as first cause, can be considered not *ad habentem tantum* but *per comparationem ad objectum*—that is, under the aspect of volitional choice and direction.[10] While formal exemplarity is sufficient to explain the analogical link between God and creatures at the level of form or essence, it is not sufficient to account for the existence of a particular thing. For example, the concept of goodness or knowledge in creatures is traceable in a causal sense to the goodness of God himself, which is the exemplar cause of created goodness. However, an individuated, subsistent being that has come to be from nothing is the result of a creative choice, distinguishing the singular from the universal form.

The concept "man" may be traceable analogically to the formal exemplarity of God, but the existence of "this man" must be a volitional exercise of God's principal efficient causality. While there is a certain general efficiency attributable to formal exemplarity, it is volition—both the divine act of choosing and the object chosen—that constitutes the efficient act in the creation of a specific thing. This is important because the creative choice of God contains already within it the finality of the nature he chooses to create, patterned on the understanding of the good contained within the object of the will. The good as understood (*ratio boni*), which is patterned on the divine goodness (the exemplar formal cause), functions as the final cause (*causa causarum*) that gives intelligibility to the entire volitional act as the goal towards which it reaches.[11] In this way, goodness, under-

---

non attribuitur alteri, quamvis omnia sint una res; et inde est quod bonitas divina dicitur causa bonorum, et vita causa viventium; et sic de aliis.... Quaedam autem ad habentem tantum, ut vita, bonitas et hujusmodi. Et haec omnia habent unum modum causalitatis communem scilicet per modum efficientis exemplaris, ut dicimus, quod a primo bono sunt omnia bona, et a primo vivente omnia viventia." *Super Sent.* lib. 1, dist. 38, q. 1, a. 1, solutio. Mandonnet/Moos, vol. 1 (1929), 898.

10. "Si ergo accipiamus diversas attributorum rationes, inveniuntur aliqua habere comparationem non tantum ad habentem, sed etiam ad aliquid sicut ad objectum, ut potentia, et voluntas, et scientia.... Sed illa quae dicuntur per comparationem ad objectum, habent etiam alium modum causalitatis, respectu scilicet objectorum, ut voluntas respectu volitorum; et sic quaeritur hic de causalitate scientiae. Constat enim quod scientia sua est causa per modum efficientis et exemplaris omnium scientiarum; sed dubium est, utrum sit causa scitorum quae sunt objecta scientiae." *Super Sent.* lib. 1, dist. 38, q. 1, a. 1, solutio. Ibid.

11. "Ad quartum dicendum, quod voluntas habet completam rationem causae, inquantum objectum ejus est finis secundum rationem boni, qui est causa causarum;

stood and willed under a given aspect, is held as the object of a divine volitional choice that is responsible for the creation of a given individuated being. It is the nature of the thing created itself that is held as the volitional object here, and by extension we can say that the *telos* or directedness of the created nature and all potencies available to it—even those of a rational creature—are already contained in the eternal and creative volition of God. As a result the power of God's will extends not only to the first act of being but necessarily encompasses all secondary acts possible for the nature created. In this way, it is the first principle that moves all to their ultimate end.[12]

Aquinas uses the metaphor of artistry to unite formal exemplarity with the proper sense of principal efficient causality found in God's creative volition.[13] In the same way that an artist holds the formal cause in his mind, making the final cause the object of his will and choosing efficient means to achieve that end, God uses his own goodness as exemplar when he chooses to create a specific nature. Although creaturely essences are modeled analogically on the divine ideas as formal cause (*ad habentem tantum*), the creative act is still a volitional choice without compulsion. In this way the existence of things does not proceed from God by natural necessity or emanation; creation is a choice—an act of divine freedom.[14] And yet God's is not

---

12. unde et imperium super alias vires habet; et ideo absolute voluntas Dei causa rerum dicitur. De scientia autem non similiter se habet sicut de voluntate, ut dictum est; nec etiam ita comparatur scientia ad scitum sicut vita ad viventem." *Super Sent.* lib. 1, dist. 38, q. 1, a. 1, ad 4. Mandonnet/Moos, vol. 1 (1929), 900.

12. "Ad aliud dicendum, quod secundum ipsum, primum principium agens et ultimus finis reducuntur in idem numero, ut patet in 12 Metaph. (text. 37): ubi ponit quod primum principium movens movet ut desideratum ab omnibus." *Super Sent.* lib. 2, dist. 1, q. 2, a. 5, exp. text.

13. "Sciendum est ergo, quod scientia secundum rationem scientiae non dicit aliquam causalitatem, alias omnis scientia causa esset: sed inquantum est scientia artificis operantis res, sic habet rationem causae respectu rei operatae per artem. Unde sicut est causalitas artificis per artem suam, ita consideranda est causalitas divinae scientiae. Est ergo iste processus in productione artificiati. Primo scientia artificis ostendit finem; secundo voluntas ejus intendit finem illum; tertio voluntas imperat actum per quem educatur opus, circa quod opus scientia artificis ponit formam conceptam. Unde scientia se habet ut ostendens finem, et voluntas ut dirigens actum et informans opus operatum." *Super Sent.* lib. 1, dist. 38, q. 1, a. 1, solutio. Mandonnet/Moos, vol. 1 (1929), 899.

14. "Ad sextum dicendum, quod sicut creaturae non exeunt a Deo per necessitatem naturae, vel potentiae naturalis, ita nec per necessitatem scientiae; sed per libertatem

an arbitrary choice: in wisdom, God chooses to make his own goodness the object of his creative action.[15]

To understand the relationship between divine goodness, choice,
and wisdom, Aquinas cites Avicenna, who says that it is because of
his knowledge and love of the good that God is said to be the cause of
things by willing this same good.[16] Aquinas likens the process of creation to the artist who models an artifact on his own formal concept.

The image of divine artistry is important for understanding Aquinas' theory of instrumental causality. We have seen that God can be
likened to an artist in the act of creation and that this form of creative
artistry is different from the artistry of a creature. Because God creates from nothing, he does not use pre-existing matter or forms outside of himself. God can be likened to an artist, but as creator he is
different from a creaturely artist in as much as he is solely responsible
for all forms of causality in his role as first principle.

The difference between God and creaturely artists has important
implications for our understanding of instrumental causality in relation to God. While a creaturely artist uses tools to accomplish a work
of art, God's role as first principle implies that the act of creative art-

---

voluntatis in qua completur ratio causalitatis; et ideo non quandocumque scivit creavit,
sed quandocumque voluit." *Super Sent.* lib. 1, dist. 38, q. 1, a. 1, ad. 6. Mandonnet/Moos,
vol. 1 (1929), 900.

15. Concerning the relationship of divine willing and divine wisdom: "Ad duodec-
imum dicendum, quod in omnibus illis quae agunt propter finem qui est extra voluntatem, voluntas regulatur secundum illum finem.... Sed voluntas Dei non dedit esse ipsi
universo propter alium finem existentem extra voluntatem ejus, sicut nec movet propter
alium finem ... quia nobilius non agit propter vilius se; et ideo non oportet ex hoc quod
non semper agat, quod habeat aliquid inducens et retrahens, nisi determinationem voluntatis suae, quae ex sapientia sua omnem sensum excedente procedit." *Super Sent.* lib.
2, dist. 1, q. 1, a. 5, ad 12. Mandonnet/Moos, vol. 2 (1929), 37.

16. "Et ideo constat quod quidquid accidit in effectu per defectum a formis artis, vel
a fine, non reducitur in scientiam artificis sicut in causam. Patet etiam quod principalitas
causalitatis consistit penes voluntatem quae imperat actum. Unde patet quod malum,
quod est deviatio a forma et a fine, non causatur per scientia Dei; sed tantum causalitatem habet respectu bonorum, secundum quod consequuntur formam divinae artis et
finem; non tamen ita quod respectu horum dicat perfectam rationem causalitatis, nisi
secundum quod adjungitur voluntati; et ideo in *littera* dicitur, quod scientia beneplaciti
est causa rerum. Et proper hoc etiam Avicenna lib. *De Intellig.*, cap. I dicit, quod inquantum Deus cognoscit essentiam suam, et amat vel vult eam, secundum quod est principium rerum, quarum vult se esse principium, fluunt res ab eo." *Super Sent.* lib. 1, dist. 38, q.
1, a. 1, solutio. Mandonnet/Moos, vol. 1 (1929), 899.

istry must not only be *ex nihilo* but also immediate. Because nothing preexistent can be involved in a properly creative act, creation necessarily proceeds directly from the eternal will of God who is the principal cause of all. This happens without the intervention of any intermediary and certainly without God himself undergoing any change.[17]

Artistry in the order of creation is different, however, not only because matter and the exemplar exist outside the artist and preexist his particular work of art but because in creaturely artistry the artist uses intermediary tools and the process of change to make the work of art. For Aquinas, created things are comprised of two elements: matter and form, both of which are produced by the first principle.[18] A creaturely artist must make use of existing matter and form, working through the process of motive change that characterizes actualization and becoming in the created world. From this perspective, it is the principle of motion that differentiates divine and creaturely artistry. Change in the world is effected through motion and presumes an existing substrate in which the change can act. Lombard is clear, however, that creation *ex nihilo* presumes no such substrate, and because God in himself is motionless, he therefore creates instantaneously from his eternity without the medium of motion.[19] Creation from nothing does not describe change effected in already existing things or the actuation of potency but the coming to be of a given thing in the most primary and essential sense. The reality of motion and change presumes this first act of being. Because God's creative act causes things to be essentially rather than causing existing things to change, it functions at a level of reality that precedes motion.

---

17. *Super Sent.* lib. 2, d. 1, q. 1, a.2, solutio; a. 5, solutio; ad 1, 9.

18. "Forma autem quae est pars rei non ponitur ab eo in idem numero incidere cum agente, sed in idem specie vel similitudine: ex quo sequitur quod sit unum principium primum extra rem, quod est agens, et exemplar, et finis; et duo quae sunt partes rei, scilicet forma et materia, quae ab illo primo principio producuntur." *Super Sent.* lib. 2, dist. 1, q. 1, exp. text. Mandonnet/Moos, vol. 2 (1929), 43.

19. "[Deus] sempiternae voluntatis novum aliquem significamus effectum, id est aeterna eius voluntate aliquid noviter existere.... Nos vero operando mutari dicimur, quia movemur: non enim sine motu aliquid facimus.... Deus ergo facere vel agere aliquid dicitur, quia causa est rerum noviter existentium, dum eius voluntate res novae esse incipiunt quae ante non erant, absque ipsius agitatione: ut actus proprie dici non queat, cum videlicet actus omnis in motu consistat, in Deo autem motus nullus est." Lombard in *II Sent.*, dist. 1, c. 3.1–2. Ad Claras Aquas, vol. 1, part 2 (1971), 331.

The concept of motion is essential for understanding Aquinas' use of the concept of instrumentality as a species of efficient causality within the created order. God as principal efficient cause acts immediately and without instrumentality to achieve his end when creating a certain nature out of nothing. Within creation, however, efficient causality as motion implies the actualization of potency towards an end. As a result we can distinguish two modes of efficient causality: that which pertains to God as first efficient cause and that which exists in things already created in the form of motion. When applied to God, the concept of instrumental efficient causality refers not to God's immediate creation of the being of a specific nature but to created efficient causality in as much as it is related to, and dependent on, God as first principle.[20] As we have seen, God holds the form of natures as the end of his creative will, as an artist holds the image he intends to fashion in the eye of his mind.[21]

Although there is no instrumentality in the act of creation, the power of God's creative artistry extends to the essence of a given nature. It follows then that the potencies of the natures he creates are contained within this same creative will; even that motion which actuates their potency, then, is not out of the reach of his will. Motion in the created order is sometimes referred to as secondary efficient causality to properly distinguish it from that form of principal efficiency that is reserved for God alone. Because the contingency of each created being naturally refers to God as first cause, the secondary efficient causality of act, potency, and motion (found within each created nature) can be understood as instrumental inasmuch as the acts specified by given natures are defined and directed by their relationship with God as first principle.

We know that Aquinas describes God's creative act using the image of an artist who chooses to depict a given form in his wisdom. Aquinas will further extend this metaphor to describe God's relationship with what he has already created using the concept of secondary

---

20. Aquinas distinguishes between principal and secondary efficient causality, at times using the term "instrumental cause" as a synonym for secondary efficient causality. See *Super Sent.* lib. 2, dist. 1, q. 1, a. 5, ad s.c. 5; idem, lib. 4, dist. 1, q. 1, a. 1, qc. 4, solutio.

21. *Super Sent.* lib. 1, dist. 38, q. 1, a. 1, ad. 6; idem, Lib. 2, dist. 1, q. 1, a. 5, ad 12; idem, lib. 1, dist. 38, q. 1, a. 1, Solutio.

instrumental efficient causality. Within the created order, divine artistry does not take the form of creation *ex nihilo* based on the exemplarity of the divine ideas. Using this first form of artistry, God makes things to be that were not before, bringing them to their first or essential act. In another way, however, God can use motive change in the created order in the way that an artist uses his tools. Natural potencies of created things are not simply created once and then left to actuate themselves according to their own lights. There is a sense in which their potencies are directed in wisdom towards the finality of creation as a whole by the divine artist. As the potency of a created nature is actuated, its motion to act is directed not only by its natural form but by the exemplarity of the divine ideas as well. Aquinas teaches that God, in the Person of the Word, moves created things as an artist moves multiple tools (like small knives: *cultelli*) instrumentally to achieve a single end. Because Aquinas is speaking of the actuation of the potency of an existing thing, these instrumental movements are necessarily accidental or secondary to the being's first act of existence.

In this way God's artistry functions not in the creative but in the instrumental sense, moving multiple accidental potencies to achieve his end. All of these potencies, despite their multiplicity, participate in the single intention of the artist and their motion as instrumental efficient causes is specified by this end. Like the tools in the hand of the craftsman, they participate in the same end, and ultimately the volitional force behind them derives from a potency that is not their own but rather that of the artist. No matter how many instruments are employed to achieve a certain end, they are still defined by the finality specified by the principal agent.[22]

In the end, there are two ways in which the relationship between God to the world can be described using the image of an artist: first, there is that divine artistry which creates from nothing without the

---

22. "Verbi gratia, ad esse cultelli exiguntur per se aliquae causae moventes, sicut faber et instrumentum ... quod cultellus factus a quodam fabro sene, qui multoties instrumenta sua renovavit, sequitur multitudinem successivam instrumentorum, hoc est per accidens; et nihil rohibit esse infinita instrumenta praecedentia istum cultellum, si faber fuisset ab aeterno." *Super Sent.* Lib. 2, dist. 1, q. 1, a. 5, ad 5. Mandonnet/Moos, vol. 2 (1929), 39.

use of instruments and is responsible for the essential existence of each created thing. Secondly, God as principal cause can be understood as an artist in relation to that which he has already created. God creates as an artist and subsequently governs what he has created in providence, as an artist working with his tools, gathering all created finalities towards an end that he has foreseen in wisdom. Broadly speaking, these two forms of artistry are sufficient to describe God's relationship to the created order at the level of nature under the mode of efficient causality. With that in mind, we move now to consider God's relationship to creation in the order of grace, where he employs the sacraments as instrumental efficient causes of human sanctification.

SACRAMENTS AS DISPOSITIVE
INSTRUMENTAL CAUSES
OF GRACE

In the sacraments, God continues to interact with the world that he has already created, and so in some sense they can be understood within the category of instrumental efficient causality. But in the sacraments God's intention is not simply to work towards natural ends through the process of natural potency and act but to achieve the renewal of the world through grace. In light of this, the purpose of the sacraments is to sanctify humanity. But how should we understand the causality at work in the sacraments? The sacraments have a supernatural purpose, and yet they make use of (already created) physical substances such as bread, water, oil, and the like. At the level of nature, these natural substances already exist in an instrumental relationship with God as first principle who directs them as an artist directs his tools. Although their purpose as sacraments is not natural in its scope, Aquinas will build on this existing instrumental relationship, describing the sacraments as instruments of sanctification.[23]

But what kind of instrument are the sacraments? Are they efficient causes of grace? If so, how are they situated as instruments with respect to the finality of the divine act at work in the sacraments if

---

23. *Super Sent.* lib. 4, dist. 1, q. 1, a. 1, qc. 4, co..

God's final intention is supernatural? A problem arises at this point with respect to the finality of sacramental effect: because the telos of sacramental action cannot be contained within natural created potencies, it seems that the instrumental action of these same created potencies cannot be sufficiently proportioned to the ultimate effect, which for the sacraments is grace itself.[24]

Part of the answer to these and other questions will be found in Aquinas' appropriation of the doctrine of analogy. Concerning the sacraments, Aquinas says that it is of the nature of an instrumental cause (sacramental or no) to be analogical. All efficient causality is directed teleologically by the final cause, which is the goal towards which an efficient cause moves. Because instrumental causes require a principal efficient cause to specify this finality to direct them towards it, their causality must be spoken of by similitude to the effect. Only a principal cause, by whose power the instrumental cause works, can be said to be cause of something either univocally or non-univocally.[25] Instrumentality, by contrast, is causal by analogy, pro-

---

24. As a result of this, many of Aquinas' predecessors and contemporaries opted to restrict the sacraments to causing only a disposition for grace. This position was proposed by many scholastic theologians in different ways. Alexander of Hales, William of Auxerre, William of Middleton, Bonaventure, and Albert all held versions of this position. This is not to say that there are not important differences among these authors. However, many of these authors are rightly concerned to avoid claiming that the sacraments caused grace in the strict sense because grace was thought to be created directly by God from nothing and infused into the soul. They tended to hold that if there was any real power in the sacramental action, it must be limited to causing a kind of disposition, condition, or occasion for the reception of grace. See John F. Gallagher, *Significando Causant: A Study of Sacramental Efficiency,* Studia Fribugensia New Series 40 (Fribourg: The University Press, 1965), 64.

25. Ad quartum dicendum quod causa univoca vel non univoca, proprie loquendo et simpliciter sunt divisiones illius causae cujus est similitudinem habere cum effectu; hoc autem est principalis agentis et non instrumentalis, ut dicit Alexander, secundum quod narrat Commentator in XI *Meta.* (text. 24). Et ideo proprie loquendo, neque instrumentum est causa univoca neque aequivoca. Posset tamen reduci ad utrumlibet, secundum quod principale agens, in cujus virtute instrumentum agit, est causa univoca, vel non univoca." *Super Sent.* lib. 4, dist. 1, q. 1, a. 4, qc. 1, solutio, ad 4. Mandonnet/Moos, vo. 4 (1947), 33–4. Earlier in this article (a. 4), Aquinas discusses causality and analogy at length, building an understanding of principle causality as causal in a univocal sense in relation to the effect. (In particular, see *Super Sent.* lib. 4, d. 1, q. 1, a. 4, qc. 4. See chap. 1, p. 37, n. 77). His discussion of instrumental causality, cited here, is framed by this larger context. Historically, the question of

portioned to the effect towards which it is moved by the principal cause. This is true of creaturely artists and their tools in the natural order and is also true of God in relation to creatures. Any instrumental action in the created order makes use of the natural potency of a thing, placing that potency at the service of a principal agent who is responsible for the action univocally speaking. An example is water being used to wash. Water has the natural power of cleansing, but the one who uses it to cleanse is principally responsible for the washing.

When considering the use of instruments in the natural order in his *Commentary on the Sentences*, Aquinas argues that the effect of an instrument can be understood in two ways: there are those effects which directly reach (*pertingere*) the final effect intended by the principal and those which do not. Depending on his purpose, a principal mover can direct an instrument to an act which may complete his ultimate intention or to an action which may simply prepare the way for the use of other instruments.

Those instrumental causes that reach the ultimate cause can be called perfective or completing (*perficere*) because the motion of the instrumental efficient cause (as moved by the principal agent) results directly in the ultimate effect. In another sense, the actual motion of the instrument may not directly result in the final effect intended by the principal agent. In this case, the instrument in question disposes or arranges (*dispositivus*) with respect to the finality towards which the principal agent has directed his intent and motive power. It does not immediately effect the ultimate intention, but it plays an essential role in the accomplishment of the final goal. Even if other instrumental means could have been selected, once the causal process has been initiated by the principal agent, the tools used in that process become necessary causes and cannot be superfluous or arbitrary because they are the tools that have been chosen by the agent or artist.

---

analogy had already been raised in the context of sacramental causality before 1245 by Alexander of Hales (in his earlier *Glossa*), who said that "cause" can only be said equivocally of the sacraments. See chap. 1, note 30. Although these issues cannot be fully addressed in the context of this present work, these texts seem to be most intelligible when the doctrine of analogy is understood ontologically, and not merely semantically. For an informative study of the subject of analogy in Aquinas and the Thomist tradition, see Joshua Hochschild, *The Semantics of Analogy: Rereading Cajetan's De Nominum Analogia* (Notre Dame, Ind.: University of Notre Dame Press, 2010), 1–32.

An example from natural instrumental agency might be the construction of a house: the saw in the hand of the builder may be used to produce a stool or bench in the perfective sense. Here the perfection of the finality is achieved from the instrumental application of the potency of the instrument. In another sense the action can be viewed from the perspective of the overall intentionality of the builder who intends not only to produce a bench but also to build an entire house. For the completion of this larger project, the natural potency of the saw alone is insufficient—further tools will be required to accomplish this end. In this sense the instrument considered in itself has no real power outside the context of its use. However, the agency and intent of the builder continue to produce the final effect, and so the instrumental action that falls short of this overall finality can be seen in two ways: as perfective of an immediate result and as dispositive for a future finality.[26]

In the *Sentences*, Aquinas uses this distinction between perfective and dispositive efficient causality to describe the instrumental causality of the sacraments. Aquinas teaches that the sacraments "reach" (*pertingere*) a certain proximate effect that takes place in the soul, even though their power as instruments does not reach the ultimate finality of the action.

Aquinas in fact attributes two separate effects to the sacraments: character and grace. He speaks first of sacramental character as that which is conferred directly by the working of the sacrament (the *res et sacramentum*) and then of grace as the final effect of the sacrament (the *res tantum*).[27] Because the overarching goal of the sacraments is the sanctification of the human person, the ultimate effect of the sacraments is not sacramental character but grace. Aquinas believes that the ultimate end of the sacramental effect—the sanctification of the soul in grace—is beyond the reach of any instrumental cause. As a result, the sacraments as instruments of sanctification can only be dispositive with respect to the finality of grace.[28]

As we progress with this study, it will become clear that the defi-

---

26. *Super Sent.* lib. 4, dist. 1, q. 1, a. 4, solutio I. See Gallagher, *Significando Causant*, 93, 100. This doctrine will change in the *Summa*.

27. *Super Sent.* lib. 4, dist. 1, q. 1, a. 4, solutio I.

28. Ibid.

nition of grace is of central importance for the way in which the instrumental causality of the sacraments is articulated. Among Thomas'
contemporaries, it was commonplace to speak of grace as something
created *ex nihilo*.[29] The development of Aquinas' thought on the nature of grace in his later writings will have a decisive effect on his understanding of efficient causality, in some ways simplifying his understanding of sacramental cause.

In the *Commentary on the Sentences*, the theme of creation and
re-creation is the overarching context for the process of justification or sanctification.[30] As a result it also contextualizes the instrumental causality of the sacraments in Aquinas' early thought. In book
one of the *Sentences*, Aquinas says that the processes of creation and
re-creation are almost entirely similar. Grace is imparted to the soul
as a created habit, which allows the soul to participate in the divine
life through the action of charity. We know that the act of creation
ex nihilo cannot involve any instrument. In the sacraments, however, we are clearly not dealing with the creation of a new subsistent
essence. Although a habit is not a subsistent being but an accident,
Aquinas does use strong ontological language to describe grace as a
new being created by God—*esse gratiae*—which is not the result of
natural potencies.[31] Aquinas characterizes the infusion of grace as a
new creative initiative on the part of God involving an already created thing. Assuming this perspective, Aquinas draws a certain comparison between the efficiency of the sacraments as dispositive instruments with respect to grace and the process of procreation, in which

29. For example, this position was held by Bonaventure, Richard of Middleton,
Henry of Ghent, Scotus, and others. See Gallagher, *Significando Causant*, 148–49. See
also Bernhard Blankenhorn, "The Instrumental Causality of the Sacraments: Thomas
Aquinas and Louis-Marie Chauvet," *Nova et Vetera* (English) 4 (2006): 255–94, 262.

30. Torrell, *Saint Thomas Aquinas: The Person and His Work*, 43.

31. "Ad tertium dicendum, quod omnino simile est de creatione et recreatione. Sicut enim Deus per creationem contulit rebus esse naturae, et illud esse est formaliter
a forma recepta in ipsa re creata, quae est quasi terminus operationis ipsius agentis; et
iterum forma illa est principium operationum naturalium, quas Deus in rebus operatur:
ita etiam et in recreatione Deus confert animae esse gratiae; et principium formale illius esse est habitus creatus, quo etiam perficitur operatio meritoria quam Deus in nobis operatur; et ita iste habitus creatus partim se habet ad operationem Spiritus sancti
ut terminus, et partim ut medium." *Super Sent.* lib. 1, dist. 17, q.1, a. 1, ad 3. Mandonnet/
Moos, vol. 1 (1929), 395–96.

the process of natural generation disposes for the immediate infusion of the human soul by God. While there is a kind of instrumentality in the natural process of procreation, the finality of the act (the creation of a new human person with a rational soul) is beyond any natural potency and therefore must be a direct act of creation.[32]

Although Aquinas does not explicitly define grace as created in the *Sentences*, he draws a certain parallel between grace and the process of procreation.[33] In procreation the process of material or natural generation is supplemented by a creative act on the part of God, who creates and infuses the human soul. Aquinas likens them in this way: the infusion of grace, which is the ultimate effect of the sacraments, is beyond the instrumental potency of the sacramental actions in the way that the creation of a human soul is beyond the potency of the human parents. In both cases, the instrumental actions cannot be perfective of the ultimate effect but only dispositive.[34] Because there can be no instrumentality in the act of creation, it is not possible for human agency to cause the existence of a new subsisting human form in the perfective sense.[35] Human instrumentality can only dispose for such an end. In the same way, Aquinas will argue that the finality of the sacraments, which is the sanctification or justification of human persons, is beyond the reach of such perfective instrumentality.

A theme that recurs without modification throughout Aquinas' works is the role of the principal cause in sacramental action. This emphasis is strong here in the *Commentary on the Sentences* and will not wane in future works. It is important to understand his insistence on dispositive instrumentality in light of this. Even in natural instrumental causality, the principal causality of God is of central importance. The theory of dispositive instrumental causality is an attempt to preserve this, given the scope of natural potency in light of the finality of grace.

Fundamentally, dispositive causality is an attempt to preserve the

---

32. *Super Sent.* lib. 4, dist. 1, q. 1, a. 4, solutio I.

33. See Gallagher, *Significando Causant*, 87–90, 98.

34. *Super Sent.* lib. 4, dist. 1, q. 1, a. 4, solutio I. See also Gallagher, *Significando Causant*, 98.

35. However, Aquinas only applies this in the case of human generation. Where the rational soul is lacking, the process of generation and corruption in the natural order can involve an instrumental agency that is properly perfective. See *Super Sent.* lib. 4, dist. 1, q. 1, a. 4, solutio I.

principal agency of God with respect to grace. For Aquinas it is not the sacraments in themselves that sanctify but rather the power of God working through them instrumentally. Because instruments are analogical causes, an action is not attributed univocally to an instrument but to the principal agent. The power in the instrument, inasmuch as it is applied to a particular work, is not the power of the instrument *per se* but is derived from the principal agent who imparts motion to the instrument.[36] Strictly speaking, we do not seek salvation from the sacraments themselves, but through them we receive salvation from God himself. Concerning instrumental agency, Aquinas distinguishes between that from which an effect comes (*a*) and that through which it is given (*per*).[37] As a result the sacraments as instrumental causes mediate (*mediantibus*) salvation (*salus*), and this salvation is received in the human person as in a subject (*sicut in subjectis*).[38]

If the sacraments are related to the final intention of God as principal agent, even in a dispositive sense, this raises the question of the relationship of the sacraments as instrumental causes to grace itself. Is grace in the sacraments somehow, so as to be contained by them in a quasi-physical sense, or must we say that the sacraments are only externally or accidentally related to the conferral of grace, as conditions upon which God chooses to confer it? Neither of these options is entirely acceptable. Hugh of St. Victor taught that the sacraments contain (*continere*) grace as medicine might be contained in a vial;[39] this evocative metaphor was popular in the Middle Ages and served to connect scriptural images of healing, such as the parable of the good Samaritan, with a primitive concept of cause.[40] Aquinas will

36. *Super Sent.* lib. 4, dist. 1, q. 1, a. 1, qc. 4, solutio.

37. *Super Sent.* lib. 4, dist. 1, q. 1, a. 4, qc. 1, solutio.

38. "Ad tertium dicendum quod in sacramentis Deus operatur salutem sicut in instrumentis, quibus mediantibus salus causatur; sed in hominibus sicut in subjectis recipientibus salutem." *Super Sent.* lib. 4, dist. 1, q. 1, a. 1, qc. 4, solutio, ad 3. Mandonnet/ Moos, vol. 4 (1947), 15.

39. Hugh of St. Victor first proposed this image. See *De sac*, I.9. This same image is used by Prevostin (d. 1210) and William of Auxerre (d. 1231). See Leeming, *Principles of Sacramental Theology*, 293–94.

40. Peter Lombard uses the Good Samaritan as his primary example of sacramental healing at the beginning of his treatment of the sacraments in book 4 of the *Sentences*. Lombard is also one of the first to use the word "cause" in relation to sacramental signs. *IV Sent.* dist. 1 c 4.2.

qualify Hugh's image of the vial of medicine to avoid the implication that grace is somehow subsisting in the sacraments. It is only when it reaches its finality in the recipient that grace can be said to be in the person *sicut in subjectis*.

Concerning the power of the principal agent, an instrumental cause contains this power not under the mode of something completed but under the modality of intention, in the way that color is contained in air. Air is necessary to conduct color to the eye but does not contain it as such in its finality. St. Thomas teaches that it is in this way that grace is in the sacraments.[41] Although grace is not in the sacraments as in a subject—that is, not subsisting as a completely actuated form—it is in the sacraments as an effect is said to be present in a dispositive instrumental cause. Like color moving through the air, it exists incompletely in a medium that conveys it towards its finality.

Some have argued that in the *Sentences*, Aquinas did not conceive of the sacraments in terms of physical motion but rather only as "moral" instrumental causes—that is, instruments which rely solely on merit to elicit a reward.[42] However, his use of the category of po-

41. *Super Sent.* lib. 4, dist. 1, q. 1, a. 4, solutio IV.

42. Theophil Tschipke has proposed that in the *Sentences* Aquinas describes the sacraments as only "moral" causes, attributing the full sense of instrumentality only to Christ's post-Cyrillian doctrine of sacramental causality in the *Summa*. Theophil Tschipke, *Die Menschheit Christi als Heilsorgan der Gottheit: Unter Besonderer Berücksichtigung der Lehre des Heiligen Thomas von Aquin*, Freiburger Theologische Studien, vol. 55 (Freiburg im Breisgau: Herder, 1940), 122–23, 143–45. In his 1953 article, Joseph Lécuyer criticized Tschipke's conclusions in this regard, showing that although the instrumentality of Christ's humanity may be largely limited to a form of meritorious causality in the *Sentences*, even at this early stage Aquinas' approach to the causality of the sacraments employs a form of real, physical causality. Joseph Lécuyer, "La causalité efficiente des mystères du Christ selon saint Thomas," *Doctor comunis* 6 (1953): 95. Although Tschipke is right to point out Aquinas' debt to Cyril in his later Christology, he undervalues Aquinas' doctrine of sacramental causality in the *Sentences*. The notion of the sacraments as moral causes—a sixteenth-century concept—seems anachronistic here and is not entirely equivalent to the concept of meritorious causality which Aquinas applies to Christ's humanity in both the *Sentences* and the *Summa*. It should be noted, however, that many Thomists from at least the time of Bañez to the early twentieth century tended to equate moral causality with Aquinas' Christological concept of meritorious causality. These concepts clearly overlap, and highlighting Aquinas' authentic sense of meritorious causality was certainly a fruitful way to deal with the challenge of moral causality during the early modern period. This book does not adopt this approach, however, and the arguments presented here and elsewhere (particularly in chapter 4) are intended to show the value of adequately distinguishing Aquinas' meritorious causality

tency to explain the presence of grace in the sacraments belies this. Aquinas' own concept of motion (derived from Aristotle) helps him to explain the manner in which power is present in an instrumental cause.[43] We know that all created things are characterized by potency and the process of becoming and that the process of actualizing this potency should be understood as motion directed towards a certain end or act. Aquinas describes motion as an act already contained in potency, although not yet accomplished: motion is act that remains partially in potency.[44]

In light of this, Aquinas' teaching on grace and sacramental instrumentality is more intelligible. If grace is the "act" or the final purpose intended by God, it comes to the fullness of its act when it reaches the goal intended by the principal mover—that is, when grace comes to subsist in the soul. Because the sacraments are motive instruments in this process (whether dispositive or no), it would be inappropriate to attribute subsistence to the "act" of grace at this instrumental stage, even though it is really present in potency within their motion. To say that an act is present in potency in this instrumental sense is not to say that it is only potentially existent. It is truly present in the intention and motion of the principal agent, both of which are imparted to the instrument. The instrumental cause does not have the power of the agent within it as something complete (*ens completum*) but through the mode of intention (*per modum intentionis*), such that the form communicated (in this case, grace) is contained within the instrument as color is contained in air. The complete species of the form is not in an instrumental agent.

Recall that instruments are only causal by analogy. Only a univocal agent (a principal cause) can contain the full form intended. The mode of intentional presence here is a flowing intentionality (*per*

as a Christological concept and his broader doctrine of merit from other, deontological and neo-occasionalist approaches popular during the modern period.

43. Some argue that the concept of dispositive cause is drawn from Avicenna. See H.-D. Dondaine, "Apropos d'Avicenne et de saint Thomas de la Causalite Dispositive à la Causalité Instrumentale," *Review Thomiste* 51 (1951), 441–44. See also Bernhard Blankenhorn, "The Instrumental Causality of the Sacraments: Thomas Aquinas and Louis-Marie Chauvet," *Nova et Vetera* (English) 4 (2006): 60.

44. "Motus est actus existentis in potentia." *Super Sent.* lib. 2, dist. 1, q. 1, a. 2, ad 1. Mandonnet/Moos, vol. 2 (1929), 19.

modum intentionis fluentis), which flows from potency to act, as the form is present in the moving cause which strives for its actuality.[45] If we recall the example of the artist, the final cause is held as the object of volitional choice and therefore directs the efficient means selected to meet that end. In this way, the *ratio* of any instrumental cause is determined by the finality towards which it is directed by the principal agent, whose power works through the instrument. In the case of the sacraments, God causes grace *per modum influentiae*—that is, God pours grace into the soul, using the sacraments as instruments through which this power flows.[46]

THE SACRAMENTS AS SIGNS

Thus far, we have said a great deal about the sacraments as causes; of course, they are not only causes but signs of the purpose to which they have been directed. One of the benefits of Aquinas' theory of sacramental instrumentality is its ability to unite the causal and signate dimensions that are constitutive of true sacramentality. While some might oppose the categories of sign and cause conceptually or attempt to treat them in isolation, even at this early stage in his *Commentary on the Sentences* Aquinas is able to describe the signate and causal value of the sacraments as different dimensions of the same motive whole, working under the direction of the principal agent.

Concerning the sacraments as signs, Aquinas says that because instruments derive their motion from the principal agent, the sacraments are not in themselves something sanctified; rather, it is the divine power hidden within them (*occultum*) which sanctifies.[47] The

45. *Super Sent.* lib. 4 dist. 1, q. 1, a. 4, Solutio IV.

46. "Ad quintum dicendum, quod ex sacramentis causatur gratia per modum influentiae; nec tamen sacramenta sunt quae influunt gratiam, sed per quae Deus sicut per instrumenta animae gratiam influit." *Super Sent.* lib. 4, dist. 1, q. 1, a. 4, solutio I, ad 5. Mandonnet/Moos, vol. 4 (1947), 34.

47. "Ad quartem quaestionem dicendum quod definitio illa Augustini, si tamen in verbis illis sacramentum definire intendit, datur de sacramento quantum ad id quod est principale in ratione ipsius, scilicet *causare sanctitatem*. Et quia sacramenta non sunt primae causae sanctitatis, sed quasi causae secundariae et instrumentales, ideo definiuntur sacramenta *sanctificationis instrumenta*. Actio autem non attribuitur instrumento, sed principali agenti, cujus virtute instrumenta ad opus applicantur, prout sunt mota ab ipso. Et ideo sacramenta non dicit esse sanctificantia, sed quod *in eis divina virtus*

sacraments cannot be "sanctified" in this sense because the act of sanctification intended for the recipient is present in potency within the motion of the sacramental instrument, not in subsistent act. In this way the power of God is said to be "hidden" (*occultum*) within the sacraments. When Aquinas uses the word *occultum*, he is speaking of the power of the principal agent, the final actuality of whose act is as yet in potency; the power, agency, and direction of the principal agent towards the final end is present in the sacramental instrument as the power or motion of the carpenter is present in the saw.

However, the power of God working towards the sanctification of human persons through the instrumentality of the sacraments is not completely hidden, even if its final end has not yet been accomplished. Recall that the sacraments are not only causes but signs. A tool in action is more than simply an inanimate object. The working of a tool also reveals something of the final cause towards which it has been put in motion. The saw in motion reveals something of the purpose of the builder. In this way, Aquinas speaks of the sacraments as both *causa* and *signum*. Like an incomplete sculpture, the final cause is as yet not fully visible.[48] While the efficient power itself may be hidden (*occultum*), the working of the instrument reveals something of the end. In this way, the signate power of the tool in act is greater than the signification of the unused tool itself. A saw found lying on the ground might signify certain things, but a saw in the hand of a carpenter who is building a house signifies not only its own act of cutting but shelter, rest, warmth, and security as well. None of these effects is yet visible, but by association with the intention of the principal agent, the saw's instrumental action reveals some of his larger purpose.

---

occulta existens sanctificat." *Super Sent.* lib. 4, dist. 1, q. 1, a. 1, qc. 4, solutio. Mandonnet/Moos, vol. 4 (1947) 15. Aquinas attributes this definition to Augustine. As we will examine shortly, one way to understand Aquinas' development of the theory of instrumental cause is as an interpretation of the received Augustinian tradition.

48. "Ad primum ergo dicendum, quod sacramentum est et causa et signum. Est quidem causa instrumentalis. Et ideo virtus agentis principalis occulte in ipso operatur, sicut virtus artis in serra. Sed inquantum est signum, est ad manifestum hujusmodi occultationem; ut sic ante significationem sit occultum, sed postquam significatio facta est actu, sit manifestum." *Super Sent.* lib. 4, dist. 1, q. 1, a. 1, qc. 4, solutio, ad 1. Mandonnet/Moos, vol. 4 (1947), 15.

Because the sacraments are both signs and causes, Aquinas teaches that both are frequently present in our sensory encounter with a thing. A sign of an effect can be encountered (*quia*), or a cause leading to an effect (*propter quid*) can be found. Aquinas says that a sign manifests something in as much as it contains it, and a cause is manifest to us in as much as it falls under our senses. And so the sacraments as signs can reveal to us the power hidden within them (*quia*), and the presence of this cause reveals the effect (*propter quid*), although the final effect is still hoped for in the future.[49] It is the power contained in the instrumental cause—not as a subsistent finality but *per modum intentionis fluentis*—that is both cause and sign. The exterior working of the instrument is a sign (*quia*) of the causal reality contained within, and, in perceiving the cause, we are led (*propter quid*) to hope for the effect, which is the ultimate sanctification of the soul in grace. In the *Sentences*, Aquinas is clear that an instrument which is taken up in the hands of a principal agent functions in some way according to its natural potencies. Although the power and intent of the principal agent can flow on to other effects beyond the reach of this potency, the relationship of a given instrument to such effects must be dispositive, rather than perfective. As a result the working of an individual instrumental cause is limited to the exercise of a given tool. And it is the working of the tool that is both sign and effect: the sacrament signifies what it effects and effects what it signifies. Sign and effect are in a sense one (or at least intrinsically related) in the action of the instrument.[50]

---

49. "Ad quintum dicendum, quod signum, quantum est in se, importat aliquid manifestum quoad nos, quo manuducimur in cognitionem alicujus occulti. Et quia ut frequentius effectus sunt nobis manifestiores causis; ideo signum quandoque contra causam dividitur, sicut demonstratio *quia* dicitur esse per signum a communi, in I *Phys.*; (a. 1, 184ª, 18 s.; 1. I, n. 6 s); demonstratio autem *propter quid* est per causam. Quandoque autem causam est manifesta quoad nos, utpote cadens sub sensu; effectus autem occultus, ut si expectatur in futurum. Et tunc nihil prohibit causam signum sui effectus dici." *Super Sent.* lib. 4, dist. 1, q. 1, a. 1, solutio, ad 5. Mandonnet/Moos, vol. 4 (1947), 13.

50. In the *Sentences*, Aquinas argues that the sacraments touch the end of grace as signs (*attingere*) but as causes they are only dispositive. In the *Summa*, he will effectively draw sign and cause even closer together by arguing the causal dimension of the sacraments also touches this same finality. See Reginald Lynch, "Cajetan's Harp: Sacraments and the Life of Grace in Light of Perfective Instrumentality," *The Thomist* 78 (2014): 94–100.

THE RECEIVED TRADITION

When considered in itself, Aquinas' theory of instrumental cause can be understood as an adaptation of various philosophical categories taken from Aristotle, Avicenna, and others. In this vein, subsequent changes in his theory of instrumental cause can be understood as speculative developments of these traditions. In another sense, however, Aquinas' theory of sacramental causality can be understood as an attempt to preserve the older Augustinian teaching, inherited by the scholastics primarily through Lombard, within current theological and linguistic categories. As was shown in chapter 1, Augustine described the sacraments as visible words or signs that manifest their interior reality. For Augustine the power of the Word is what sanctifies the soul, and inasmuch as it flows through the physical things used in the sacraments, those same things become signs of its presence.[51] Augustine saw the sacraments fundamentally as signs through which the power of God flows into the soul. The power at work here is God's alone and is not limited to the sacrament in its natural potencies and material limitations.[52] When Aquinas proposes his own theory of instrumental causality, he articulates a similar concept by speaking of the power in the sacraments coming "from" (*a*) God and

---

51. "*Iam vos mundi estis propter verbum quod locutus sum vobis.* Quare non ait, mundi estis propter Baptismum quo loti estis, sed ait, *propter verbum quod locutus sum vobis*; nisi quia et in aqua verbum mundat? Detrahe verbum, et quid est aqua nisi aqua? Accedit verbum ad elementum, et fit Sacramentum, etiam ipsum tamquam visibile verbum.... Unde ista tanta virtus aquae, ut corpus tangat et cor abluat, nisi faciente verbo: non quia dicitur, sed quia creditur? Nam et in ipso verbo, aliud est sonus transiens, aliud virtus manens. *Hoc est verbum fidei quod praedicamus,* ait Apostolus, *quia si confessus fueris in ore tuo quia Dominus est Iesus, et credideris in corde tuo quia Deus illum suscitavit a mortuis, salvus eris. Corde enim creditur ad iustitiam, ore autem confessio fit ad salutem.* Unde in Actibus Apostolorum legitur: *Fide mundans corda eorum...* quo sine dubio ut mundare possit, consecratur et Baptismus. Christus quippe nobiscum vitis, cum Patre agricola, *dilexit Ecclesiam, et seipsum tradidit pro ea.* Lege Apostolum, et vide quid adiungat: *Ut eam sanctificaret,* inquit, *mundans eam lavacro aquae in verbo.* Mundatio igitur nequaquam fluxo et labili tribueretur elemento, nisi adderetur, *in verbo ...* quamvis nondum valentem corde credere ad iustitiam, et ore confiteri ad salutem. Totum hoc fit per verbum, de quo Dominus ait: *Iam vos mundi estis propter verbum quod locutus sum vobis.*" *Jo. Ev. Tr.* 80.3 CCL 36. See also *Contra Faustum* CSEL 25, 19.16.

52. See Emmanuel J. Cutrone, "Sacraments," in *Augustine through the Ages,* ed. Allan D. Fitzgerald (Grand Rapids, Mich.: Eerdmans, 1999), 741, 745.

"through" (*per*) the sacraments. The sacrament may not have the capacity to perfect the finality of the power that moves through it according to its material elements, but the power moving through it reaches its finality in the human soul just the same, under the principal agency of God.

Concerning the effect of the sacraments in relation to visible signs, Augustine taught that grace moved through outward signs, even the sacramental actions of an unworthy minister, as light through an unclean place or water through an aqueduct.[53] There are some similarities here between Augustine's aqueduct and Aquinas' image of color moving through air, although we should not assert that the two models are completely congruent. Aquinas' theory of instrumental causality is different from Augustine's explanation of the sacraments as visible words in many respects. Nevertheless, an important feature of Aquinas' sacramental theory is its ability to articulate the sense of the Augustinian tradition in later scholastic categories. While other earlier scholastics struggled to describe the causality of the sacraments without compromising the principal agency of God with respect to grace, Aquinas' theory of instrumentality allows him to preserve the notion of *vis fluens* in the sacraments—a power principally attributable to God alone that flows through the sacraments, making them causes only with respect to his power and his final intention.

While ostensibly about the presence of Christ in the Eucharist, the Berengarian controversy forced a more detailed discussion of the interrelation between sacramental sign, presence, and effect that affected the reception of Augustine's sacramental doctrine in the West and set the stage for more detailed technical discussions of the nature of sacramental causality during the scholastic period, where the interpretation of Augustinian sacramentality would remain of central importance. Although Aquinas' theory of instrumentality can be seen as a reception of the Augustinian teaching that the power of the Word flowing through the sign makes the sacrament, there are other more extrinsicist interpretations current in the Middle Ages which eventually feed into the nominalist tradition. While most of these authors

---

53. See *Jo. Ev. Tr.* 5.15 CCL 36 and *De Baptismo* CSEL 51, 3.10.15. See also William Harmless, "Baptism," in Fitzgerald, *Augustine through the Ages*, 88.

claim Augustine, Aquinas' theory of instrumental causality is uniquely suited to describe the power flowing through the sacraments.

There is no doubt that for Augustine God is the cause of grace
and that the sacraments are signs of this interior and invisible reality. However, it is not clear what role the signs (or sacraments) themselves play in the exercise of this causal power. It seems that Peter
Lombard was the first to introduce the idea of the sacraments as in
some sense causes of grace themselves, as a development of the Augustinian doctrine of sign.[54] Peter Lombard develops Augustine's
teaching on sign in the fourth book of his *Sentences* (appropriately ti-
tled *de Doctrina Signorum*). Lombard cites Augustine as saying that
the sacraments are signs of "sacred things" and the "visible forms
of invisible grace."[55] Lombard teaches that because sacraments are
properly called signs of this invisible grace, they manifest the cause
at work as well because the sacraments were not instituted to signify grace alone but to sanctify.[56] Along with that of many other scholastics, Aquinas' teaching on dispositive instrumentality appears as a
commentary on this very text (*Sent. IV* d. 1) and is proposed as a development of Lombard's notion of the sacraments as both signs and
causes within the Augustinian tradition.[57]

54. See Lombard, *IV Sent.*, dist. 1, c. 4. Gallagher states: "The statements of Augustine may be reduced to defining the sacrament as '*signum rei sacrae.*'" Gallagher, *Significando Causant*, 59.

55. "Quid sit sacramentum. Augustinus in libro X De civitate Dei: 'Sacramentum
est sacrae fei signum .' Dicitur tamen sacramentum etiam 'sacrum secretum.'... Item,
sacramentum est invisibilis gratiae visibilis forma." Lombard, *IV Sent.*, dist. 1 c. 2. Ad
Claras Aquas, vol. 2 (1981), 232. A textual note in the *Ad Claras Aquas* edition (1981) of
Lombard's text attributes this last quotation, "invisibilis gratiae visibilies forma," to Augustine's *Quaestiones in Heptat.* III, q. 84. CSEL, 281. The first quotation does appear
in a slightly different form in *De civ.* 10.5: "sacramentum id est sacrum signum." CSEL
40–I, 452. See also a parallel text in the *Summa Sententiarum* tract iv c. 1. PL 176: 117a–b.
Pourrat, 42.

56. "Sacramentum enim proprie dicitur, quod ita signum est gratiae Dei et invisibilis gratiae forma, ut ipsius imaginem gerat et causa exsistat. Non igitur significandi tantum gratia sacramenta instituta sunt, sed et sanctificandi." Lombard, *IV Sent.*, dist. 1 c.
4.2. Ad Claras Aquas, vol. 2 (1981), 233.

57. In light of this, the following assertion made by M.-D. Chenu is clearly false:
"[Augustine's distinction between *res et signa*] became hardly more than an artificial
framework kept as a heading in the *Sentences* of Peter Lombard and of all of his commentators, including Saint Thomas. Yet, this division ... served to retain an atmosphere of
symbolism from which even the most rationalistic Aristotelians were unable to escape. In

We can see Aquinas' Augustinian influence clearly when he discusses the infusion of grace into the soul earlier in his *Commentary on the Sentences*, where Aquinas uses the notion of instrumental cause to defend Augustine's teaching that God is the life of the soul.[58] While some might claim that this would rule out any kind of created medium, Aquinas uses instrumentality to describe divine life in the form of grace's coming to fruition in the soul as light which originates in the sun, passes through the air and reaches its act or fruition in a body which is illumined. For Aquinas, God is the principal exemplar and the light passing through the air is the instrumental efficient cause, the finality of which is reached in the illumination of the body.[59] This

---

the writings of Saint Thomas, this symbolism never explicitly took shape as a conscious systematic theory." Marie-Dominique Chenu, *Toward Understanding Saint Thomas*, trans. A.-M. Landry and D. Hughes (Chicago: Henry Regnery Company, 1964), 55–56. A careful examination of Aquinas' teaching on instrumentality and Lombard's text shows the rich connection between Augustine and the sacramental doctrine of Lombard and the early Aquinas. This continuity will be retained in Aquinas' later works as well. Chenu asserts here that the Augustinian distinction between the finality of the sacrament and the outward signs was all but lost during the Middle Ages. However, we have seen that the reception of Augustine's sacramental doctrine in the Middle Ages was significantly more complicated than this. Further, Lombard clearly articulates the importance of the connection between the sacraments as signs and as causes (*IV Sent.*, dist. 1 c. 4.2) In fact, Lombard's argument for the sacraments as causes is intrinsically dependent on his understanding of their role as signs, a concept he derived directly from, and explicitly attributes to, Augustine. We have seen that Aquinas follows Lombard in this much and develops his interpretation in important ways. Further, it is precisely Aquinas' use of the category of instrumental efficient causality that allows him to preserve the connection between sign and cause without either compromising the sovereignty of God or lapsing into nominalism. Aristotle is certainly no enemy of symbolism here.

58. Augustine is cited by Aquinas in *Super Sent.* lib. 1, dist. 17, q. 1, a. 1, arg. 2. Aquinas cites "*de verbis Apostoli*, serm. XVIII et XXVIII." Mandonnet/Moos, vol. 1 (1929), 392. The editors of the *Parma* edition claim can also be found in *Sermo* 156.6: "Caro enim sibi non est vita; sed anima carnis est vita. Anima sibi non est vita: sed Deus est animae vita." PL 38:853. See also Aquinas' response to arg. 2, cited below.

59. An objector states: "Item, sicut anima se habet ad corpus ut vita ipsius, ita se habet Deus ad animam, ut dicit Augustinus, *De verbis Apostoli*, serm XVIII et XXVIII. Sed anima non vivificat corpus per aliquam formam mediam. Ergo nec Spiritus anctus animam per habitum medium. Ergo nec spiritus sanctus animam per habitum medium." *Super Sent.* lib. 1, dist. 17, q. 1, a. 1, arg. 2. Mandonnet/Moos, vol. 1 (1929), 392. Aquinas responds: "Ad secundum dicendum, quod anima comparatur ad corpus non tantum ut causa agens, secundum quod est motrix corporis, sed etiam ut forma; unde formaliter seipsa facit vivere corpus, secundum quod vivere dicitur esse viventium. Deus autem non est forma ipsius animae vel voluntatis qua formaliter vivere possit; sed dicitur vita

teaching recalls Aquinas' previous description of sacramental instrumentality where he described the *vis fluens* moving through the sacraments as color moving through air to be received in the eye; in this way grace is "contained" in the sacraments not as a fully actualized subsistent form but as the power of the principal agent acting through the instrument to achieve its intended effect.[60] Aquinas' teaching on sanctification and participation in the divine nature through grace is connected strongly with his theory of sacramental instrumentality, even here in the *Sentences*. Although these ideas are not yet fully developed, the connection between grace, sacramental instrumentality, and beatitude will not lose its importance in Aquinas' mature work, nor will Aquinas lose touch with the Augustinian tradition.

The implicit connection between Aquinas' theory of sacramental causality and Augustine's sacramental theory can be seen more clearly at the end of Aquinas' explanation of his theory of dispositive instrumentality in the *Sentences*, which he offers in part as an explanation of the doctrine received from Augustine. Aquinas cites Augustine's explanation of Baptism as an example of the way in which his own theory of dispositive instrumental causality works: the water of Baptism touches (*tangere*) the body, but the water purifies (*abluere*) the heart.[61] In applying this example to the sacraments as instrumen-

---

animae sicut principium exempliter influens vitam gratiae ipsi. Similiter dicendum de luce, quod lux potest dupliciter considerari. Vel prout est in ipso corpore lucido, et sic se habet ad illuminationem aeris ut principium efficiens, nec illuminat nisi per formam luminis influxam ipsi diaphano illuminato; vel prout est in diaphano illuminato, et sic est forma ipsius, qua formaliter est lucidum. Deus autem dicitur esse illuminans lux per modum lucis quae est in ipso corpore lucenti per se, et non per modum quo illuminatum formaliter illuminatur a forma lucis in ipso recepta. Sed illi lumini recepto assimilatur caritas vel gratia recepta in anima." *Super Sent.* lib. 1, dist. 17, q. 1, a. 1, solutio, ad 2. Mandonnet/Moos, vol. 1 (1929), 395.

60. See *Super Sent.* lib. 4, dist. 1, q. 1, a. 4, Solutio IV.

61. "Et hoc est quod Augustinus dicit quod aqua baptismi *corpus tangit et cor abluit*. Et ideo dicitur quod sacramenta efficiunt quod figurant. Et hunc modum justificandi videtur Magister tangere in littera (8). Dicit enim quod homo non quaerit salutem in sacramentis quasi ab eis, sed per illa a Deo. Haec enim praepositio *a* denotat principale agens; sed haec praepositio *per* denotat causam instrumentalem." *Super Sent.* lib. 4, dist. 1, q. 1, a. 4, solutio I. Mandonnet/Moos, vol. 4 (1947), 33. Recall Augustine's formulation: "Unde ista tanta virtus aquae, ut corpus tangat et cor abluat?" *Jo. Ev. Tr.* 80.3 CCL 36. Franciscus Diekamp argues that this is a prelude to what will later be referred to as physical causality by the Thomistic commentators. No doubt he is relying on Aquinas' own interpretation of this passage (cited here) as an instance of instrumental causality

tal causes, Aquinas follows one of his Dominican contemporaries: as was shown in chapter 1, Roland of Cremona (d. 1259) also used efficient causality to interpret Augustine in this way, describing the water of Baptism as touching (*tangere*) the body, and sanctifying (*sanctificare*) the soul by the power of the Word within it.[62] Furthermore, Roland seems to be the first to describe the sacramental process in terms of efficient causality. Roland teaches that the sacraments cannot contain grace except in the sense that an effect is contained in its cause. Therefore we can properly attribute the act of justification to the sacraments after the manner of an efficient cause.[63] Roland sees himself as following Augustine in describing this efficiency as a power (*virtus*).[64] For Roland, any kind of extrinsic interpretation of this power is ruled out. It is neither a political nor a rhetorical form of persuasion; it is a kind of "physical" potency in the sense that coldness (*frigidus*) is imparted by water.[65]

---

to make this claim. Franciscus Diekamp, *De Sacramentis, tum in Communi tum in Specie et de Novissimis*, Adolphus Hofmann, ed. *Theologiae Dogmaticae Manuale: quod Secundum Principia S. Thomae Aquinatis*, vol. 4 (Paris: Desclée, 1946), 47. Further, the use of the phrase *virtus aquae* is significant because it ascribes a certain power to the water in reference to the power of God. This necessitates a nonunivocal sense of power and efficiency with regard to the principal agency of God and the finality of grace, which Aquinas artfully articulates.

62. "Quam, cum aqua tangit corpus, sanctificat animam, ita aliquid debet esse in oleo et balsamo, per quod, cum oleum et balsamum tangit frontem, sanctificatur anima vel confirmatur." *In IV Sent.*, dist. 1; fol. 89va. Text as cited in Ephrem Filthaut, *Roland von Cremona, O.P., und die Anfänge der Scholastik im Predigerorden: Ein Beitrag zur Geistesgeschichte der älteren Dominikaner* (Vechta i. O.: Albertus Magnus Verlag der Dominicaner, 1936), 168. See chapter 1 in this volume.

63. *In IV Sent.*, dist. 1; fol. 79va. Roland seems to be contending with the thought of William of Auxerre (d. 1231), who argued that the sacraments were material causes, rather than efficient. Filthaut, *Roland von Cremona*, 165. The notion that the sacraments were material causes was also taught by Hugh of St. Victor. Haring, "Berengar's Definitions of *Sacramentum* and Their Influence on Mediaeval Sacramentology," 126–27.

64. *In IV Sent.*, dist. 1; fol. 85ᵃ⁻ᵇ. See Filthaut, *Roland von Cremona*, 167.

65. "Es ist keine Qualität im moralischen, sondern in wirklich physischen Sinne … die nicht in das Gebiet der Final-, sondern der Wirkursache gehört. Das nun durch die Taufformel (Form) qualifizierte Wasser (Materie) berührt gemäss der ihm verliehenen Kraft den Täufling und wirkt verändernd auf den 'spiritus vitalis' ein, der durch den ganzen Körper verzeigt ist." Filthaut, *Roland von Cremona*, 167. Filthaut notes the importance of Roland's teaching on sacramental instrumentality, insisting that it must be interpreted in a physical, and not a moral, sense as the power at work in Baptism sanctifies the whole person. Filthaut sees this as in continuity with Augustine's teaching.

For Aquinas, one of the principal challenges was to connect the concept of sacramental cause with that of sign without compromising divine agency or inadequately describing the role of the sacraments themselves as either extrinsic or incomplete in their relation to the causality of grace. There seems to be no one in the medieval period who sought to diminish God's causal role in the sacraments. However, a number of other theories were proposed (in contradistinction to Aquinas) which inadequately describe the role of the sacraments in the causal process. In order to introduce his own theory in distinction 1 of the fourth book of his *Sentences* commentary, Aquinas presents two other theological models for sacramental cause popular in the mid-thirteenth century. The first is the idea that the sacraments are causes *"sine qua non."* Sacraments are efficacious only because God has ordained that they play a role in his plan to justify the human person. Aquinas offers the example of a leaden coin that by royal decree is given value in the eyes of the king.[66] The second example is a version of dispositive causality: in this model, the sacraments effect character (*res et sacramentum*) by means of efficient causality; grace is not caused efficiently, but the sacraments are disposing causes (*causae disponentes tali dispositione quae est necessitas*). Under this model the sacraments impart the necessary disposition for the reception of grace, presuming the person has no impediment. Aquinas says that most theologians believe this position to be sufficient.[67]

66. Aquinas does not cite specific theologians in the *Sentences*. However, Bonaventure, Fishacre, and others proposed a *sine qua non* causal model similar to the one described here by Aquinas. Bernhard Blankenhorn, "The Place of Romans 6 in Aquinas' Doctrine of Sacramental Causality: a Balance of History and Metaphysics," in *Ressourcement Thomism: Sacred Doctrine, the Sacraments, and the Moral Life*, ed. Reinhard Hütter and Matthew Levering (Washington, D.C.: The Catholic University of America Press, 2010), 136. This theory remained popular after Aquinas. Durand of Saint Pourcain (d. 1332) used the example of the leaden coin as well, and it is later taken up by those who believe the sacraments are only moral causes of grace. Gallagher, *Significando Causant*, 76–77, 153.

67. *Super Sent.* lib. 4, dist. 1, q. 1, a. 4, solutio I. Aquinas does not cite specific theologians here, and the theory is more difficult to trace to specific thinkers than the "king and lead coin" example. However, there were a number of contemporary theologians who believed that the sacraments caused a disposition of some kind (either by some form of efficient causality or in a less specific sense), while the actual causal responsibility for grace remained God's alone. For example, arguing against those who would say that the sacraments are only conditions for grace *sine qua non*, William of Auxerre

Both of these theories are proposed as valid by the Franciscan school in the *Summa Halensis*, which was being actively edited at Paris during the time that Aquinas was completing his commentary on the *Sentences*.[68] Both theories of sacramental causality described by Aquinas—*sine qua non* and dispositive causality—are proposed by the *Summa Halensis* as valid explanations of sacramental efficacy.[69] Concerning the first, Aquinas clearly teaches that *sine qua non* causality is categorically unacceptable because if the sacraments are only causes *sine qua non*—that is, conditions without which the reception of grace is impossible—sacramental causality is reduced to an accidental property, no different from the sacraments of the Old Law. Understood in this way, the sacraments are accidental and extrinsic to the actual cause worked by God. They do not cause grace strictly speaking but only promise that grace will be caused as a divine response to their use. They are only causes in a legal sense.

In rejecting the *sine qua non* approach, Aquinas aligns himself with the dispositive approach which was popular at the time. Existing theories of dispositive causality were certainly preferable to *sine qua non* causality because an actual intrinsic change in the person is effected through the conferral of the character. At the beginning of *Solutio I*, Aquinas describes existing theories of dispositive cause as separating the causation of the *res et sacramentum* and the *res tantum*: the sacraments cause the disposition for grace (*res et sacramentum*), but grace itself (*res tantum*) is caused only by God.[70] Dispositive

---

(d. 1231) posits that it is the character that calls for grace as a disposition in the soul. Alexander of Hales (d. 1245) develops this using the category of efficient cause: the sacraments are not efficient causes of grace as such (which is created directly by God) but rather effect the character, which then disposes for grace. See Gallagher, *Significando Causant*, 70–71.

68. Aquinas became a bachelor of the Sentences in 1252 and completed his commentary on the *Sentences* sometime after 1256. Torrell, *Saint Thomas Aquinas: The Person and His Work*, 328, 332. During this time, the Franciscan school in Paris was actively editing the *Summa Halensis*. The sacramental teaching found in this *Summa* was drawn largely from the previous work of William of Middleton and was being incorporated into the *Summa Halensis* by the Franciscan editors around the time that Aquinas was concluding his commentary on the *Sentences*.

69. *Summa Theologica* (Halensis), IV, qu. 5, a. 5, III. Willibrord Lampen, ed., *De Causalitate Sacramentorum iuxta Scholam Franciscanam, Florilegium Patristicum tam veteris quam medii aevi auctores complectens*, 26 (Bonn: Peter Hanstein, 1931), 9.

70. *Super Sent.* lib. 4, dist. 1, q. 1, a. 4, solutio I.

models of this kind did not always clearly connect the potency of the sacramental motion as an instrument to the finality of grace. Aquinas' initial description of dispositive causality is similar to the position described in the *Summa Halensis*, where it is very clear that the sacraments cause, via efficient causality, a disposition that prepares for the reception of grace; grace itself, however, is caused only by God.[71]

Because the sacraments only cause a disposition in the soul (which may be associated with the character or the *res et sacramentum*), Aquinas argues that there are in fact two separate lines of causality which result: the causing of the disposition and the causing of grace.[72] In this understanding, however, a further occasionalism is risked: sacramental character presents the necessary disposition or occasion, and God causes grace univocally. Although certain similarities remain, the version of dispositive instrumental causality that Aquinas presents in the body of Solutio I as his own teaching is distinct from this. While Aquinas will retain the division between character as *res et sacramentum* and grace as *res tantum* in his own reply, he will use his theory of instrumentality to define the term "dispositive" as a form of instrumental action in reference to and moved by the single, overarching intention of a principal mover. Understood in this way, their very definition as dispositive instruments is necessarily in reference to this finality.

For Aquinas, the sacraments, even considered as disposing causes, do more than provide a kind of moral disposition for the reception of grace. Aquinas' early theory of instrumentality describes dispositive causality as a form of natural instrumentality, operative in the construction of a house by an architect: all tools employed by the architect are directed towards his final purpose and share, in some sense, in that finality. However, this finality may well exceed the scope of many of the individual tools involved: a saw, for example, touches its proper end as a perfective instrument (the table) but is related to the overarching instrumental finality of the architect (the house) as a dispositive instrument—something which participates as a real in-

---

71. "Sacramenta sunt causae per modum materialis disponentis vel efficientis, large sumendo. Disponunt enim hominem et aptiorem reddunt ad gratiae susceptionem, et etiam gratiam infusam ad operandum expeditiorem." *Summa Theologica* (Halensis) IV q. 5 a. 5, III, resp. Lampen, *De Causalitate Sacramentorum*, 9.

72. *Super Sent.* lib. 4, dist. 1, q. 1, a. 4, solutio I.

strument in the larger purpose of the architect without itself touching the finality.[73]

Although Aquinas is not yet able to describe sacramental motion as a form of perfective instrumentality, the necessary participation of a dispositive cause in the finality of the principal agent places the sacraments clearly within the category of instrumental efficient motion as it is described in the *Sentences*. Although the potency of the saw does not touch the finality of the house directly, it does so dispositively because its instrumental motion has been actuated by the power and intentionality of the architect. For Aquinas, the sacraments are perfective instrumental causes of sacramental character and dispositive instrumental causes of grace. Although this second category may seem to lack the force of the first, the distinction between dispositive and perfective causality is introduced by Aquinas within the general category of instrumental causality as a whole and both remain species of efficient instrumentality. By contrast, in the *Summa Halensis* the "disposition" in question is the result of an efficient cause, not an instrumental cause in itself.

Although Aquinas' theory of instrumental causality will eventually transcend the distinction between dispositive and perfective instrumentality, in the *Sentences* Aquinas already employs the category of instrumental causality in a way that is more in keeping with Roland of Cremona's use of efficient causality than the dispositive approach current among some of his Franciscan contemporaries. Cremona's description of grace contained in the sacraments as an effect within its efficient cause did much to preserve the Augustinian doctrine of sacramental efficacy. By describing the sacraments as dispositive instrumental causes in the *Sentences*, Aquinas preserves something of Cremona's interpretation of the Augustinian doctrine of *vis fluens*, in which grace flows through the sacraments as an effect through the motion of an efficient cause. Although his mature teaching will surpass his early doctrine on this point, Aquinas' approach to sacramental causality in the *Sentences* moves beyond other versions of dispositive causality popular at the time, which make no meaning-

73. Ibid. The carpentry analogy which Aquinas employs here will develop in the *Summa*. See Lynch, "Cajetan's Harp," 13–16.

ful connection between the sacraments and the finality of grace within the category of efficient causality.

GRACE AND RE-CREATION

In the *Sentences*, Aquinas uses the language of disposition to describe sacramental instrumentality for a variety of reasons. Although he inherits the term from his predecessors, his application of the idea is principally an attempt to preserve the causal sovereignty of God as first principle. To this end, the connection between creation and re-creation is very important for Aquinas. If grace is a new act of creation from nothing, there can be no instrumentality involved in the proper sense. As a result we have seen Aquinas compare the instrumentality of the sacraments to the infusion of the soul into the body at conception.

In distinction 17 of the first book of Aquinas' *Commentary on the Sentences*, Aquinas argues that creation and re-creation are similar in all ways.[74] Both are immediate and both lack instrumentality in the full sense.[75] In both creation and re-creation, God confers being to nature through form. In creation, God gives the form of a nature to a created thing. In a similar way, God gives new being through grace in re-creation, in which God the Holy Spirit operates through the medium of charity within the person to reach the effect of love.[76] In this way, grace is present as an accidental form: an accident can impart its qualities to the body in which it inheres, as when an illumined

---

74. "Ad tertium dicendum, quod omnino simile est de creatione et recreatione." *Super Sent.* lib. 1, dist. 17, q. 1, a. 1, ad 3. Mandonnet/Moos, vol. 1 (1929), 395–96.

75. Although the early Aquinas did acknowledge the possibility of angelic mediation in the act of creation, he acknowledges that this is contrary to revelation. *Super Sent.* lib. 2 d. 1, q. 1, a. 3.

76. "Ad tertium dicendum, quod omnino simile est de creatione et recreatione. Sicut enim Deus per creationem contulit rebus esse naturae, et illud esse est formaliter a forma recepta in ipsa re creata, quae est quasi terminus operationis ipsius agentis; et iterum forma illa est principium operationum naturalium, quas Deus in rebus operatur: ita etiam et in recreatione Deus confert animae esse gratiae; et principium formale illius esse est habitus creatus, quo etiam perficitur operatio meritoria quam Deus in nobis operatur; et ita iste habitus creatus partim se habet ad operationem Spiritus sancti ut terminus, et partim ut medium." *Super Sent.* lib. 1, dist. 17, q.1, a. 1, ad 3. Mandonnet/Moos, vol. 1 (1929), 395–96.

thing becomes bright or when whiteness inhering in a thing makes it white.[77] Although the creative action of God is immediate, the action of this habit is in one sense instrumental (*medius*) because it involves an elicited human potency.[78] Although charity is not itself infinite, it is a form infused in the soul under the efficiency of God, who is infinitely powerful.[79] In this way it is clear that there is a sense in which God in the person of the Holy Spirit can work through the medium of instrumentality to achieve an effect, the act of which the instrument (the infused habit) seems to "touch" in a perfective sense. However, because Aquinas still treats the infusion of grace as a new act of creation, he is prevented from describing sacramental instrumentality as instrumentality *simpliciter*. There must be some qualification attached which preserves the immediacy and transcendence of divine action in this case.

Aquinas uses a startlingly reified expression to describe grace in this context (*esse gratiae*) that does not appear after his *Sentences* commentary.[80] His meaning is clear enough from the context, however: Aquinas is referring to the being of the accidental form infused by God into the soul. By emphasizing the dimension of *esse* in grace, Aquinas is able to preserve its divine origin, even if its being is accidental and not essential. Aquinas does not develop the implications of the accidental status of grace here in the *Sentences*, but later he will use this distinction between accidental and substantial being to qualify the comparison between creation and re-creation—all but univo-

77. *Super Sent.* lib. 1, dist. 17, q. 1, a. 1, solutio.; lib. 1, dist. 17, q. 1, a. 1, solutio, ad 2.

78. See *Super Sent.* lib. 1 dist. 17, q. 1, a. 1, solutio, ad 1. In the *Sentences*, Aquinas defines grace as a kind of infused habit. This concept will develop in his later works.

79. "Ad quintum dicendum, quod aliquid dicitur facere dupliciter: vel per modum efficientis, sicut pictor facit parietem album; vel per modum formae, sicut albedo facit album. Facere igitur de peccatore justum vel Deo conjunctum, est ipsius Dei sicut efficientis, et ipsius caritatis sicut formae. Unde non potest concludi quod caritas sit virtutis infinitae, sed solum quod est effectus virtutis infinitae." *Super Sent.* lib. 1, dist. 17, q. 1, a. 1, solutio, ad 5. Mandonnet/Moos, vol. 1 (1929), 396.

80. The phrase *esse gratiae* appears multiple times in distinction 17 of the first book of the *Sentences* which is referred to here. Outside of this, it appears once in distinction 40 and once in distinction 46 of book 1. It appears only once in book 2, after which point it does not recur: *Super Sent.* lib. 2, dist. 26, q. 1, a. 1, solutio, ad 4. This phrase also appears in contemporary theological texts such as the *Summa Halensis*: Lib. 2, pars 1, Inq. 1, tract. 1, sec. 1, q. 2, Titulus 2, membrum 2, c. 1, solutio. *Summa Theologica* (Halensis), vol. 2 (Rome: ad Claras Aquas, 1928), 25–26.

cally stated here—to develop a mode of divine creative interaction with existing substrates using the language of instrumentality.

An interesting prelude to this later development is the language Aquinas uses to describe charity in the soul here in distinction 17 of the first book of the *Sentences*. At this stage, the relationship between charity and grace is not defined very clearly. This is primarily because Aquinas wishes to emphasize both that charity as the life of God in the soul (following Augustine) and that it is through a kind of instrumentality that the soul is brought to the act of supernatural love through an influx of new life.[81] In this way grace is infused as whiteness in a white thing or light in something illumined.

As Aquinas' thought on these matters continues to develop, we will find that his theory of instrumentality develops alongside his theory of grace and that the modification of the comparison between creation and re-creation in grace is essential for this development. We know that God can be understood as an artist in the act of creation and in his subsequent relation to the world through secondary instrumental causality. We know that in some sense we can speak of our life in grace as a new creation.[82] Because this new creation takes place within an existing creature, however, there is room for some kind of instrumentality, allowing for divine action to function artistically and instrumentally in recreating the world in Christ. However, the mode of this re-creation—and the kind of instrumentality associated with it—will be further developed in Aquinas' mature work within the context of motive change in the created order, not as a fresh creation *ex nihilo* proceeding without instrumentality from the first principle.

CHRISTOLOGICAL INSTRUMENTALITY

There are many developments that emerge within Aquinas' thought after the completion of the *Sentences*. The category of dispositive causality is outmoded by Aquinas' approach to instrumentality in the *Summa*, and this change parallels further developments in the doc-

---

81. See *Super Sent.* lib. 1, dist. 17, q. 1, a. 1, solutio, ad 4, 5, 6.
82. "If anyone is in Christ, he is a new creation; the old has passed away, behold, the new has come." 2 Cor. 5:17 RSV.

trine of grace. Beyond this, the *Summa* is notable for the degree to which it roots sacramental causality in the instrumentality of the Incarnation itself. Not all of these connections are as well developed in the *Sentences*. Nevertheless, elements of Aquinas' mature theory are discernable even at this early stage.

The *Summa* clearly describes both the humanity of Christ and the sacraments themselves as true instrumental causes—functioning as tools or secondary efficient instrumental causes—operating under the creative power of God and working towards the re-creation of the human person in grace. In the *Summa*, Aquinas presents the humanity of Christ as a "conjoined instrument"—as the hand is to the body, so is the humanity of Christ to his divinity, the human nature of Christ being used instrumentally to accomplish the work of redemption.[83] By extension, the sacraments of the Church are understood as "separated instruments"—as a stick in the hand, directed by the purposes of the one who wields it.[84] At this mature stage, Aquinas exhibits a deepened awareness of the Christic dimension of sacramental instrumentality as a form of divine artistry, interacting with

83. "Respondeo dicendum quod, sicut dictum est, sacramentum operatur ad gratiam causandam per modum instrumenti. *Est autem duplex instrumentum, unum quidem separatum, ut baculus; aliud autem coniunctum, ut manus.* Per instrumentum autem coniunctum movetur instrumentum separatum, sicut baculus per manum. Principalis autem causa efficiens gratiae est ipse Deus, ad quem comparatur humanitas Christi sicut instrumentum coniunctum, sacramentum autem sicut instrumentum separatum. Et ideo oportet quod virtus salutifera derivetur a divinitate Christi per eius humanitatem in ipsa sacramenta." *ST* III Q. 62 a. 5 co. (emphasis mine). I. Backes argues that, although Aquinas' mature thought is indeed influenced by Greek Christology, this distinction between separate and conjoined instrumentality is his own inovation. Ignaz Backes, *Die Christologie des hl. Thomas v. Aquin und die griechischen Kirchenväter* (Paderborn: Schöningh, 1931), 285. See Paul Crowley, "Instrumentum Divinitatis in Thomas Aquinas: Recovering the Divinity of Christ," *Theological Studies* 52(September, 1991): 458n19. For a recent study that frames Aquinas' engagement with these issues in historical context, see Corey Barnes, "Christological Composition in Thirteenth Century Debates," *The Thomist* 75 (2011): 173–206, and "Thomas Aquinas's Chalcedonian Christology and its Influence on Later Scholastics," *The Thomist* 78 (2014): 189–217. See also *Christ's Two Wills in Scholastic Thought: The Christology of Aquinas and Its Historical Contexts* (Toronto: Pontifical Institute of Mediaeval Studies, 2012), 180–290. Barnes treats the relationship between the two wills of Christ at length, developing the causal implications of this. Barnes, *Christ's Two Wills in Scholastic Thought*, 224–90, and also treats the reception history of this issue after Aquinas in later scholasticism. Ibid., 291–328.

84. *ST* III Q. 62 a. 5 co. Text as in note 83.

created reality through the medium of created tools. Beyond the artistic employment of inanimate tools, the anthropological dimension of this instrumentality is raised by the role of priestly intention, the end of grace, and the humanity of Christ himself. The nature of the Incarnation itself, as a union of the power of the divine nature with the created potency of humanity, raises the question of anthropological instrumentality. Although there are many factors that influence the subsequent development of Aquinas' thought, in the *Sentences* a number of key elements of his mature thought on these issues are already visible.

Early in the *Sentences*, Aquinas argues that, while the divinity of Christ effects grace, his humanity functions in the order of merit with regard to this same end.[85] However, this does not mean that the humanity of Christ is a moral cause in the modern sense, functioning under the modality of meritorious or rhetorical persuasion. Concerning our resurrection in relation to Christ's, Aquinas argues that the sacred humanity functions in relation to the divinity of Christ as an instrumental cause, the divinity itself being the principal efficient cause in the univocal sense.[86] Here, Aquinas employs a sense of instrumental efficient causality that he has used elsewhere in the *Sentences*: God as principal and exemplary cause is effective in the univocal sense. Instruments participate in this analogically. Although this general sense of instrumentality is drawn from both Platonic and Aristo-

---

85. "[Christus] gratiam dedit, inquantum Deus, effective, et inquantum homo, per modum meriti. Unde ad significandum redundantiam gratiae ipsius in nos per modum operationis, facta est missio visibilis ad ipsum in Baptismo: quia tunc ipse nihil accipiens a baptismo, tactu suae mundissimae carnis vim regenerativam contulit aquis, efficienter ut Deus, et meritorie ut homo." *Super Sent.* lib. 1, dist. 16, q. 1, a. 3, solutio. Mandonnet/Moos, vol. 1 (1929), 376. See also Dondaine, "Apropos d'Avicenne et de saint Thomas de la causalite dispositive a la causalite instrumentale," 451.

86. Aquinas argues that the principal cause at work here is God himself, who raised Christ from the dead. "Et per hunc modum resurrectio Christi est causa nostrae resurrectionis; quia illud quod facit resurrectionem Christi, qui est causa efficiens univoca nostrae resurrectionis, agit ad resurrectionem nostram, scilicet virtus Divinitatis ipsius Christi.... Sed ipsa resurrectio Christi virtute Divinitatis adjunctae est causa quasi instrumentalis resurrectionis nostrae; *operationes enim divinae agebantur mediante carne Christi quasi quodam organo*, sicut ponit exemplum Damascenus in 3 lib. (de Fid. orthod., cap. 15), de tactu corporali quo mundavit leprosum, Matth. 8." *Super Sent.* lib. 4, dist. 43, q. 1, a. 2, Solutio I. Parma/Bourke, vol. 7 (1948), 1061. See also Crowley, "Instrumentum Divinitatis in Thomas Aquinas," 459–63.

telian sources, it is clear that it involves a specifically Aristotelian kind of physical motion towards an end specified by the principal agent. In both the *Summa* and the *Sentences*, Aquinas describes the passion as meritorious, and the intrinsically meritorious nature of this sacrifice will distinguish the Thomistic approach from other nominalistic and idealistic theories in later centuries.

In the *Sentences* Aquinas does describe the humanity of Christ as meritorious, in as much as it functions as an instrument of his divinity.[87] Questions remain, however, about the manner in which this instrumentality functions in relation to the sacraments as instrumental causes and about the relationship between this Christological instrumentality and the finality of grace. Although the *Summa* employs the concepts of conjoined and separated instruments to describe this process, in the *Sentences* Aquinas is not explicit on this point.[88] Much of his language in distinction 43 conforms to the general pattern of principal and instrumental causality that is woven into the metaphysical fabric of the *Sentences*. However, in distinction 43 Aquinas describes the instrumentality of Christ's humanity in a more specific sense with the term *organum*. In this context Aquinas cites Damascene, who describes the power of Christ's divinity working through his humanity as an instrument or *organum* in the case of earthly miracles such as the cure of a case of leprosy in Matthew 8.[89] Although Aquinas benefits from Damascene's theological exegesis in this particular case, his broader use of the concept of *organum* reflects a well-developed understanding of Aristotelian anthropology.

Although the term *organum* is of more limited significance in classical Latin,[90] the Greek ὄργανον is more closely associated with instrumentality in the speculative sense.[91] In philosophical usage,

---

87. See note 86.

88. M.-Benoît Lavaud shows the implications of the development of Aquinas' approach to the instrumentality of Christ's humanity from the *Sentences* to the *Summa* for the sacraments. M.-Benoît Lavaud, "Saint Thomas et la Causalité Physique Instrumentale de la sainte humanité et des sacrements," *Revue Thomiste* 32 (1927): 292–316.

89. See note 86.

90. The term *organum* appears most readily in ecclesiastical Latin in reference to a musical instrument. In later usage it refers directly to the musical instrument known today by the same name. In the text of the Vulgate it is listed with the harp and the human voice as an instrument used in praise of God. See Gn 4:21; I Paralipomenon (1 Chr) 15:16; II Par. (2 Chr) 5:13; Judith, 15:15; Job, 21:12; Ps 136:2 (Iuxta LXX); Wis 19:17.

ὄργανον has a more technically precise semantic field in reference to anthropology. In the *Republic* and elsewhere, Plato uses *organon* in a specifically anthropological sense to refer to an organ of sense apprehension.[92] Following this, Aristotle used the term to describe the body or its different parts in relation to the soul,[93] referring specifically to the hand in relation to the body as an "instrument of instruments" in *de Anima*.[94] The notion of both the body and the hand as instruments of the soul will become important for Aquinas not only as anthropological concepts but in Christological and sacramental usage as well, where Christ's humanity and the sacraments both function as instruments of his divinity, as a stick in the hand.

In the early context of the *Sentences*, Aquinas' use of *organum* in the case of the sacraments may appear to be only a Latinized citation

---

Charlton Lewis and Charles Short, eds. *A Latin Dictionary.* Text as in *Biblia Sacra: Iuxta Vulgatam Versionem,* ed. Robert Weber and Roger Gryson, 5th ed. (Stuttgart: Deutsche Bibelgesellschaft, 2007). However, the term has some reference in classical Latin to a tool, particularly in the context of Columella's work on Agriculture, *De Re Rustica.* See Columella, *De Re Rustica,* 3.13.12. *Perseus Digital Library,* www.perseus.tuffts.edu (accessed May 5, 2013). In Christian antiquity, similar usage of the concept of *organum* as instrument or tool is found in the writings of early Church Fathers such as Ignatius of Antioch, who described the animals in the arena as "tools through which the martyr becomes a perfect sacrifice to God." 2 Clem. 18:2 uses the term to describe the "tools of the devil." See Ignatius' Letter to the Romans 4:2. William F. Arndt and F. Wilbur Gingrich, *A Greek-English Lexicon of The New Testament and Other Early Christian Literature: A Translation and Adaptation of Walter Bauer's Griechisch-Deutsches Wörterbuch zu den Schriften des Neuen Testaments und der übrigen urchristlichen Literatur,* 4 th revised and augmented ed. (Chicago: The University of Chicago Press, 1971), 582.

91. The Latin term *organum* is originally derived from the Greek ὄργανον, which carries a more technically precise semantic field in philosophical usage. While the reference to musical instrumentation is certainly present in the Greek, the concept of ὄργανον as an instrument or tool for making or doing something is more common. *A Greek-English Lexicon,* with revised supplement, (*LSJ*), ed. Henry George Liddell and Robert Scott (Oxford: Clarendon Press, 1996), 1245.

92. *Republic* 508b, 518c. *Theaet.* 185c. *Phaedrus* 250b. *Tim.* 45b. *LSJ,* 1245.

93. *PA* 643a11, 645b14. *GA* 716a24. *LSJ,* 1245.

94. *De An.* 432a2. See also *PA* 687a21. Aristotle also uses the term to describe the organs of locomotion: the feet walking. *GA* 732b28. He also describes internal functions such as digestion *GA* 788b24, and respiration *PA* 664a29, using *organon.* Ὄργανον is of course also the collective title of a group of Aristotle's major logical works: *Categories, On Interpretation, Prior Analytics, Posterior Analytics, Topics,* and *On Sophistical Refutations.* See Richard McKeon, *The Basic Works of Aristotle* (New York: Random House, 2001).

of Damascene's Greek. However, when the larger usage of *organum* in the *Sentences* is taken into account, Aquinas seems to show a broader knowledge of the technical meaning of ὄργανον in Greek philosophy and uses the Latin *organum* to delineate this, independent of his exposure to Damascene. Furthermore, Aquinas' use of *organum* in the *Sentences* is distinct from the larger category of *instrumentum*—which Aquinas uses to refer to instrumental causality in a general or specifically metaphysical sense. When *organum* is used, it can be seen to have specific anthropological overtones in the Aristotelian sense. In his natural anthroplogy, Aquinas follows Aristotle in describing the soul as a motor in relation to the body—that is, form specifying matter provides the formal principle to govern the actuation of potency and physical motion. In this context the early Aquinas cites *De Anima* and refers to a kind of instrumental relationship within the body-soul composite: in operations in which the soul is the principal agent, the instrumental mediation of the body is necessary for the completion of the task. For Aquinas, as the form of the body, the soul determines its matter and as motor it determines the *organum*, which are moved as by an artist making use of a proper instrument.[95]

It seems that Aquinas uses the term *organum* primarily in its instrumental sense in reference to individual sense organs, prefering to use the term *corpus* to refer to the body as a whole. He also uses *organum* to refer to the sensitive appetites, describing individual senses as instruments which convey impressions of reality to the soul.[96] For Aquinas, individual bodily powers such as the voice are also understood as a kind of *organum*—an instrument functioning on behalf of the soul.[97] Even the concepts of separated and conjoined instruments, which Aquinas will apply explicitly to sacramental Christology in the *Summa*, are present implicitly in Aquinas' natural anthropology of *organum* in the *Sentences*. He speaks of the senses and other

95. "Et hanc positionem improbat Philosophus in 1 *De anima*, text. 53, ostendens quod anima est forma corporis et motor ejus. Oportet autem ut determinatae formae determinata materia debeatur, et determinato motori determinatum *organum, sicut quaelibet ars in agente utitur propriis instrumentis*: unde haec anima non potest esse forma et motor nisi hujus corporis." *Super Sent.* lib. 2, dist. 19, q. 1, a. 1, co. (emphasis mine). Mandonnet/Moos, vol. 2 (1929), 482.

96. *Super Sent.* lib. 2, dist. 17, q. 2, a. 1, solutio.

97. *Super Sent.* lib. 2, dist. 8, q. 1, a. 4, qc. 5, solutio.

bodily parts and capacities with a fixed function as *organa affixae*.[98] Beyond this, however, Aquinas clearly applies *organum* to parts of the body with variable functions, such as hands,[99] and to external instruments able to work by the power of the one who wields them. These can be either animated or inanimate instruments such as servants or carpentry tools, respectively.[100] From this it is clear that Aquinas tends to use the term *organum* to reference specific anthropological concepts drawn from Aristotle and not simply as a general synonym for instrumental causality. *Organum* is distinct from his broader doctrine of instrumentatality as a kind of subspecies of specifically anthropological instrumental causality.

Although he is not yet able to fully apply this model to Christology and the sacraments, in using the term *organum* to refer to the humanity of Christ, Aquinas implicitly references a model of instrumental causality drawn not from the Neoplatonist cosmology of the *Liber de Causis* and other similar sources but from Aristotelian anthropology. In addition, Aquinas' application of *organum* to Christology and the sacraments must necessarily be understood as a reference not only to Damascene's Christology but to Aquinas' own understanding of *organum* at the level of natural anthropology. When employed in the context of Christological instrumentality, Aquinas' use of the term *"organum"* implicitly positions his Christology in reference to the Aristotelian anthropology he has already employed elsewhere in the *Sentences*.

Curiously, however, although the instrumentality of Christ's humanity is made far more explicit in the *Summa*, the word *organum* is not employed.[101] Instead, the broader concept of instrumental cau-

---

98. Aquinas describes the concupiscible powers in this way. *Super Sent.* lib. 2, dist. 21, q. 1, a. 2, arg. 5. Aquinas also describes muscles and nerves as *organa affixae*. *Super Sent.* lib. 2, dist. 14, q. 1, a. 3, solutio, ad 4.

99. *Super Sent.* lib. 2, dist. 1, q. 2, a. 5, solutio, ad 3.

100. "Uno modo quando illud quod ordinatur ab operante ut causa operati est causa ejus secundum virtutem aliam a virtute operantis, quam tamen ab ipso recipit: et hoc oportet esse instrumentum operantis, inquantum est motum ab operante, vel per imperium, sicut servus, vel motu corporali, sicut res inanimatae, ut securis. Unde philosophus dicit in VIII *Ethic.*, cap. XI, quod servus est sicut *organum animatum, et organa sunt sicut servi inanimati.*" *Super Sent.* lib. 2, dist. 13, q. 1, a. 5, solutio (emphasis mine). Mandonnet/Moos, vol. 2 (1929), 341.

101. Elsewhere in his mature Christology, however, Aquinas continues to use the

sality is invoked using the term *instrumentum*, and the anthropological context for Christological causality in the sacraments must be deliberately explained. In the *Sentences*, however, while *instrumentum* is used to describe the causality of the sacraments themselves,[102] the choice of the word *organum* in relation to the humanity of Christ already implies an intuition of the same anthropological instrumentality although it remains nascent and unarticulated in its theological implications.

Why does Aquinas choose not to articulate more explicitly the instrumentality of Christ's humanity in the *Sentences*? Despite his understanding of Aristotelian anthropology, one reason is of course his lack of exposure to other sources within Greek Christology. (In particular, the work of Cyril of Alexandria will be especially influential.)[103] Beyond this, however, there remain issues surrounding grace, instrumentality and supernatural ends that are very much unresolved at this stage. Aquinas cites these issues explicitly as his reasons for proposing the doctrine of dispositive instrumentality in the case of the sacraments.[104] Although he does not say so, the same set of concerns would seem to prevent him from adopting a perfective model of Christological causality with respect to grace in the *Sentences*. In the *Summa*, the humanity of Christ as the arm and the sacraments as the stick in the hand both function to effect the sanctification of the person in grace. The unqualified presentation of this doctrine assumes that both the humanity of Christ and the sacraments are not dispositive but perfective instrumental causes in the true sense. By describing the humanity of Christ as an *organum* of his divinity, Aquinas is able to reference the natural anthropology already at work elsewhere in the *Sentences* without entangling his Christology in the broader is-

---

term "*organum*," quoting Damascene. "Secundum quod corpus est animae instrumentum, non quidem extrinsecum et adventitium, sed proprium et coniunctum. *Unde Damascenus dicit humanam naturam esse organum verbi.*" *De Unione Verbi*, a. 1 co. (emphasis mine). Torrell argues that *De Unione* dates from the Spring of 1272. Torrell, *Saint Thomas Aquinas: The Person and His Work*, 336–37.

102. *Super Sent.* lib. 4, dist. 1, q. 1, a. 1, qc. 4, solutio.

103. See Theophil Tschipke, *Die Menschheit Christi als Heilsorgan der Gottheit.*; Backes, *Die Christologie des hl. Thomas v. Aquin und die griechischen Kirchenväter.*

104. *Super Sent.* lib. 4, dist. 1, q. 1, a. 4, solutio I.

sue of sacramental instrumentality and re-creation, concepts still very much under construction at this early stage. As a result, Aquinas is able to clearly articulate the kind of anthropological instrumentality at work in the hypostatic union and hint at its sacramental implications without arguing that this same instrumentality is a direct instrumental cause of grace through the sacraments.

3

From the *Sentences* to the *Summa*

This is the second of two chapters devoted to the primary texts of Aquinas. In the first we discussed Aquinas' early doctrine as it appears in his *Sentences* commentary, where Aquinas proposes a theory of dispositive instrumental causality to explain the efficacy of the sacraments. This present chapter will discuss the further development of Aquinas' thought on sacramental instrumentality. In the previous chapter a substantial amount of time was given to the underlying principles that contextualize Thomas' doctrine of instrumentality, such as creation from a single first principle and the contingent relationship of created things that forms the root of the doctrine of instrumental cause. In the interest of expediency, we will not explore these same fundamental principles in each of Thomas' subsequent works; although there may be interesting points of contrast between the *Sentences* and Aquinas' mature work even here, the bulk of this doctrine is unchanged, at least insofar as it concerns us at present. Instead, we will focus our attention on the way in which Thomas' doctrine of sacramental instrumentality develops over the course of his later teaching. Specifically, we will notice the manner in which his doctrine on grace and re-creation develops in conjunction with his theory of sacramental instrumentality.

As we have already mentioned in the historical section of this work, St. Thomas does not use the word "dispositive" when describing sacramental cause in his mature works. Some interpreters of Aquinas did not believe that this terminological change was significant; this opinion can be found even among twentieth-century scholars.[1] It will be shown here that, as was first noticed by Cajetan, the absence of the word "dispositive" in the mature works of Aquinas in fact indicates an important development in his sacramental theory.

This chapter will begin by examining two works that post-date the *Sentences* commentary and yet still retain the language of "dispositive instrumental cause" when speaking of the sacraments: *De Veritate* and *De Potentia*.[2] While the terminology remains unchanged here, there are several important changes that prepare the way for a more fully developed sense of instrumentality that does not need to limit itself to dispositive action.[3] Following this, we will examine the *Tertia Pars* of the *Summa Theologiae*, where the term "dispositive cause" does not appear.

Hermeneutically, Aquinas' approach to sacramental causality raises questions of textual interpretation and commentatorial reception. It

---

1. We have already studied these issues earlier in this book at length. Capreolus and De Ferrara, along with many other early Thomists, argued for dispositive causality. In the twentieth century, M. Gierens argued that there is no significant development in Aquinas' thought on this matter. See Gierens, "Zur Lehre des hl. Thomas uber die kausalität der Sacramente," *Scholastik* 9 (1934): 321–45. This theory is successfully refuted by John F. Gallagher. See his *Significando Causant: A Study of Sacramental Efficiency*, Studia Fribugensia New Series 40 (Fribourg: The University Press, 1965), 120–34, 125n2. Bernard Leeming and others argue for dispositive causality primarily because of its perceived usefulness for the emerging field of ecclesiology, rather than out of a concern for the original intent of Aquinas or certain of his commentators. See Bernard Leeming, *Principles of Sacramental Theology* (Westminster, Md.: Newman, 1963), 314–40. John F. Gallagher also responds convincingly to Leeming on certain points. See Gallagher, *Significando Causant*, 133n3.

2. St. Thomas commented on the *Sentences* in Paris under St. Albert the Great, 1254–56; after the completion of this initial formation, he remained in Paris as a Regent Master, 1256–59, during which time he authored the *De Veritate*. The *De Potentia* was written during Aquinas' Roman period 1265–68. Notably, Aquinas also authored the *Prima Pars* of the *Summa Theologiae* during this time. Jean-Pierre Torrell, *Saint Thomas Aquinas:The Person and His Work*, vol. 1, trans. Robert Royal (Washington, D.C.: The Catholic University of America Press, 1996), 328.

3. The development of Aquinas' theory of sacramental causality could be traced through all of his major works. Given the length of this book, we will only be able to treat a selection of his writings. The contents of this selection are determined in part by our desire to portray the importance of the doctrine of grace and the theory of obediential potency in Aquinas' sacramental theology.

was careful study of this question in the *Sentences* and the *Summa* that first brought these textual developments to light. It was not until the sixteenth century that this development was noticed by the Thomistic commentatorial tradition. However, Aquinas' approach to sacramental causality in the *Summa* is made possible in part by changes in his approach to grace. Correspondingly, the degree to which this textual development is appreciated by different commentators affects their respective approaches to grace in relation to potency, and sacramental grace in particular. The second part of this chapter will examine the doctrine of grace in connection with the concept of potency in the later commentatorial tradition. The chapter will close by considering the effect of sacramental instrumentality on the interpretation of the subspecies of sacramental grace among different commentators.

DE VERITATE AND DE POTENTIA DEI

Both the *De Veritate* and the *De Potentia Dei* represent significant steps forward in Aquinas' thought on sacramental cause. Although Thomas still teaches that the sacraments are dispositive instrumental causes in both works, he manages to resolve many of the underlying speculative issues that contributed to his teaching on dispositive causality in the first place.[4] Specifically, Aquinas will develop his teaching on grace with respect to the act of creation and re-creation in relation to existing material potencies. In the *De Potentia*, the concept of instrument in the proper sense will be clarified in light of potencies both human and divine. Although Aquinas mentions the sacraments in both the *De Veritate* and the *De Potentia*, he does not explicitly apply the results of these developments to the issue of sacramental causality as yet: he chooses to retain the language of dispositive cause despite the fact that his underlying principles have developed significantly.

The *De Veritate* is one of Aquinas' earlier works, originating from his first years as a master in theology at Paris after the completion of his *Commentary on the Sentences*.[5] Although some scholars in the ear-

---

4. For a description of the sacraments as dispositive instrumental causes, see *De Ver.* q. 27 a. 4 ad 3, ad 12. *De Pot.* q. 3 a. 4 ad 8.

5. St. Thomas commented on the *Sentences* from 1254–56; he wrote the *De Veritate* between 1256–59. Torrell, *The Person and His Work*, 328.

ly twentieth century argued that the *De Potentia* was written during this same period, Torrell maintains that it was composed much later.[6] Despite its later date of composition, however, it is important to consider the *De Potentia* along with the *De Veritate*. Both of these works provide detailed treatment of certain specific issues which later come to fruition in the full systematic treatment found in the *Contra Gentiles* and the *Summa Theologiae*. Neither the *De Veritate* nor the *De Potentia* is a complete systematic work like the *Sentences,* the *Contra Gentiles,* or the *Summa*. There is no systematic treatment of larger topics such as grace, redemption, and creation. By their nature they treat specific questions and do so with a fair amount of depth, although they lack the more comprehensive treatment of these issues found in Aquinas' systematic works. As a result, the developments found in these texts fall within specific areas of Aquinas' thought.

Question twenty-seven of the *De Veritate* treats the topic of grace at length in relation to accidental potency and instrumentality; it is this subject that will principally concern us here. An interesting development that is present here is the concept of the instrumentality of the sacred humanity of Jesus Christ, a notion that seems to have come to Aquinas in part from some of the Greek Fathers.[7] In the *De Veritate*, Aquinas attributes this version of incarnational instrumentality to Damascene several times in his treatment of the sacraments as

6. There has been some confusion about the dating of the *De Potentia*. Some earlier scholars (such as Mandonnet) believed that it was composed in 1259, following almost directly on the *De Veritate*. Gallagher cites Mandonnet but is aware of the possibility of a later date. Gallagher, *Significando Causant,* 110. Torrell, however, places its composition in Aquinas' Roman period, around 1265–66. Notably, Aquinas also authored the *Prima Pars* of the *Summa Theologiae* during this time. Torrell, *The Person and His Work,* 328, 160–62. This later date makes the *De Potentia* more akin to the *Contra Gentiles* than to the *De Veritate*.

7. See Gallagher, *Significando Causant,*107. For a comprehensive study of this subject, see Theophil Tschipke, *Die Menschheit Christi als Heilsorgan der Gottheit: Unter Besonderer Berücksichtigung der Lehre des Heiligen Thomas von Aquin,* Freiburger Theologische Studien 55 (Freiburg im Breisgau: Herder, 1940). For more recent commentary on the same theme, see Bernhard Blankenhorn, "The Instrumental Causality of the Sacraments: Thomas Aquinas and Louis-Marie Chauvet," Nova et Vetera 4 (2006): 255–94 and Blankenhorn, "The Place of Romans 6 in Aquinas' Doctrine of Sacramental Causality: A Balance of History and Metaphysics," in *Ressourcement Thomism: Sacred Doctrine, the Sacraments, and the Moral Life,* ed. Reinhard Hütter and Matthew Levering (Washington, D.C.: The Catholic University of America Press, 2010).

causes of grace.[8] Aquinas first introduces the concept of the humanity of Christ as an instrument (*organum*) in his *Commentary on the
Sentences*.[9] It should be noted that, while Aquinas does introduce this
concept of incarnational instrumentality in the *De Veritate*, it does
not affect his conclusions significantly. Aquinas still argues for sacramental causes as dispositive instruments in the *De Veritate*, and the
way in which his argument proceeds does not change ostensibly from
the *Sentences*.[10] In the *De Veritate* Aquinas essentially re-articulates
the same argument for the sacraments as dispositive instrumental
causes that he first proposed in the *Sentences*. Because instruments
taken up in the hand of a builder are used according to their natural
potencies, we cannot attribute perfective instrumentality to natural
instruments when considering a supernatural act.[11]

What prepares the way for future developments in Aquinas' theory of the sacraments as instrumental causes is the development of
his understanding of grace with respect to the act of creation. Recall
that, at the end of our treatment of the *Sentences*, Aquinas drew a very
strong parallel between creation and re-creation, arguing that the *esse
gratiae* was given to the soul as an accident—a kind of habit which
enables the supernatural act of charity as a participation in God's own

---

8. See *De Ver.* q. 27 a. 3 ad 7 and a. 4 resp.

9. "Quandoque autem illius actionis qua effectus producitur, non est principium
primo et per se ipsa forma secundum quam attenditur similitudo, sed principia illius
formae; sicut si homo albus generaret hominem album, ipsa albedo generantis non est
principium generationis activae; et tamen albedo generantis dicitur causa albedinis
generati, quia principia albedinis in generante sunt principia generativa facientia albed-
inem in generato; et per hunc modum resurrectio Christi est causa nostrae resurrectionis; quia illud quod facit resurrectionem Christi, qui est causa efficiens univoca nostrae
resurrectionis, agit ad resurrectionem nostram, scilicet virtus divinitatis ipsius Christi,
quae sibi et patri communis est; unde dicitur Roman. 8, 2: qui suscitavit Jesum Christum a mortuis, vivificabit mortalia corpora nostra. Sed ipsa *resurrectio Christi virtute divinitatis adjunctae est causa quasi instrumentalis resurrectionis nostrae*; operationes enim
divinae agebantur *mediante carne Christi quasi quodam organo*, sicut ponit exemplum
Damascenus in 3 Lib. de tactu corporali quo mundavit leprosum, Matth. 8." *Super Sent.*
lib. 4 d. 43 q. 1 a. 2 qc. 1 co. (emphasis mine).

10. An argument for dispositive instrumental causality virtually identical to that
which appears in the *Sentences* can be found in *De Ver.* q. 27 a. 4 ad 3, ad 12 and a. 4 resp.

11. Aquinas uses the same image that appeared in the *Sentences* (*Super Sent.* lib. 4 d.
1 q. 1 a. 4 Solutio I): an artist or builder uses a saw to make a stool, which falls within the
natural potency of the saw as an instrument. But when we consider the finality of grace,
natural instrumentality can only be dispositive. *De Ver.* q. 27 a. 4 resp.

life. Aquinas insists that grace must be an act of creation because it is beyond the capacity of any natural potency. Grace is communicated through a renewed act of creation, and the human act of charity rises to God under the impulse of the Holy Spirit. While we have seen that there is a kind of implicitly perfective instrumentality at work in Aquinas' understanding of charity as it is expressed in the *Sentences*, his emphasis on grace as re-creation prevents him from applying a perfective form of causality to the instrumental motion of the sacraments because, as he has said elsewhere in the *Sentences*, the act of creation from nothing escapes the use of any instrumentality, except in the dispositive sense.

While Aquinas will retain the language of dispositive cause in the *De Veritate* when speaking of the sacraments, there is an important development in his theology of grace here that will pave the way for future developments in sacramental instrumentality.[12] In the *De Veritate*, Aquinas affirms a number of propositions that he has already spelled out in the *Sentences*. For example, he describes grace as a kind of created form in the soul. Grace in this sense is not an extrinsic acceptance of the creature by God but a created accident.[13] However, there is a significant terminological development concerning grace here in the *De Veritate*. In response to an objector who claims that grace cannot be deduced from the potency of created matter, Aquinas responds by developing the implications of the accidental being of grace (an idea also already present in the *Sentences*). Because accidents subsist in an already existing substance, grace is not created in the strict sense of the word because this would imply the creation of a new subsistent being from nothing. Rather, Aquinas says that grace is "concreated." Aquinas uses this language to describe the manner in which grace is brought about as an accidental form of being. In this case God's creative act does not bring something to be from nothing but works from within the accidental potencies of an already existing nature. Aquinas is clear that creation properly speaking is reserved for substances (*rei subsistentis*). But because created substance has the property of potency or becoming (*fieri*), accidental potency is a necessary feature of its being. This accidental potency cannot be

---

12. See Gallagher, *Significando Causant*, 102–9.
13. *De Ver.* q. 27 a. 1.

created from nothing because it does not have being *per se* but rather has its being in another. The being an accident has is not from matter (*ex qua:* that is, it is not individuated by matter as a new substance). Rather, its being is in matter, on which it depends, and through the change of which (the actuation of accidental potency) its being is educed (*per cuius mutationem in esse educuntur*).[14]

Concreation, therefore, applies properly to the coming-to-be of accidental properties in already existing substances, from whose potencies this new accidental being can be drawn forth by God's creative power. While the idea of concreation is mentioned several times in the *Sentences*, Aquinas does not apply the concept to sacramental grace until the *De Veritate*.[15]

As a result of this qualification, Aquinas will modify his comparison between creation and re-creation. In creation there can be no instrumentality because there is nothing for the instrument to operate with or in. Re-creation, however, presumes the existence of something on which the instrument can operate.[16] In this way, Aquinas admits that creation and re-creation are not in fact similar in all things—a qualification of his earlier claim in the *Sentences*. In this he is building on principles already in place in his *Sentences* commentary; recall that, even in the *Sentences*, Aquinas taught that grace was an accidental property.[17] At no time was it ever assumed that grace

14. "Ad nonum dicendum, quod illa ratio non est usquequaque sufficiens. Nam creari proprie est *rei subsistentis*, cuius est proprie *esse et fieri*: formae autem non subsistentes, sive substantiales sive accidentales, non proprie creantur, sed concreantur: sicut nec esse habent per se, sed in alio: et quamvis non habeant materiam ex qua, quae sit pars eorum, habent tamen materiam in qua, a qua dependent, et per cuius mutationem in esse educuntur; ut sic eorum fieri sit proprie subiecta eorum transmutari. Secus autem est de anima rationali, quae est forma subsistens; unde proprie ei creari convenit." *De Ver.* q. 27 a. 3 ad 9 (emphasis mine). This reasoning would also apply to nonsubsistent substantial forms.

15. Aquinas does use the concept of concreation in the *Sentences*, but the connection with the causality of sacramental grace is not developed. In addition to distinguishing it from the creation proper to substance, Aquinas uses concreation to describe the infused virtues, (*Super Sent.* lib. 3 d. 23 q. 2 a. 5 co) and the manner in which the *lumen gloriae* is imparted to angels (*Super Sent.* lib. 3 d. 14 q. 1 a. 3 qc. 2 co. and *Super Sent.* lib. 4 d. 50 q. 1 a. 1 co).

16. "Ad decimumquintum dicendum, quod creatio nihil praesupponit circa quod posset fieri instrumentalis agentis actio; recreatio vero praesupponit; et ideo non est simile." *De Ver.* q. 27 a. 4 ad 15.

17. *Super Sent.* lib. 1 d. 17 q.1 a. 1 ad 3.

was created as a subsistent form. The real development here in the *De Veritate* is his admission that this accidental status distances grace from properly creative acts. While grace was a *habitus creatus* in the *Sentences*, in the *De Veritate* it is now *concreatus*.[18]

In the *De Potentia* Aquinas develops the principle of concreation which, while already present in the *Sentences* in germ, is applied directly to grace in the *De Veritate*. In the *De Potentia* Aquinas restates the principle that accidents, properly so called, are not created but rather concreated; they are concreated as something in an existing creature.[19] As we have seen, the major contribution of the *De Veritate* is the qualification of the comparison between the infusion of grace into the soul and the act of creation *ex nihilo*. While there are important parallels to be drawn between the act of creation and the concreation of grace, the two are not entirely congruent. This incomplete correspondence between creation and re-creation removes one of the principal objections to the involvement of created instrumental causality in the production of grace in the soul, although this development alone does not fully resolve the question of sacramental instrumentality.

In *De Potentia*, however, a new parallel arises. At this point Aquinas is very clear that grace is concreated using the potency of matter. Although Aquinas still holds to dispositive causality, he uses a more developed version of his original comparison between the causing of grace and the infusion of the human soul at conception: the infusion of grace can be likened to creation because it has no cause within the subject.[20] Here, the similitude between grace and creation is no longer framed in the language of creation *ex nihilo*. Although Aquinas strongly affirms that grace cannot be educed from the potency of matter by any natural agent, by focusing our attention on the potency of matter Aquinas has effectively directed the conversation away from creation

18. Ibid.

19. See *De Pot.* q. 3 a. 3 ad 7.

20. See *De Pot.* q. 3 a. 8 ad 3. Aquinas uses the language of potency—both divine and created—to speak about the difference between God and the world using the language of proportion and proper proportionality. He concludes that, although grace is not properly created because it does not subsist, "infusion of grace is like creation in that grace has no cause in the subject, neither efficient, nor matter in which it would be potentially, and from which it would be drawn by a *natural* agent." Gallagher, *Significando Causant*, 111 (emphasis mine).

per se and towards the nature of the interaction between created and uncreated potencies. The comparison between grace and the creation of a soul remains, but Aquinas has almost entirely changed the context in which this comparison is offered. By developing his understanding of created and uncreated potency, Aquinas is able to articulate the concept of concreation more fully in light of this.

An example of this can be seen in the comparison between the causality of the sacraments and of miracles. In the *De Potentia*, Aquinas says that both are examples of the same kind of instrumentality: in miracles angels or men are used instrumentally as spiritual creatures to effect the divine intention, which does not remain in them but passes through them as light through the air or motion in an instrument. The formal cause, or the finality of the principal cause's intent, is passing through the instrumental efficiency of the secondary agent (*per modum formarum imperfectum*). Aquinas says that what is accomplished through the instrumentality of spiritual creatures such as angels and human beings by miracles is accomplished through corporeal created things in the sacraments. With this comparison, Aquinas has returned to an example of sacramental causality here that first appeared in the *Sentences*.[21] It is now clear, however, that the instrumentality at work does not merely dispose for a later action on the part of God. It is part of the motive cause itself, initiated by the principal agent, which is eventually perfected in the causing of grace in the subject. The causality of the sacraments does not stop with the production of the sacramental character, which then disposes for the reception of grace in the way that natural generation disposes for the infusion of the soul. The instrument is part of a single causal process, initiated by God as principal agent, in which the instrument participates because it contains within it the finality of the act in the form of the principal agent's intention, even if its own act does not touch the finality of grace itself.[22] This notion is only intimated in the *Sentences*, where the argument is made that the sacraments "contain" grace *per modum intentionis fluentis*.[23]

---

21. See *Super Sent.* lib. 4 dist. 1 q. 1 a. 4, solutio IV.

22. *De Pot.* q. 6 a. 4 co.

23. *Super Sent.* lib. 4 dist. 1 q. 1 a. 4, solutio IV. "Ad quintum dicendum, quod ex sacramentis causatur per modum influentiae gratia: nec tamen sacramenta sunt quae

From the *Summa Contra Gentiles* onward, the word "dispositive" will no longer appear in Aquinas' treatment of sacramental instrumentality. Instead, the sacraments are simply referred to as instrumental causes of grace. By this stage, there are many factors contributing to this shift in the development of Aquinas' thought. As we have previously noted, however, refinements in Aquinas' doctrine on grace are of primary interest to us here. Final causes specify act and potency as the idea held in the mind of the agent (or artist), and so it should not surprise us that the finality of grace is of central importance for defining and ordering the causal process that leads to its actualization.

SUMMA THEOLOGIAE

When speaking of sacramental instrumentality in the *Sentences*, Aquinas distinguished between those instrumental causes that were perfective and those that were merely dispositive in relation to the final end of the principal mover. The central issue was the scope of the natural potency of the instrument. This question was particularly heightened in the context of grace, where the final end is inherently supernatural. The distinguishing mark of a perfective instrumental cause was its ability to reach or touch (*pertingere*) the finality of the principal agent's intention. In the *Summa Theologiae*, there is no mention of either perfective or dispositive instrumentality. The sacraments are instrumental causes of grace *simpliciter*. In speaking of sacramental cause in the *Summa*, Aquinas cites the same passage from Augustine's commentary on John that he first cited in the *Sentences*: the water of Baptism touches (*tangit*) the body and washes (*abluit*) the heart.[24]

---

influunt gratiam, sed per quae Deus sicut per instrumenta animae gratiam influit." *Super Sent.* lib. 4 dist. 1 q. 1 a. 4, solutio I ad 5. As such, "real power is said to be in the angel or man acting as instrument; power there in a passing way. He is more than a sign used to designate the subject of the miracle. For that no power need be in the angel or man above his normal power." Gallagher, *Significando Causant*, 113. Recall Aquinas' original argument against the *sine qua non* position, which he says reduces the sacraments of the New Law to mere signs, and therefore no different from the sacraments of the Old. *Super Sent.* lib. 4 dist. 1 q. 1 a. 4, solutio I.

24. *In Ioann.* Tract. LXXX, super XV, 3. CCL 36: 529. However, the category of dispositive causality does remain in play in non-sacramental contexts in some of Aquinas' later works, such as his commentary on the *Metaphysics*, V, lec. 2, n. 767.

Because the heart can only be cleansed by grace, Aquinas concludes that the sacraments are causes of this grace.[25] In the *Sentences* he presented his teaching on sacramental instrumentality as an interpretation of this passage from Augustine, using the image of touching (*tangit*) as a way of describing the dispositive nature of sacramental causes with respect to the finality of grace.

In the *Summa*, Aquinas retains the image from Augustine but drops the language of dispositive cause. This changes the way in which his language of sacramentality conforms to this Augustinian image. In the *Summa*, Aquinas simply asserts that the sacraments are causes of grace and feels no need to qualify this statement. At the outset, he repeats the counterexample of the leaden coin that he used in the *Sentences*, reiterating his argument that this position reduces the sacraments to mere signs. The sacraments of the New Law must be not only signs, but causes, of grace. In the *Sentences* he followed this by introducing a version of dispositive causality, popular among certain theologians of his time. This example is absent from the *Summa*, however. Only the extrinsicist leaden coin stands as a counterpoint to Thomas' theory of instrumentality.[26] Following this, Aquinas distinguishes two kinds of causes: principal and instrumental, with no further division within the category of instrument. A principal agent operates by the power of its form, in the way that a fire heats something by its own heat. In this way, only God can be considered the cause of grace because grace is nothing other than a participation by similitude in the divine nature.[27] An instrumental cause, by contrast, does not work by the power of its own form but only through the motion which is imparted to it by the principal agent. Because of this the effect is not attributed to the instrument but to the principal agent.

---

25. "Sed contra est quod Augustinus dicit, *super Ioan.*, quod aqua baptismalis *corpus tangit et cor abluit*. Sed cor non abluitur nisi per gratiam. Ergo causat gratiam: et pari ratione alia Ecclesiae sacramenta." *ST* III q. 62 a. 1 s.c. (Emphasis found in the following texts cited from the *Summa* is retained from the Pauline edition.) See Thomae de Aquino, Sancti, *Summa Theologiae*, Editiones Paulinae (Torino: Comerciale Edizioni Paoline s.r.l., 1988).

26. *ST* III q. 62 a. 1 co.

27. Daria Spezzano treats this concept as a feature of Aquinas' mature teaching on grace and related issues. Spezzano, *The Glory of God's Grace: Deification according to St. Thomas Aquinas* (Ave Maria, Fla.: Sapientia Press, 2015), 130–51.

Here there is little to distinguish this doctrine from that found in the *Sentences*. The bench is not attributed to the axe but to the skill and knowledge that exists in the carpenter. It is in this way that the sacraments of the New Law cause grace: by being summoned by divine command to cause grace.[28] To support this, Aquinas cites Augustine, who says that divine power operates "through" the sacraments. In this way the sacraments can be considered proper instruments because they operate through the power of another.[29] One can also notice a more streamlined concept of artisanship at work here: the axe is a tool in the hand of a natural artist that is directed instrumentally to achieve the finality of the bench. Likewise, an instrument (even a created nature) in the hands of the divine artist is a tool in the same way, directed instrumentally to the end chosen by the artist. The difference between these two examples has less to do with the limitations of the natural finality of the tool than it does with the difference between the principal agents.[30]

In the *Sentences* Aquinas spoke of the sign value of the sacraments in terms of the working of the instrument itself—that is, the saw or axe in motion. In the *Summa,* this concept is not nullified, but *here Aquinas* describes sacramental instruments as signs of the power of their principal agents. He says that principal causes are not signs of their effects properly speaking because their power is frequently hidden. Instruments, however, if their action is visible, are properly called signs of the effect that is hidden within them. In this way they cannot be causes alone but are signs and causes inasmuch as they are

28. "Causa vero instrumentalis non agit per virtutem suae formae, sed solum per motum quo movetur a principali agente. Unde effectus non assimilatur instrumento, sed principali agenti: sicut lectus non assimilatur securi, sed arti quae est in mente artificis. Et hoc modo sacramenta novae legis gratiam causant: adhibentur enim ex divina ordinatione ad gratiam in eis causandam. Unde Augustinus dicit, XIX *contra Faust.: Haec omnia,* scilicet sacramentalia, *fiunt et transeunt: virtus tamen,* scilicet Dei, *quae per ista operatur, iugiter manet.* Hoc autem proprie dicitur instrumentum, per quod aliquis operatur. Unde et *Tit.* 3, 5 dicitur: *Salvos nos fecit per lavacrum regenerationis.*" Ibid. See also Humbert Bouëssé, "La causalité efficiente instrumentale de l'Humanité du Christ et des Sacrements chrétiens," *Revue Thomiste* 39 n. 83 (1934): 374n13.

29. *ST* III q. 62 a. 1 co.

30. For a more comprehensive treatment of this issue, see Reginald Lynch, "Cajetan's Harp: Sacraments and the Life of Grace in Light of Perfective Instrumentality," *The Thomist* 78 (2014): 66–71.

moved by the principal agent. In this way sacraments are instruments in the full sense because they are ordered to the holiness of another (*aliquid sacrum*) as both signs and causes.[31] Some have questioned whether the mature doctrine of Aquinas (as interpreted by Cajetan and Bañez) conveys the unity between sacramental sign and cause with the clarity with which it is expressed in the *Sentences*.[32] However, Aquinas is clear in the *Summa* that the sacraments are instruments in the full sense of the term because they are both signs and causes.[33]

Aquinas expands on the connection between sign and cause by returning to the image of Baptism first proposed by Augustine. For Aquinas there is a sense in which an instrument has two actions: one proper to its form and one which is properly instrumental and proportioned to the power of the principal agent. The two are inherently interrelated, of course, because the perfection of an instrumental action depends on the exercise of the proper action of the instrument: an axe cannot act as the instrumental cause of a bench unless it exercises its proper action. In the same way the sacraments in their bodily nature exercise a proper effect on the body, which they touch (*tangere*). They operate instrumentally by divine power on the soul. Just as the water of Baptism washes the body by its proper power, it washes the soul in as much as it is an instrument of divine power. The sacrament of Baptism, as an instrumental cause of grace under the aegis of divine power, requires the exercise of the instrument's proper form (bodily washing) to be efficacious as an instrument of the principal agent's intent (spiritual washing). Aquinas argues that this dependence of instrumentality on the exercise of natural function is fitting

31. "Ad primum ergo dicendum quod causa principalis non proprie potest dici signum effectus, licet occulti, etiam si ipsa sit sensibilis et manifesta. Sed causa instrumentalis, si sit manifesta, potest dici signum effectus occulti: eo quod non solum est causa, sed quodammodo effectus, inquantum movetur a principali agente. Et secundum hoc, sacramenta novae legis simul sunt causa et signa. Et inde est quod, sicut communiter dicitur, *efficiunt quod figurant*. Ex quo etiam patet quod habent perfecte rationem sacramenti: inquantum ordinantur ad aliquid sacrum non solum per modum signi, sed etiam per modum causae." *ST* III q. 62 a. 1 ad 1.

32. See Leeming, *Principles of Sacramental Theology*, 314–15, 324.

33. In the *Sentences* the sacraments "touch" grace perfectively as signs, but as causes they are merely dispositive. In the *Summa* these categories are united more closely and the movement of the instrument becomes both sign and cause in the perfective sense. See Lynch, "Cajetan's Harp," 88–100.

because of the unity between body and soul.[34] It is the hylomorphic character of the human person that makes the use of sacraments as instrumental causes fitting. God could effect grace in other ways, but the use of sensible signs is a fitting means of interacting with the human person, even when elevated in grace.

Concerning the sacraments as proper (and not dispositive) instrumental causes, it is important to notice the change in Aquinas' position from the *Sentences* commentary. While the division between those acts proper to the form of the instrument (the axe cutting) and those which are not so proportioned (the causing of grace) is retained, Aquinas no longer refers to the relationship that exists between the axe and the finality of the artist's intent as a kind of disposition. While it is true that the proper form of the instrument (the axe cutting) does not reach (*pertingere*) the finality of the artist's intent, in the *Summa* Aquinas defines the relationship of the axe in motion to the finality of the act as instrumental in the proper sense, and this is because the power at work in the instrument is not its own but is that of the principal agent. Where before instrumentality was applied in the perfective sense to the immediate effect of the instrument's motion (the wood as cut) and dispositively to the larger intent of the artist (the house built), Aquinas has shifted the meaning of instrumentality to refer properly to the relationship between the axe in motion and the completion of the stool. Because of this conceptual shift, it is no longer necessary to speak of dispositive causality.

Because of this, Thomistic commentators like Cajetan speak of the relationship between the natural form of the tool (the water of Baptism or the carpenter's axe) and its instrumental use in terms of artistry. For Cajetan, there is a difference between a nature moving accord-

34. "Ad secundum dicendum quod instrumentum habet duas actiones: unam instrumentalem, secundum quam operatur non in virtute propria, sed in virtute principalis agentis; aliam autem habet actionem propriam, quae competit sibi secundum propriam formam; sicut securi competit scindere ratione suae acuitatis, facere autem lectum inquantum est instrumentum artis. Non autem perficit actionem instrumentalem nisi exercendo actionem propriam; scindendo enim facit lectum. Et Similiter sacramenta corporalia per propriam operationem quam exercent circa corpus, quod tangunt, efficiunt operationem instrumentalem ex virtute divina circa animam: sicut aqua baptismi, abluendo corpus secundum propriam virtutem, abluit animam inquantum est instrumentum virtutis divinae; nam ex anima et corpore unum fit. Et hoc est quod Augustinus dicit, quod *corpus tangit et cor abluit.*" *ST* III q. 62 a. 1 ad 2.

ing to its natural form and the direction of that natural motion towards the end intended by an artist. He uses the example of a harp, which, while capable of making noise in the hands of a nonharpist, can only make music in the hand of a musician. When taken up by the musician, the harp does not make both noise and music. Only the artistry intended by the principal agent is attributable to the instrumental motion at this point.[35] The natural form of sacramental elements (such as baptismal water) and their instrumental effects (such as cleansing the soul in grace) can be understood in this way. Cajetan says that there is a sense in which even the sacramental signs, which still display the signate value of their natural forms in a certain way (the natural form of water signifies cleansing), can be understood in light of the single motion of this artistic harmony.[36]

In the *Sentences* Aquinas already indicated that instrumental causes were of their nature analogical, proportioned not to their own formal acts but to the intention of the principal agent.[37] Here we have a

35. "Nec te moveat quod Auctor iungit motui instrumenti virtutem seu vim, ex ipsa adiunctione insinuans differentiam inter instrumenti motum, et virtutem de qua est quaestio.... Quod ut melius intelligas, distingue motum quo potest instrumentum moveri, in motum simplicem, et motum virtuosum. Est siquidem instrumenti simplex motus ille ad quem ex parte moventis sufficit potentia motiva.; ex parte vero termini, naturalis effectus instrumenti. Motus autem *virtuosus* est ille qui ex parte moventis, ultra potentiam motivam, exigit artem, seu aliquid proportionale arti; ex parte vero termini, ducit ad effectum principalis agentis, puta artis, seu alicuius proportionaliter se habentis sicut ars se habet ad instrumenta sua. Exemplum utriusque motus perspice in cithara: cuius fides si moveantur a non-musico, sonabunt tantum; si vero moveantur a musico, efficient non solum sonum, sed sonum musicum, qui est effectus proprius artis musicae. Ubi patet quod simplex motus percussionis illarum: motus vero qui ab arte procedit, ad effectum artis ducit, utpote vim artis in se habens; et propterea motus virtuosus appellatur." Cajetan, *Commentary on ST* III q. 62 a. 5, n. 4.

36. "In motu virtuoso instrumenti, ut dictum est, quod instrumentum agit per solum motum quo movetur a principali agenti. Ratione autem solius formalis distinctionis inventae inter motum et virtutem in motu virtuoso instrumenti apponitur motui instrumenti vis seu virtus: et non ad denotandum quod sint duae res; sed quod haec duo coeuntia in instrumento, inveniuntur constituentia illius motum virtuosum. Et hic est quem sacramentalia signa a Deo sortiuntur, cum sacramenta conferuntur ... tunc sacramentalia signa et verba moverentur simplici motu tantum, utpote a solo homine, et nihil aliud efficerent nisi corporalem ablutionem. Cum vero quis hominem abluit servatis servandis iuxta institutionem Christi, moventur tunc sacramentalia signa motu virtuoso, utpote a Iesu Christo (*ipse est* enim *qui baptizat*), et *corpus tangendo abluunt cor,* ut Augustinus dicet." Cajetan, *Commentary on ST* III q. 62 a. 5, n. 4.

37. "Ad quartum dicendum, quod causa univoca vel non univoca, proprie loquendi

more mature articulation of that same original idea. The act of the instrument according to its proper form clearly could not touch the finality of the principal agent's action. Water washing the body does not of itself touch the heart. But in this respect the instrument is functioning according to its own power and not as an instrument in the proper sense. As an instrument, however, it does wash the heart because of the power of God at work within it. When the water functions as an instrument in this way, it is moved in a single motion by the principal agent to effect a larger purpose. In this regard Aquinas is unambiguous in the *Summa*: the sacraments are instrumental causes of grace in an unqualified manner. It is specifically through the instrumental use of the sacraments that God cleanses the soul in grace. Here in his mature writings, Aquinas is now able to fully articulate his doctrine of instrumentality as an interpretation of the received Augustinian doctrine. He does this in a way that both preserves the causal univocity of God with respect to grace, while at the same time fully integrating the sacraments into the causal process of God's intention as instrumental causes, as analogical participants in divine power.

The end toward which the sacraments are directed as instrumental causes is grace. This finality is said to be connatural with human nature although it entirely surpasses any natural potency. In a similar way, the instrumentality of the sacraments is fitted both to the sign value and the proper form of physical things that is appetible to the natural human intellect (such as water washing), while at the same time being directed towards a supernatural effect in the soul that is entirely beyond the natural reach of either the proper form of the instrument or the potency of the human person who receives grace. By comparison, however, the instrumental use of the sacraments by the power of God has a kind of connaturality to it; it appears as an analogical extension of the action of the principal agent in the order of efficient causality, rather than a simple equivocation in which God responds to a sign with absolutely no intrinsic value, such as a king who

---

et simpliciter sunt divisiones illius causae cujus est similitudinem habere cum effectu; haec autem est principalis agentis et non instrumentalis, ut dicit Alexander, secundum quod narrat Commentator. Et ideo proprie loquendo, neque instrumentum est causa univoca neque aequivoca. Posset tamen reduci ad utrumlibet, secundum quod principale agens, in cujus virtute instrumentum agit, est causa univoca, vel non univoca." *Super Sent.* lib. 4 dist. 1 q. 1 a. 4 qc. 1 ad 4.

chooses to reward a subject who presents him with a leaden coin. In this way, Aquinas' mature concept of instrumentality is more aptly fitted to the natural form of the tool. The water really washes spiritually, when used by God as an instrument.

Although in many circles the term "obediential potency" is not regularly associated with the sacraments, when the natural form of a created thing (such as water) is put to a purpose beyond the scope of its nature to serve the will of God in wisdom, as an instrument it experiences an elevation in relation to the finality intended by God.[38] Aquinas' own language intimates this in the *Summa* when he says that the sacraments cause grace instrumentally out of obedience to the divine will.[39]

The end to which the sacraments are directed is the sanctification of the human person. For Aquinas, this sanctification cannot be understood in an extrinsic or forensic sense; it is a participation in the divine nature. In light of this, it is the divine will that calls the water of Baptism to serve this supernatural end instrumentally, and the soul responds obedientially to the will of God in grace. Because grace is a participation in God's nature, God himself is the final end of the sacraments. He is both final cause and principal efficient cause of the sacramental motion that draws the human creature back to him in grace. Cajetan best describes the relationship between principal and instrumental causality in light of this: God must be the sole principal cause of grace because it is in his nature that the human subject, in whom the finality of grace adheres, is called to participate. In service of this end, God summons (*adhibet*) the sacraments as instruments and through (*per*) them causes grace.[40]

38. In the *Summa*, Aquinas describes the sign value of the natural forms of the sacraments (their proper form) in relation to divine wisdom: it is in accord with divine wisdom that grace be conferred under sacramental signs appropriate to the human condition. "Est ex conditione humanae naturae, cuius proprium est ut per corporalia et sensibilia in spiritualia et intelligibilia deducatur. Pertinet autem ad divinam providentiam ut unicuique rei provideat secundum modum suae conditionis. Et ideo convenienter divinia sapientia homini auxilia salutis confert sub quibusdam corporalibus et sensibilibus signis, quae sacramenta dicantur." *ST* III q. 61 a. 1 co.

39. "Et hoc modo sacramenta novae legis gratiam causant: adhibentur enim ex divina ordinatione ad gratiam in eis causandam.... Hoc autem proprie dicitur instrumentum, per quod aliquis operatur." *ST* III q. 62 a. 1 co.

40. "Quoad tertium, ponitur primo distinctio bimembris de causa agente: scilicet

For both the sacramental instruments and human nature, the reality of grace is present as an elevation of each in response to divine power. The human person participates in divine life, and the sacraments attain this end as instruments. The water that washes the body and the rational nature that knows and loves the truth of God are both elevated beyond the scope of their natural form by the will of God and under the impulse of his power. The water, as an instrument of God's power, serves his intended end by which the human soul participates in divinity. Although both natures are elevated, the distinction is made between them in terms of instrument and end, both defined in reference to God as principal agent. The water serves as an instrument through which God reaches his intended end; human beings live in this finality as an elevation of the potencies of their personhood. Although this elevation is entirely gratuitous, it is also fitting and therefore demonstrates not only the mercy but the goodness and wisdom of God, operative not only in nature but in grace.

GRACE, INSTRUMENTALITY, AND OBEDIENTIAL POTENCY

In the *Summa*, Aquinas applies the doctrine of instrumental causality to natural sacramental causes in the context of supernatural ends without the qualification. For the commentatorial tradition, the concept of obediential potency is important in this regard and is used broadly to explain the attainment of supernatural ends by created natures in a variety of different contexts. When commenting on the first article of the *Summa Theologiae*, Cajetan defines obediential potency as an apti-

---

principali, et instrumentali. – Secundo, ponitur causae principalis conditio, qua distinguetur ab instrumentali, scilicet: Principalis causa est quae agit virtute suae formae, cui assimilatur effectus. Et iuxta hoc membrum ponitur una conclusio: *Solus Deus est causa principalis gratiae*. Probatur. Solus Deus est cuius est participata similitudo gratia. Ergo solus Deus est gratiae causa principalis. Antecedens est Petri Apostoli. Consequentia patet ex conditione causae principalis. – Tertio, ponitur conditio causae instrumentalis. Et iuxta hoc membrum ponitur alia conclusio, scilicet: *Sacramenta sunt causae agentes instrumentaliter ad gratiam*. Probatur. Causa instrumentalis est quae non agit virtute suae formae, sed per solum motum quo ab agente principali movetur. Sed sacramenta Deus adhibet ut per ea causet gratiam. Ergo sunt causae instrumentales." Cajetan, *Commentary on ST* III q. 62 a. 1, n. 2.

tude for the realization within a thing of that which God may decree.[41] It is God's sovereignty as first principle over created beings which gives created things an inherent obedience to his will that runs deeper than the natural scope of any individual created nature. In *De Virtutibus*, Aquinas argues that this obediential potency applies not only in the case of humans before the vision of God but to all created things.[42]

If we recall the image of divine artistry found in the *Sentences*, God's act of creation is essentially a volitional engagement with the exemplarity of his own goodness. God's creative act is *ex nihilo* and immediate and so involves no instrumentality. Of course God chooses to create in complete freedom, but he does not do so arbitrarily. He models created things after the exemplar of his own goodness and in so doing displays his wisdom. Because he creates through volitional efficiency, working towards a finality held in *intentio* (which is his own goodness), God as creator can be called an artist. To be an artist in this sense is to make or create under the finality of some aspect of the good. Further, he continues to act as an artist within the created order, shaping natural things to reach his intended purposes. It is this second mode of interaction which opens up the possibility of instrumentality as a form of divine artistry in which natural potencies are directed to divine purposes. In this we can see the wisdom of artistry displayed in the ordering of things in a fitting manner, first in accord with the divine nature, second in accord with the nature of things. Although in the *Sentences* Aquinas speaks of God as an artist in both senses, in the *Summa* he is able to speak more freely of God as an artist in the second sense, even within the context of grace. In the *Sentences*, the second mode of artistry—which involves the instrumentality of cre-

41. "Vocatur autem *potentia obedientialis*, aptitudo rei ad hoc ut in ea fiat quidquid faciendum ordinavit Deus." Cajetan, *Commentary on ST* I* Q. 1, a. 1, n. IX (Leonine ed. 4:8). See also Lawrence Feingold, *The Natural Desire to See God according to St. Thomas Aquinas and His Interpreters*, 2nd ed., Faith and Reason: Studies in Catholic Theology and Philosophy series (Naples, Fla.: Sapientia Press, 2010), 101.

42. "In tota creatura est quaedam obedientialis potentia, prout tota creatura obedit Deo ad suscipiendum in se quidquid Deus voluerit. Sic igitur et in anima est aliquid in potentia, quod natum est reduci in actum ab agente connaturali; et hoc modo sunt in potentia in ipsa virtutes acquisitae. Alio modo aliquid est in potentia in anima quod non est natum educi in actum nisi per virtutem divinam; et sic sunt in potentia in anima virtutes infusae." *De Virtutibus* Q. 1, a. 10, ad 13. See also Steven A. Long, "On the Possibility of a Purely Natural End for Man," *The Thomist* 64 (2000): 213–14.

ated natures—is already fully present with respect to God's providen-
tial governance, which directs natural potencies towards their natural
ends; the supernatural end of grace is qualified, however, by the category of dispositive causality. In the *Summa* Aquinas speaks of God
as an artist in the second sense within the category of act and potency, applying the concept of instrumental causality to natural potency
without qualification even in relation to supernatural ends.

God can move the potency of created things on a natural and a
supernatural level. Even in the case of grace, however, the obedience
of created things to the will of God is not arbitrary. Because God as
artist creates natures and further directs their potency to his ends in
wisdom, the obedience of created natures to God's supernatural purposes usually elicits acts that exhibit a certain connaturality: although
beatitude is entirely above human nature, in a certain sense the rational soul is fitted (in an entirely passive and supernatural manner)
to receive this gift.[43] In the case of miracles, God does interact in an
equivocal manner with creatures, bringing about a change that is entirely without natural precedent.[44] A miracle does not actuate any
potency within the nature (obediential or otherwise) but rather in-
tervenes in created nature according to its own power. In grace, however, God interacts with the human person in a connatural manner,
educing from the potency of humanity's own nature a participation
in the divine nature.[45]

43. A. Riches has argued that, "Aquinas's anthropology has often been read as if it
were straightforwardly bound to the Aristotelian axiom of proportionality.... If we in-
sist on a connatural *finis* of human nature as definitive of that nature, then Christ cannot be the revelation of 'man to himself' since Christ's hypostatic transcendence fails on
this rule to satisfy the terms of connaturality." Aaron Riches, "Christology and duplex
hominis beatitudo: Re-sketching the Supernatural Again," *International Journal of Systematic Theology* 14, no. 1 (January 2012): 54. In this and in what follows, the concept of
obediential potency (which will be shown to be an incarnational concept for Aquinas)
demonstrates that the classical approach to man's twofold end from within the Thomistic commentatorial tradition can attribute a kind of connaturality to man's final, supernatural end without denying the proportionality of his natural end. Indeed, this further
connaturality of grace presumes and depends upon the integrity of nature.

44. Confusing obediential potency with the miraculous is an unfortunate mistake,
all too common in the twentieth century. See Steven A. Long, *Natura Pura: On the Recovery of Nature in the Doctrine of Grace* (New York: Fordham University Press, 2010),
28–51; "On the Possibility of a Purely Natural End for Man," 214.

45. For a discussion of the concept of connaturality in this context, see Réginald

This principle extends to all natural things according to the mode of divine artistry. Building on Aquinas, Garrigou-Lagrange describes the obediential potency of created things before God as similar to the obedience of a material cause in the hands of an artist: "Even in the natural order the form of a statue is educed from the potentiality of the wood, inasmuch as the wood obeys the carver, or the clay the potter."[46] Although there is a sense in which the wood does have the passive natural potency to serve as the material cause of the statue, it lacks the intrinsic potency to achieve this end through self-actuation. In relation to the wood, the statue can be called a connatural end because the intrinsic properties of the wood's nature are well-fitted to express this end under the impulse of artistic motion.

The passive potency of nature that is properly called "obediential" is somewhat different, however. When describing grace itself as a response to divine motion, Aquinas first recalls the metaphysical relationship between the human person and divine power at the level of natural potency: human nature is moved to its natural end by the first mover. Unlike the intervention of an external efficient cause, this movement functions in a way that is intrinsic to the nature itself. The actuation of human potency requires this movement, which directs it towards the achievement of its natural end.[47] There is a certain obedience present here, as the human nature finds its fulfillment and actuation through docility to divine motion. In a similar way, to achieve beatitude human nature needs the movement of God in grace to specify the end and to initiate and sustain the movement of the person towards the end.[48] Because the end of beatitude is beyond the acts proper and naturally proportioned to human nature, obedience to this beatitudinal motion cannot be natively educed from the scope of natural human potency. Although natural potency (as nat-

---

Garrigou-Lagrange, *Grace: Commentary on the Summa Theologica of St. Thomas, Ia IIae, Q. 109–14*, trans. The Dominican Nuns of Corpus Christi Monastery, Menlo Park, Calif. (St. Louis: Herder, 1952), 120, 132, 307–08. See also Steven A. Long, "Obediential Potency, Human Knowledge, and the Natural Desire for God," *International Philosophical Quarterly* 37 no. 1 (1997): 51–3.

46. Garrigou-Lagrange, *Grace*, 307.

47. *ST* Iª IIae Q. 109, a. 6, co.

48. On the relationship between nature and supernature in this context, see Long, *Natura Pura*, 26–27.

ural) is exceeded in this context, the concept of obedience to divine motion remains.

This kind of obediential potency has been called a "nonaversion" to the initiative of the divine will.[49] This is not to say, however, that in grace the person is moved towards an end that is entirely alien to human nature. Just as the hands of the potter actuate the passive potency of the clay and move it towards a connatural end, in grace divine motion moves the human soul to supernatural acts of faith, hope, and charity as ends which are at once both supernatural and connatural. Cajetan argues that there is a sense in which obediential potency builds on the connatural ends of nature, such that the human person has a certain aptitude for beatitude that a lion lacks. Cajetan claims that, while the end of beatitude is not natural according to mode, subjectively speaking it is natural in the sense that faith and love are intellectual acts for which human nature has potency in the obediential sense.[50] In the wisdom of God, therefore, there is a "fitness" between grace and human nature. This in no way denotes a natural aptitude for grace (properly speaking) within human nature; the supernatural elevation of the human person in this way reflects the gratuitous intention of God.[51] This gratuitous self-communication is in keeping with God's wisdom and goodness. All created things participate analogically in the perfection of the divine goodness according to their natures. But no creature has a natural participation in the divine nature (*Deitas*), and so for God to make available to us a participation in his own

49. Garrigou-Lagrange, *Grace*, 308–9.

50. "Unde ad *primum* Scoti dicitur, quod Augustinus non dixit quod sit *naturae* hominum. Aliud est enim potentiam esse naturae, et aliud esse naturalem: primum enim significat *subiectum* potentiae, secundum autem *modum* potentiae. Et ideo primum est verum in proposito: secundum vero falsum. Potentia siquidem illa obedientialis ad fidem et caritatem, est in natura hominum, quia intellectiva est: non autem in natura leonina, quoniam sibi repugnant." Cajetan, *Commentary on ST*, Iᵃ Q. 1, a. 1, n. X (Leonine ed., 4:8). See also Long, "On the Possibility of a Purely Natural End for Man," 214–16.

51. "Thus by its formal reason the obediential power signifies nothing but a non-aversion. However, God, by conferring his supernatural gifts does indeed perfect thereby the nature of the soul, raising it to a superior order. Thus these gifts of grace are, at one and the same time, completely gratuitous, in no sense due to us, and perfectly becoming to our nature, with a fitness which is not, however, natural but supernatural, at once most sublime, most profound, and gratuitous.... This is the very mystery of the essence of grace, which is simultaneously something freely given and something which renders us pleasing." Garrigou-Lagrange, *Grace*, 309.

nature is properly supernatural. However, because his goodness is infinite and diffusive of itself, to grant a supernatural participation in his own divinity is fitting. Therefore, because this elevation is a supernatural furthering of a creature's analogical participation in divine goodness, it is at once both fitting and entirely gratuitous.[52]

Aquinas insists that there can be no cause for grace apart from God and that no creature can be disposed for grace according to its natural form. However, because grace moves the will to accept a supernatural good, there is a sense in which God himself has prepared the person for the gift of grace through the first gift of a rational nature capable of being moved by God to freely will the good.[53] In this

---

52. Aquinas argues that the Incarnation is in keeping with God's goodness, which is diffusive of itself (*ST* III^a Q. 1, a. 1, co.). Creatures have different capacities to receive this communication of goodness, according to their form. The form of the human soul, because of its capacity for spiritual things, is uniquely fitted to be perfected in grace, just as faith builds upon the human intellect's natural capacity for the truth (*ST* I^a II^{ae} Q. 1.), hope upon the will's desire for goodness (*ST* I^a II^{ae} Q. 17, a. 2, Q. 18, a. 1.), and charity upon the uniquely human capacity for friendship, of which it is the supernatural perfection (*ST* I^a II^{ae} Q. 23, a. 1.). As a result, Garrigou argues that supernatural perfection offered in grace is uniquely fitted to the human person: "Iam enim agendo ut auctor naturae, Deus communicat creaturis aliquam participationem analogicam suarum perfectionum, scilicet esse, vivere, intelligere. Corpora inanimata conveniunt analogice cum Deo prout sunt *entia*; plantae autem et animalia prout sunt *viventia*, homines prout sunt *intelligentes*. Sed nulla creatura, habet naturaliter participationem *Deitatis*, seu naturae divinae ut *divina* est. Unde ut Deus sese communicet secundum id quod est sibi magis intimum, debet nobis praebere participationem suae naturae divinae, ut divina est, seu suae intimae vitae supernaturalis; et hoc ei convenit ratione suae infinitae bonitatis summo modo diffusivae.... Nam ratio humana ex se sola non potest cognoscere vitam Dei intimam ... nec proinde convenientiam eiusdem communicationis. Insuper etsi summum bonum sit essentialiter diffusivum sui, non necessario sed libere semetipsum diffundit, nam "bonitas Dei est perfecta et esse potest sine aliis, cum nihil ei perfectionis ex aliis accrescat" [*ST* I q. 19, a. 3].... Ergo elevatio hominis ad finem supernaturalem est conveniens et simul gratuita." Réginald Garrigou-Lagrange, *De Revelatione per Ecclesiam Catholicam Proposita*, 5th ed., vol. 1 (Roma: F. Ferrari, 1950), 389.

53. "Si loquamur de gratia secundum quod significat auxilium Dei moventis ad bonum, sic nulla praeparatio requiritur ex parte hominis quasi praeveniens divinum auxilium, sed potius quaecumque praeparatio in homine esse potest, est ex auxilio Dei moventis animam ad bonum. Et secundum hoc, ipse bonus motus liberi arbitrii quo quis praeparatur ad donum gratiae suscipiendum, est actus liberi arbitrii moti a Deo, et quantum ad hoc, dicitur homo se praeparare, secundum illud Prov. XVI, *hominis est praeparare animum*. Et est principaliter a Deo movente liberum arbitrium, et secundum hoc, dicitur a Deo voluntas hominis praeparari, et a domino gressus hominis dirigi." *ST* I^a II^{ae} Q. 112, a. 2, co.

way, grace remains connatural to the person despite its essentially supernatural character. This supernatural participation in divine goodness is fitting because it is intrinsic to the person: Cajetan argues that, although the capacity for beatitude cannot be explained by any natural potency or the extrinsic movement of a secondary cause, human nature can be said to be disposed because of its obediential potency for the vision of God.[54]

For Aquinas, the connatural relationship between nature and grace is founded on the Incarnation itself. Here, Aquinas uses the concept of obediential potency to describe the relationship between the divinity and humanity of Jesus Christ.[55] Likewise, the relationship between nature and grace, in which our humanity is joined to divinity, can be framed in similar terms.[56] Aquinas argues that because

54. "Ad evidentiam huius difficultatis, scito quod apud nos potentia aut est naturalis, aut violentia, aut *obedientialis*.... Vocatur autem *potentia obedientialis*, aptitudo rei ad hoc ut in ea fiat quidquid faciendum ordinaverit Deus. Et secundum talem potentiam, anima nostra dicitur in potentia ad beatitudinem pollicitam, et finem supernaturalem, et alia huiusmodi." Cajetan, *Commentary on* ST Iª Q. 1 a. 1, n. IX (Leonine ed., 4:8) .

55. "In anima humana, sicut in qualibet creatura, consideratur duplex potentia passiva: una quidem per comparationem ad agens naturale; alia vero per comparationem ad agens primum, qui potest quamlibet creaturam reducere in actum aliquem altiorem, in quem non reducitur per agens naturale; et haec consuevit vocari *potentia obedientiae* in creatura. Utraque autem potentia animae Christi fuit reducta in actum secundum hanc scientiam divinitus inditam." ST IIIª Q. 11, a. 1, co. See Thomas Joseph White's recent description of this in *The Incarnate Lord: a Thomistic Study in Christology*, Thomistic Ressourcement Series, vol. 5, ed. Matthew Levering and Thomas Joseph White (Washington, D.C.: The Catholic University of America Press, 2015), 113. H. Bouëssé treats the relationship between volition and causal motion in the cases of principle and instrumental causality, specifically in relation to the relationship between the divine and human natures in Christ. Bouëssé, "La causalité efficiente instrumentale de l'Humanité du Christ et des Sacraments chrétiens," 378–87.

56. In this I agree with A. Riches who, along with N. Healy, stresses the importance of Christology for understanding the relationship between nature and grace. However, my use of obediential potency (Aquinas' own term) to describe the hypostatic union and the nature/grace relationship frames these issues in a somewhat different light, consistent with the approach of the Thomistic commentators. See Aaron Riches, "Christology and duplex hominis beatitudo-Resketching the Supernatural Again," *International Journal of Systematic Theology* 14 (January 2012): 44–69. See also Nicholas Healy III, "Henri de Lubac on Nature and Grace: A Note on Some Recent Contributions to the Debate," *Communio* 35 (2008): 564. As cited by Riches, "Christology and duplex ominis beatitudo," 45n2. To this end, Thomas Joseph White rightly emphasizes the necessity of maintaining the integrity of nature in the context of the hypostatic union. White, *The Incarnate Lord*, 126–43, 153–70.

of the nature of the Incarnation and the grace of union (which precedes sanctifying grace in the case of Christ's humanity), sanctifying grace must enable the assumed human nature to "touch" (*attingere*) God.[57]

Aquinas uses his mature doctrine of instrumentality here. Unlike the sacraments, however, which function as inanimate instruments, Christ's human nature functions instrumentally according to its form, as an animate instrument, in which the powers of intellect and will remain capable not only of being moved but of self-motion.[58] It is these operations, intrinsic to human nature, which "touch" God through the grace of the Incarnation.[59] For Aquinas this follows implicitly from the principle of the communication of idioms. The initial grace of union implies a further union of intellect and will with divinity in the context of sanctifying grace. Aquinas argues that this union in grace is possible for the humanity of Christ because of a passive potency latent within human nature itself, which predisposes the human nature assumed by the Word to respond in obedience to divine motion even if the end specified thereby is not proportioned to its natural form.

Aquinas calls this passive potency "obediential."[60] Although divine motion undergirds the movement of all natural forms towards their connatural ends, in the case of the hypostatic union it is this passive obediential potency that makes human nature responsive to divine motion even beyond the actuation proper to its natural form.

57. *ST* III^a Q. 7, a. 1, co. Text as in note 64.

58. "Ad tertium dicendum quod humanitas Christi est instrumentum divinitatis, non quidem sicut instrumentum inanimatum, quod nullo modo agit sed solum agitur, sed tanquam instrumentum animatum anima rationali, quod ita agit quod etiam agitur. Et ideo, ad convenientiam actionis, oportuit eum habere gratiam habitualem." *ST* III^a Q. 7, a. 1, ad 3.

59. *ST* III^a Q. 7, a. 1, co.. Text as in note 64. See also Roger Nutt, "On Analogy, the Incarnation, and the Sacraments of the Church: Consideration from the *Tertia pars* of the *Summa theologiae*," *Nova et Vetera* (English) 12, no. 3 (2014): 1000–1004.

60. "Respondeo dicendum quod, sicut prius dictum est, conveniens fuit ut anima Christo per omnia esset perfecta, per hoc quod omnis eius potentialitas sit reducta ad actum. Est autem considerandum quod in anima humana, sicut in qualibet creatura, consideratur duplex potentia passiva, una quidem per comparationem ad agens naturale; alia vero per comparationem ad agens primum, qui potest quamlibet creaturam reducere in actum aliquem altiorem, in quem non reducitur per agens naturale; et haec consuevit vocari potentia obedientiae in creatura." *ST* III^a Q. 11, a. 1, co.

For Aquinas, the doctrine of obediential potency has clear Christo-logical overtones and is intrinsically connected to the doctrine of perfective instrumental causality. The intellect and will of Christ's humanity are moved to act obedientially by divine motion—as an animate instrument—toward union with divinity.   ·

Correspondingly, in the graced Christian soul it is the human in-tellect and will that are moved by God beyond the form of human na-ture to "touch" beatitude as their object.[61] In the *Summa*, Aquinas ap-plies his mature doctrine of instrumentality (which we have already examined in the context of sacramental causality) to human nature in relation to divine motion. All created motion—be it the movement of inanimate objects or the movement of intellect and will towards their object—can be reduced to the motion of God as simple first mover. Even in created natures, which are moved to their proper act by their form, divine motion is required to achieve their natural per-fection. Aquinas argues that the creature relies upon God first for the form according to which it moves and subsequently for the motion to bring it to act. All formal perfection derived by the motion from potency to act within creation depends on God who is first act. Al-though the form of each created nature has an efficacy from God for a determined act, in the case of beatitude the soul has no such efficacy. The intellect is moved by God through grace to this new supernatu-ral act.[62] Although Aquinas himself does not explicitly apply the term

---

61. *ST* I[a] II[ae] Q. 109, a. 5, ad 3. Similarly, Aquinas argues that the infused virtues that come from grace do in fact produce authentic human acts which attain the end of beati-tude. *ST* II[a] II[ae] Q. 23, a. 2. More will be said about the intrinsic quality of graced human actions in chapter 4 in the context of Christic and human merit.

62. "Videmus autem in corporalibus quod ad motum non solum requiritur ipsa for-ma quae est principium motus vel actionis; sed etiam requiritur motio primi moventis. Primum autem movens in ordine corporalium est corpus caeleste. Unde quantumcum-que ignis habeat perfectum calorem, non alteraret nisi per motionem caelestis corpo-ris. Manifestum est autem quod, sicut omnes motus corporales reducuntur in motum caelestis corporis sicut in primum movens corporale; ita omnes motus tam corpora-les quam spirituales reducuntur in primum movens simpliciter, quod est Deus. Et ideo quantumcumque natura aliqua corporalis vel spiritualis ponatur perfecta, non potest in suum actum procedere nisi moveatur a Deo. Quae quidem motio est secundum suae providentiae rationem; non secundum necessitatem naturae, sicut motio corporis cae-lestis. Non solum autem a Deo est omnis motio sicut a primo movente; sed etiam ab ipso est omnis formalis perfectio sicut a primo actu. Sic igitur actio intellectus, et cuius-cumque entis creati, dependet a Deo quantum ad duo, uno modo, inquantum ab ipso

"obediential potency" to the disposition of the soul for grace, many of his commentators do because of the necessary similitude that exists between the perfection of Christ's humanity according to the mode of the hypostatic union and the union of the Christian soul with God through sanctifying grace.

The similitude between the hypostatic union and the supernatural perfection of the soul in grace is increased when we consider that for Aquinas the archetype of the effect of grace on the soul is the Incarnation. Building on the grace of union which renders the humanity of Christ (and by extension the sacraments) an instrument of his divinity with respect to the intended end of sanctification for the Christian soul,[63] the plenitude of sanctifying grace in Christ's human nature is the source of grace for Christians and causes grace in the souls of believers. This plenitude not only serves as an efficient cause of grace but is the source of sanctifying grace for the Christian soul. Implied here is a kind of formal or exemplary causality, in which heat is the cause not only of smoke but of more heat, functioning not only as the cause of the effect but imparting something of its form to the effect as well.[64] In this sense, the effect of sanctifying grace on the hu-

---

habet formam per quam agit; alio modo, inquantum ab ipso movetur ad agendum. Unaquaeque autem forma indita rebus creatis a Deo, habet efficaciam respectu alicuius actus determinati, in quem potest secundum suam proprietatem, ultra autem non potest nisi per aliquam formam superadditam, sicut aqua non potest calefacere nisi calefacta ab igne. Sic igitur intellectus humanus habet aliquam formam, scilicet ipsum intelligibile lumen, quod est de se sufficiens ad quaedam intelligibilia cognoscenda, ad ea scilicet in quorum notitiam per sensibilia possumus devenire. Altiora vero intelligibilia intellectus humanus cognoscere non potest nisi fortiori lumine perficiatur, sicut lumine fidei vel prophetiae; quod dicitur lumen gratiae, inquantum est naturae superadditum. Sic igitur dicendum est quod ad cognitionem cuiuscumque veri, homo indiget auxilio divino ut intellectus a Deo moveatur ad suum actum." *ST* Iᵃ IIᵃᵉ Q. 109, a. 1 co.

63. *ST* IIIᵃ Q. 7, a. 13, Q. 7, a. 1 ad 3, Q. 8, a. 1, ad 1, Q. 62, a. 5, co..

64. "Respondeo dicendum quod necesse est ponere in Christo gratiam habitualem, propter tria. Primo quidem, propter unionem animae illius ad verbum Dei. Quanto enim aliquod receptivum propinquius est causae influenti, tanto magis participat de influentia ipsius. Influxus autem gratiae est a Deo, secundum illud Psalmi, *gratiam et gloriam dabit dominus*. Et ideo maxime fuit conveniens ut anima illa reciperet influxum divinae gratiae. Secundo, propter nobilitatem illius animae, cuius operationes oportebat propinquissime attingere ad Deum per cognitionem et amorem. Ad quod necesse est elevari humanam naturam per gratiam. Tertio, propter habitudinem ipsius Christi ad genus humanum. Christus enim, inquantum homo, est mediator Dei et hominum, ut dicitur I Tim. II. Et ideo oportebat quod haberet gratiam etiam in alios redundantem,

manity that Christ has assumed through the grace of union serves as a model for the effects of grace in our nature.

Although the concept of obediential potency can be applied to all created natures, in the context of grace and the human person it takes on a Christic quality, enabling the human person to image analogically the incarnate union of flesh with the Divine Word as it is united to and participates in the divine nature in sanctifying grace. With the help of grace, beatitude becomes a kind of connatural end that perfects the human person intrinsically. Although grace is entirely beyond the potency proper to human nature, its connaturality with human nature is important because it allows a renewed sense of divine artisanship to come to the fore that is not dependent on the parallel between creation and re-creation. Aquinas has already eschewed a direct comparison between creation and re-creation in grace, opting instead for the language of potency.

Bañez and other Thomists will use the connaturality that exists between grace and the natural potencies of a rational nature to further establish the claim that the infusion of grace is not similar to the act of creation *ex nihilo*. Because grace is educed from the potency of human nature, a segment of its causal motion will be properly situated within the created order. For this reason, when considered anthropologically Aquinas' doctrine of grace preserves the intrinsic character of graced human action and portrays the theological virtues as authentic human acts.[65] God is the principal efficient cause of grace—but where the potency of nature is involved, it is fitting that there be some form of secondary efficiency. In as much as this secondary efficiency is spoken of in reference to the finality of divine intent, it is a species of instrument. Because the question of the imme-

---

secundum illud Ioan. I, *de plenitudine eius omnes accepimus, gratiam pro gratia*." *ST* III^a Q. 7, a. 1, co. In *ST* III^a Q. 56, a. 1, ad. 3, Aquinas refers explicitly to the effects of Christ's resurrection as exemplary for our own. Based on this and other texts, H. Bouëssé argues that the hypostatic union is an archetype for our earthly and heavenly life in Christ. Bouëssé, "La causalité efficiente instrumentale de l'Humanité du Christ et des Sacrements chrétiens," 371. See also *ST* III^a Q. 7, a. 7, ad 3, a. 10, co, Q. 8, a. 5, co, Q. 9, a. 3, ad 2, Q. 13, a. 1, ad 2. Aquinas distinguishes between those effects which reveal only the cause, such as smoke, and those which reveal something of the essence of the cause, such as fire caused by fire. See *ST* I^a Q. 45, a. 7, co.

65. In the next chapter, we will examine the relationship between this form of graced instrumentality and the Thomistic doctrine of merit.

diate and noninstrumental character of creation is removed from the conversation, it only remains for Aquinas to explain the manner in which an instrument (such as a sacrament) can be used to achieve a supernatural end. Like the relationship between nature and grace, Aquinas' solution to this question is rooted in the hypostatic union. We have already seen that in the *Summa* Aquinas describes the union of Word and flesh in instrumental terms: the humanity of Christ is a conjoined instrument of his divinity. Although this involves an obediential elevation of Christ's humanity, this union in itself is not the finality towards which the instrumentality of the Incarnation is directed; rather, the purpose of the Incarnation is the divinization of the human person in grace. To this end, the sacraments as separated instruments are understood as extensions of the instrumental dimension of the hypostatic union, extending the obediential elevation of nature that was first made present in the Incarnation to all the baptized. Accordingly, because of the supernatural end in view, it is fitting that a similar obedience and connaturality can be seen in the sacraments themselves as they move towards this end as efficacious signs.

When speaking of the instrumental causality of the sacraments, Domingo Bañez argues that, prescinding from any discussion of meritorious causality (as in the case of Christ's passion), there must be a kind of efficient causality in the sacraments that works as a natural cause under the direction of an artist.[66] Following Aquinas, Bañez uses the example of a pencil moved by an artist to produce an image. The pencil attains to or touches (*attingere*) the production of the im-

66. Building on the teachings of the Fathers and III Constantinople, Humbert Bouëssé argues that the realism of the Incarnation implies some form of efficient, physical causality in order to describe the nature and effect of the hypostatic union in relation to the redemption of humanity as the finality of the Incarnation; he treats the distinction between instrumental and meritorious causality in this context. Humbert Bouëssé, "La causalité efficiente instrumentale et causalité méritoire de la sainte humanité du Christ," *Revue Thomiste* 44 (1938): 256–98. See also Humbert Bouëssé, "De la causalité de l'Humanité du Christ," in *Problémes actuels de christologie*, ed. Humbert Bouëssé and Jean-Jacques Latour (Paris: Desclée de Brouwer, 1965), 147–77. E. Hugon also comments on the distinction between meritorious and physical causality, providing a genealogy of opinion on the matter among Thomists and other theologians. Edouard Hugon, "La causalité instrumentale de l'humanité sainte de Jésus," *Revue Thomiste* 13 (1905): 44–68.

age under the motion of the artist; so too do the sacraments touch (*attingere*) the production of grace in as much as they are instruments moved by the Holy Spirit.[67] Recall that the distinction between dispositive and perfective causality in the *Sentences* was based on the instrument's ability to reach or touch (*pertingere*) the finality of the principal agent's intention.[68] Here Bañez uses the same language of reaching or touching (*attingere*), recalling implicitly the distinction found in the *Sentences* to indicate that the causality of the sacraments is not dispositive but rather perfective, touching the finality of God's intention as a pencil touches the finality of a picture.

A mature understanding of Aquinas' doctrine of grace helps Bañez to make this claim. For Bañez, the comparison between the infusion of grace and the act of creation is not helpful. Following Cajetan he argues that, instead of understanding grace as something created from nothing, it should be conceived of as a supernatural *habitus* educed from the potential obedience of the subject. He reinforces the importance of distancing this conception of grace from a direct comparison with the infusion of the human soul, arguing that it would be incorrect to say that the human soul is educed from the obediential potency of the subject simply because it is produced in matter by God. In this case the soul could not depend on the subject for its potency or becoming (*fieri*) or its conservation in being (*conservari*). But grace, which is a supernatural accidental quality, is produced within a subject because it depends on that subject for potency or becoming (*fieri*) and its conservation in being (*conservari*).[69] In

---

67. "Quinta conclusio: Secundum sententiam divi Thomae, necesse est ponere in sacramentis duplicem rationem causae efficientis: alteram moralem per modum meriti et redemptionis, quam ponit magister Cano; alteram per modum causae efficientis instar causarum naturalium vel artificialium; ut sicut revera penicillus attingit ad productionem imaginis quatenus movetur ab artifice, ita sacramenta attingant ad productionem gratiae quatenus sunt instrumenta et movetur a Spiritu Sancto." Bañez *in* III, q. 62, a. 1. Bañez, Domingo Bañez, *Comentarios Ineditos a la Tercera Parte de Santo Tomas*, vol. 2, *De Sacramentis: QQ. 60–90*, ed. Vincente Beltran de Heredia, Biblioteca de Teologos Españoles, vol. 19 (Salamanca: 1953), 47.

68. *Super Sent.* lib. 4, dist. 1, q. 1, a. 4, solutio I.

69. "*Tertio* arguitur. Gratia creatur a Deo; sed ad creationem solus Deus concurrit et nullo modo creatura neque instrumentaliter quidem: ergo sacramenta non possunt concurrare ad gratiam. Ad hoc respondeo negatur major, quia creatio simpliciter est ex dicatur quod sequitur quod anima rationalis non creatur a Deo quia etiam producitur

this, Cajetan preceded Bañez, arguing that, when we speak of the sacraments, grace cannot properly be called created.[70] For Cajetan, the change that takes place in a soul when it moves from lacking grace to being in the grace of God is attained (*attingere*) instrumentally by the sacraments. Building on this, Bañez implies that it is the soul's obediential potency for grace that enables the sacraments to function as true instrumental causes of grace.[71]

Previously, we noted that Thomas had already taken an important step away from the direct comparison between grace and the act of creation in the *De Veritate* and *De Potentia* by stipulating that grace is concreated rather than created in the proper sense, indicating that the accidental quality of grace subsists in an already existing (and already created) substance.[72] This notion of existing in an already subsistent thing is a helpful point of clarification, and Bañez makes full use of this in describing the potency of grace in relation to sacramental cause.

Even in the *Sentences*, grace is described implicitly as an accidental quality or *habitus*. The move to the terminology of concreation in the *De Veritate* indicates an intention to speak of sacramental causality in light of grace as an accidental property, shedding the unqualified comparison between grace and the creation of the rational soul. Because grace is an accident existing in something, the comparison between grace and creation must be modified. The language of potency, further developed in the *De Potentia* and other mature works, shifts the focus of sacramental causality away from creation entirely and to-

---

in materia a Deo, et videtur educi de potentia obedientiali ipsius subjecti: respondetur negando paritatem rationis, nam anima rationalis ita producitur a Deo, quod non dependet a subjecto in fieri et conservari. At vero gratia, quae est quaedam qualitas et accidens supernaturalis, ita producitur in subjecto, quod dependet ab illo in fieri et conservari." Bañez, *Comentarios Ineditos a la Tercera Parte de Santo Tomas*, vol. 2 (Salamanca: 1953), 50. See also Garrigou-Lagrange, *Grace*, 308.

70. Cajetan, *Commentary on ST* IIIª Q. 62 a. 1, n. VI (Leonine ed., 12:21). See Lynch, "Cajetan's Harp," 76–77. In a secondary way, one could speak of grace as created in an imprecise sense (*immiscere*), in as much as God is able to give grace immediately to the soul apart from the sacraments. But insofar as sacramental instrumentality is concerned, the use of the category of creation, even in a metaphorical sense, is inadmissible. Cajetan, *Commentary on ST* III q. 62 a. 1, n. VI (Leonine ed. 12:21).

71. Bañez, *Comentarios Ineditos*, 50. Text as in note 69.

72. See *De Ver.* q. 27 a. 3 ad 9, *De Pot.* q. 3 a. 3 ad 7.

wards the relationship between natural potency and grace as an elevation of human nature. This shift was identified by the commentatorial
tradition. Cajetan clearly teaches that true sacramental instrumentality is only possible if grace is not an act of creation in the proper sense,
and Bañez further elucidates the connection that exists between sacramental instrumentality and the obediential potency of the soul before God in grace.

The obedience of the human soul to God in the order of grace results in an elevation of the entire human nature that, while not within the scope of its natural potency, elicits a mode of acting and living in grace that is connatural to the person. In this way the dynamic
of grace is instantiated within (and in a certain sense dependent on)
natural powers in a way that the rational soul is not dependent on
matter. As a result of this, certain commentators are reluctant to use
even the language of concreation when speaking of grace; rather, it
seems more fitting to them to speak simply of grace as educed from
the potentiality of the rational soul.[73]

The doctrine of obediential potency allows us to say that, when
God "re-creates" in grace, he does so in a connatural manner, and because he chooses to work through an obediential engagement with
natures he has already created, he educes a participation in his own
nature from within an existing created rational nature. For this reason, the language of participation is perhaps preferable to that of
re-creation because it preserves the sense of proportion implicit in
the connaturality of grace. In grace, God in his wisdom chooses to
elevate human nature in grace in a way that he does not choose to
elevate the nature of an irrational creature. We can notice in passing
that, when the categories of creation and re-creation are conflated, it
is also difficult to adequately describe this connaturality: if God infuses grace in the same way that the soul is infused into the body at its
conception, there can be no meaningful connection between grace
and the natural potencies of a creature. True, this procreative analogy
preserves the distinction between natural potency and the power of
God, but it offers us no way to explain the fittingness or wisdom operative in God's decision to elevate the human person in grace. Un-

---

73. Garrigou-Lagarrange, *Grace*, 308.

derstood in this way, elevation in grace would seem to be equally in-congruous were it to befall a human person or a lion.

It was Aquinas' early understanding of re-creation in grace (as the soul infused into the body) that limited his understanding of sacra-mental causality to dispositive instrumentality. In his mature work Aquinas has effectively situated the causality of grace within the po-tency of an existing nature, and the concept of instrumentality can now be used in a fuller sense to explain the causing of grace through the sacraments. As Bañez has said, prescinding from discussions of moral or meritorious causality, the nature of grace and its relation-ship to the human soul requires some discussion of physical instru-mentality (that is, the potency of a natural instrument).[74] For Bañez, Aquinas' mature doctrine of sacramental causality requires that we approach grace from within the category of obediential potency.

By extension, the sacramental elements themselves exhibit a simi-lar obedience when employed by God as efficacious signs to effect the obediential elevation of the person in grace. Because Aquinas argues that all created things have the capacity to respond obedientially to God, the connaturality that marks the obediential response of the hu-man person in grace can be seen in the sacraments themselves when they function as perfective instrumental causes. Like the human per-son, natural elements such as water have passive obediential potencies that are specific to a given created nature.[75] When the sacraments are understood as perfective causes of grace, they are moved by the power of God, rather than the power of their own natural form. As has been shown, however, this motion is not arbitrary or extrinsic to the nature but actuates the proper operation of the nature itself as a tool or in-strumental cause of the end proportioned to the power of the prin-cipal agent. The water of Baptism washes the body and cleanses the heart. The language of obediential potency allows us to say something about the wisdom of God as an artist, making use of created instru-ments in the order of grace, that was not entirely possible in the cate-gories employed by Aquinas in his earliest thought on the subject.

---

74. See note 67. The doctrine of merit in relation to the sacraments will be dis-cussed in the following chapter.

75. Long, "On the Possibility of a Purely Natural End for Man," 214.

SACRAMENTAL GRACE
AND INSTRUMENTALITY:
JOHN OF ST. THOMAS

It is clear that much of Aquinas' development on the subject of sacramental causality is dependent on changes within his approach to grace itself. Once Aquinas moves away from using the category of creation to describe the infusion of grace within the soul, he is able to articulate a perfective theory of causality in which the sacraments are instrumental causes of grace in an unqualified sense. Understanding the sacraments as perfective instrumental causes in this way requires Aquinas to situate grace itself more directly within the categories of act and potency. In this context, grace comes to be viewed as something educed from the soul, not as an actuation of the soul's own potency but as an obediential response to divine initiative. Clearly grace and sacramental causality are interrelated for Aquinas, and developments in his approach to grace enable his articulation of the doctrine of perfective sacramental instrumentality in his later writings. Although it is not clear that developments in sacramental causality had a corresponding influence on Aquinas' general doctrine of grace in the same way, the gradual appreciation for perfective sacramental instrumentality that began to emerge did affect the way in which the more specific subspecies of sacramental grace was interpreted in the Thomistic school.[76]

In the early scholastic period, sacramental grace was not always adequately distinguished from sanctifying and habitual grace.[77] While Aquinas himself clearly distinguishes between sanctifying grace and the grace of the virtues and gifts in both the *Sentences* and the *Summa*,[78] the relationship of sacramental grace to these categories is subject to interpretation. In the *Sentences* Aquinas builds on the medicinal imagery of Hugh of St. Victor, describing the grace imparted by

---

76. For a comprehensive study of sacramental grace among Thomistic commentators, see George Shea, "A Survey of the Theology of Sacramental Grace," *Proceedings of the CTSA* (1953): 81–130.

77. Ibid., 98–99.

78. *Super Sent.* IV d. 1, q. 1, a. 4, solutio 5; d. 7, q. 2, a. 2, solutio 2, ad 2; solutio 3. Shea, " A Survey of the Theology," 90 n. 33. *ST* III^a Q. 62, a. 2.

the sacraments primarily as a remedy for sin.[79] In the *Summa*, however, Aquinas emphasizes the perfective role of the sacraments—and the grace they impart—situating sacramental grace within the broader teleology of Christian life.[80] While Aquinas will retain Hugh of St. Victor's medicinal analogy, in the *Summa* he connects the sacraments themselves more clearly to the virtue of religion in which they perfect the human person in the worship of God.[81] The idea of religion is a significant component of Aquinas' anthropology, which uses the concept to describe the human capacity—and obligation—to establish a correct relationship with God.

Although justification comes only through grace, Aquinas does not describe religion as a result of the gift of grace but as a natural virtue under the general virtue of justice. It is constitutive of human nature itself that it is defined by its relationship to its creator. By extension, the teleology of human nature is not directed towards its own autonomous ends. Its actuation in virtue reflects the image and likeness of its creator. What the grace of justification does to the human person, therefore, is not something extrinsic to human nature but perfective in a supernatural sense of human nature itself. The sacraments, accordingly, are not only efficient instrumental causes of this justification but signs and rituals in which the graced person exercis-

---

79. "Sed contra est quod Hugo de sancto Victore dicit (I *de Sacram.*, p. 9, c. 3 ; L. 176, 319) [sic] quod sacramenta sunt vasa medicinalia. Sed omnis medicina est in remedium alicujus morbi. Ergo et omne sacramentum est in remedium alicujus defectus spiritualis." *Super Sent.* IV d. 2, q. 1, a. 1, s.c. Mandonnet/Moos, vol. 4 (1947), 75. See also *Super Sent.* IV prolog.; d. 2, q. 1, a. 2, s.c.; a. 3, solutio. The majority of scholastics during the twelfth and thirteenth centuries viewed the sacraments primarily as remedies for sin. Shea, "A Survey of the Theology," 88. However, Shea notes that, while Aquinas' early thought is generally consistent with this, there are signs that he sees the sacraments as more than remedies even in the *Sentences* (88n26).

80. C.A. Schleck, "St. Thomas on the Nature of Sacramental Grace," (two parts) *The Thomist* 18 (1955): 21; 244.

81. "Gratia autem sacramentalis ad duo praecipue ordinari videtur: videlicet ad tollendos defectus praeteritorum peccatorum, inquantum transeunt actu et remanent reatu; et iterum ad perficiendum animam in his quae pertinent ad cultum Dei secundum religionem Christianae vitae." *ST* III^a Q. 62, a. 5, co. See also *ST* III^a Q. 63, a. 1, co.; Q. 65, a. 1, co. See also Shea, " A Survey of the Theology," 91. Concerning perfection in the Christian religion as an end of the sacraments, Aquinas seems to qualify this in the case of the sacrament of Penance, which he argues is primarily concerned with the remedy for sin. *ST* III^a Q. 63, a. 6, co.

es intrinsically the virtue of religion as a fulfillment of justice according to nature and a further participation in divine life that anticipates
beatitude.

The presentation of sacramental instrumentality in the *Summa* affects the way in which the sacraments themselves are understood as
causes in relation to the perfection of the whole person in grace. Because sacramental grace is the direct result of sacramental instrumentality, the way in which it is understood can be expected to shift as
well. Accordingly, earlier commentators within the Thomistic tradition approached sacramental grace very differently from later commentators who saw the sacraments to be perfective causes. When
commenting on Aquinas' early approach on sacramental causality
in the *Sentences*, Capreolus argues that only sacramental grace can
be the direct or perfective end of the sacraments: sanctifying grace
is caused only dispositionally.[82] Although in the *Sentences* Aquinas
does clearly distinguish sacramental grace from sanctifying grace and
the grace of the virtues and gifts, Capreolus' position is dependent
on his understanding of the implications of the theory of dispositive
causality. In this he clearly associates sacramental grace with the sacramental character, which in the dispositive model is caused directly
by the sacraments, forming a disposition to receive sanctifying grace.
Capreolus' approach necessarily situates sacramental grace as something independent from sanctifying grace, preceding it in the order
of reception.[83] Elsewhere in the *Sentences*, however, Aquinas seems to
contradict this by claiming that sacramental grace presumes the presence of sanctifying grace.[84]

Cajetan understands sacramental grace in light of the sacraments
as perfective instrumental causes. In defining sacramental grace, Cajetan recalls Aquinas' distinction in the *Prima Secundae* between the

---

82. "Similem sententiam ponit, 3 p., q. 62, art. 1, et *de Veritate*, q. 27 a. 4; nisi quod
in praedictis locis videtur dicere quod sacramenta pertingunt effective instrumentaliter
ad ipsam gratiam, non faciendo mentionem de dispositione. Sed intelligendum est
quod pertingunt ad gratiam sacramentalem effective; ad gratiam vero gratum facientem,
solum dispositive, ut exponit Petrus de Palude (4. *Sentent.*, dist. 1, q. 1)." Capreolus, *Defensiones Theol.*, lib. 4 d. 1, 2, 3, q. 1 a. 1 concl. 3. See Johannis Capreoli, *Defensiones Theologiae Divi Thomae Aquinatis*, vol. 6, 4.

83. Shea, "A Survey of the Theology," 94.

84. *Super Sent.* IV d. 1, q. 1, a. 4, qu. 5.

grace of divine aid (*gratuitum divinum auxilium*) and sanctifying grace itself (*gratiam habitualis doni*). Cajetan argues that, because Aquinas describes sacramental grace as a form of "divine aid," it is more appropriate to consider it as such than as a form of habitual grace.[85] In this Cajetan counters Peter of Palude, an early Thomist who argued that sacramental grace was a habitual grace (distinct from the habit of sanctifying grace itself).[86] Against Capreolus, Cajetan argues strongly that the perfective teleology of the sacraments affects Aquinas' understanding of sacramental grace. Cajetan is clear that sacramental grace is caused perfectively by the sacraments.[87] There is a sense in which Capreolus might agree with this, in as much as he identified sacramental grace with the character imparted as the immediate effect of sacramental instrumentality. For Cajetan, however, such a

85. "In Prima Secundae Auctor, dividendo gratiam, distinxit contra habituale donum gratiae, gratuitum divinum auxilium. Ac per hoc, sub genere gratiae communiter dictae locavit duo genera seu species gratiarum, scilicet gratiam habitualis doni, et gratiam divini auxilii. Et propterea, cum hoc in loco expresse dicat gratiam sacramentalem addere divinum auxilium, non est ad aliud genus gratiae e regione positum, scilicet donum habituale, divertendum: sed, planum litterae sensum sectando, sentiendum est quod gratia sacramentalis distinguitur specie a gratia virtutum et donorum, non sicut habitus ab habitu, sed sicut gratuitum divinum auxilium a gratuito habituali dono; et per hoc, esse speciem gratiae communiter dictae, ut in responsione ad tertium dicitur; et dividi in plures species, iuxta specificam pluralitatem effectuum, ut inferius qu. LXXII, art. 7, ad 3, dicitur." Cajetan, *Commentary on ST* III³ Q. 62, a. 2, n. II (Leonine ed., 12:23.) See also note 87. Cajetan's claim that Aquinas describes sacramental grace as a form of divine aid is in reference to the corpus of question 62, on which he is commenting: "Sicut igitur virtutes et dona addunt super gratiam communiter dictam quandam perfectionem determinate ordinem ad proprios actus potentiarum, ita gratia sacramentalis addit super gratiam communiter dictam, et super virtutes et dona, quoddam *divinum auxilium* ad consequendum sacramenti finem." *ST* III³ Q. 62, a. 2, co. (emphasis mine). While Cajetan does not specify which question or article in the *Prima Secundae* he is referring to, the Leonine editors reference *ST* I³ II³ᵉ Q. 109, a. 10; Q. 110, a. 2 in this regard. For an interpretation of Cajetan on this point, see Shea, "A Survey of the Theology," 104–5.

86. Palude, *In IV Sent.*, d. 2, q. 3, a. un. As in Shea, " A Survey of the Theology," 96n57.

87. "Dicitur quod sacramentum instrumentaliter *attingit* gratiam sacramentalem; et non oportet recurrere ad dispositionem praeviam ad gratiam. Quidquid enim, secundum aliorum opinionem ut probabiliorem, dixerit Auctor in IV *Sent.*... Gratia sacramentalis non ponitur dispositio, sed, ut patebit, nullum habituale donum addit supra gratiam gratum facientem" (emphasis mine). Cajetan, *Commentary on ST* III³ Q. 62, a. 1, n. VI (Leonine ed., 12:21.)

conflation of grace and sacramental character is expressly ruled out by the structure of Aquinas' argument, which clearly specifies that grace and character form two separate ends of sacramental action.[88] Cajetan argues that sacramental grace cannot be a mere disposition for sanctifying grace or a habit distinct from the habit of sanctifying grace. Rather, each sacramental grace must be understood as an actual grace: divine *auxilium*.

For those commentators who accept Cajetan's theory of perfective sacramental causality, it was clear that the approach of previous Thomists such as Capreolus to sacramental grace was insufficient. Among later Thomists, however, Cajetan's theory of sacramental grace was not universally accepted. While Cajetan understood sacramental grace as a kind of actual grace, John of St. Thomas and the Salmanticenses associated sacramental grace with the category of sanctifying grace. Much of the difference between John of St. Thomas and Cajetan on this point hinges on the interpretation of the term *auxilium* in the *Prima Secundae*. While Cajetan held that *auxilium* always indicates actual grace, John of St. Thomas argues that Aquinas himself applies the term to the concept of sanctifying grace in question 109. Here, sanctifying grace is described as divine *auxilium* without which the person is unable to overcome sin. John of St. Thomas argues that in this context habitual grace is an internal divine motion within the soul that constitutes an habitual gift of God and that sacramental grace is a modality of this motion.[89]

---

88. "Videbis quod sub gratiae nomine hoc in loco non comprehenditur character, cum distinguatur contra characterem." Cajetan, Commentary on *ST* IIIª Q. 62, a. 1, n. I (Leonine ed., 12:20.)

89. "Nec sufficit responsio Cajetani super istum articulum, quod licet in libris sententiarum aliter expressisset D. Thomas, tamen cum in praesenti articulo dicat quod sacramentalis gratia addit super gratiam virtutem et donorum auxilium divinum, et apud D. Thomam divinum auxilium non sumitur pro habituali, set pro actuali dono, ut in prima secundae, quaest. CXI patet, ideo ex hoc loco debit dici, quod sacramentalis gratia solum addit aliquid actuale, extendens gratiam donorum et virtutum ad aliquem specialem effectum.... Nec per divinum auxilium intelligere potest S. Thomas aliquam divinam motionem ad agendum, sed aliquid permanens, sanans, seu reparans defectus peccati, cum connotatione ad auxilium, ut speciales effectus operetur ad speciales fines ordinatos. Nec apud S. Thomam novum est, per ly auxilium intelligere donum habituale: nam in prima secundae, quaest. CIX, art. VII inquirit S. Thomas, an possit homo resurgere a peccato sine auxilio gratiae, et respondet negative ; intelligit autem per auxilium gratiae, tam donum habituale quam motionem internam, ut explicat in calce

Concerning the relationship of sacramental grace to sanctifying grace, John of St. Thomas holds that there is no real distinction between sacramental grace and habitual grace such that sacramental grace would be a new and distinct habit. Neither is sacramental grace simply a form of actual grace given as a transitory gift from God. Rather, sacramental grace is a permanent gift received intrinsically in the soul. Understood in this way, this gift is only formally distinct from sanctifying grace.[90] The formal distinction between sacramental grace and sanctifying grace is modal. Sacramental grace is part of the habitual gift of sanctifying grace, which itself has both remedial and deifying qualities—healing the wounds of human nature and imparting supernatural effects—perfecting sanctifying grace according to distinct modalities according to the distinct ends of the individual sacraments within the reality of sanctifying grace.[91] In this, we see the value of Aquinas' own shift from a remedial to a perfective model of grace at work. By placing sacramental grace within the category of habitual/sanctifying grace, John of St. Thomas is able to describe sacramental grace as part of the teleological fabric of the Christian life

corporis articuli dicens: 'Et ideo requiritur auxilium gratiae ad hoc, quod homo a peccato resurgat, et quantum ad habituale donum, et quantum ad interiorem Dei motionem.'" John of St. Thomas, *Cursus Theologicus: De Sacramentis*, Disp. XXIV, Art. II., Dub. 1, sec. 11, t. 9 (Paris: Vivès, 1886), 286–87.

90. "Et dicimus, quod non est aliquid distinctum tamquam res a re, seu novus habitus, nec solum aliquid actuale per modum transeuntis datum a Deo, sed aliquid formaliter distinctum a gratia habituali et virtutem, et permanenter receptum in anima. Et quidem quod sit aliquid permanens in anima, videtur clare colligi ex S. Thoma in primis is in isto articulo, ubi inquit: 'Gratiam sacramentalem dari in remedium aliquorum defectuum, qui ex peccatis praeteritis causantur, secundum quod peccata traseunt actu, et remanent reatu.' Defectus autem illi sunt quid permanens in anima: ergo oportet quod tollantur per aliquid permanens, et non per modum transeuntis se habens, et per aliquid intrinsicum ei, qui habet defectum, et indiget remedio." John of St. Thomas, *De Sacramentis*, Disp. XXIV, Art. II., Dub. 1, sec. 9, t. 9 (Paris: Vivès, 1886), 285–86. *Salmanticenses, Cursus theologicus*, t. 17, *De Sacramentis in communi* (Paris, 1881), Disp. IV, Dub. IX, nn. 134–148. See also Shea, " A Survey of the Theology,"112–13.

91. "Gratiae sacramentales in quantum sacramentales, ordinantur vel ad diversos defectus reparandos in homine, vel ad diversos effectus supernaturales, et pertinentes ad vitam christianam, efficiendos ab ipso homine." John of St. Thomas, *De Sacramentis*, Disp. XXIV, Art. II., Dub. 1, sec. 13, t. 9 (Paris: Vivès, 1886), 287. "Ut ergo essentia gratiae sacramentalis non distinguatur specie ab essentia gratiae habitualis, et donorum ac virtutum oportet, quod sit aliquid permanens, perficiens ipsam gratiam, non tamquam res seu habitus distinctus, sed ut modus, aut formalitas." John of St. Thomas, *De Sacramentis*, Disp. XXIV, Art. II., Dub. 1, sec. 12, t. 9 (Paris: Vivès, 1886), 287.

of sanctification. Unlike the gift of prophesy, which is the result of a transient gift of actual grace, sacramental grace is a permanent and intrinsic gift that works towards the habitual sanctification of the intellect and will of the rational soul in virtue. This habitual action of the Christian life, which is made possible by the power of grace and is a special share in the grace of Christ, emerges in the graced activity of the rational soul as an imitation of Christ.[92]

This approach to sacramental grace has implications for the doctrine of instrumentality within the context of graced anthropology. John of St. Thomas argues that sacramental grace must have a permanent effect, restoring the human soul according to nature and rendering it capable of supernatural acts. In this respect, a passing actual grace—like the gift of prophesy—is not sufficient. The prophet acts as an instrumental cause in relation to God's principal causality, and because the grace he receives is actual and not habitual, the words he utters are not necessarily the product of his will. When sacramental grace is considered as a mode of sanctifying grace, there is a certain reversal: because the Christian life is intrinsically sanctifying, it is marked by a kind of graced human activity that is not solely the product of divine instrumentality interspersed in the midst of human activity but proceeds from the intellect and will of the graced rational soul as an authentic human act.[93] In this sense, while the sacraments themselves are instrumental causes, their effects render the hu-

---

92. "Et deinde, quia operatur homo per illam gratiam secundum quod vivit vita christiana, et secundum communicationem peculiarum ex gratia Christi, hoc autem quod est habere in se vitam christianam secundum imitationem gratiae Christi, non est solus actualis concursus, sed aliquid permanens. Adde quod per gratiam sacramentalem operatur homo ad libitum, quando vult: ergo debet aliquid permanens esse in homine, quo operetur ut vult, et non solum aliquid per modum transeuntis, sicut prophetia, quae ideo non est in manu prophetae ut illa utatur quando voluerit, quia non per modum habitus, sed actualis concursus datur." John of St. Thomas, *De Sacramentis*, Disp. XXIV, Art. II., Dub. 1, sec. 14, t. 9 (Paris: Vivès, 1886), 288.

93. "Ad effectus vero efficiendos ab ipso homine non sufficit actualis concursus Dei, nisi supponat in homine formam, seu perfectionem cui accommodatur ille concursus, quia cum non sit Deus solus qui operatur, sed homo, et non operetur homo ut instrumentum, sed etiam ut causa principalis, si quidem gratia sacramentalis non datur sicut potestas ad efficiendum praecise, sed ad debite efficiendum, homo autem debite non efficit, nisi per actus voluntatis et intellectus: inde est quod oportet dari ei gratiam sacramentalem, ut operetur ad modum causae principalis." John of St. Thomas, *De Sacramentis*, Disp. XXIV, Art. II., Dub. 1, sec. 13, t. 9 (Paris: Vivès, 1886), 287. "Et deinde, quia

man soul capable of performing authentic human acts—of which it is itself the principal cause—that are directed towards supernatural ends within the new deifying horizon of sanctifying grace. Because the motion of sanctifying grace does not compromise human freedom, the principal agency of the human intellect can move the person to supernatural action through the habit of grace intrinsically.[94]

As has been shown in the context of sacramental instrumentality, it is the form of the principal agent that governs the operation of the instrument. John of St. Thomas' concern for the principal agency of the human will preserves the integrity of human action in the context of habitual grace, where the primary agency of the human intellect and will can already be seen to be operative in the infused virtues where faith, hope, and charity become authentically human acts in the full sense, made possible by our conformity to Christ in grace. John of St. Thomas further positions sacramental grace in a nonrivalrous relationship with this supernatural habit, where sacramental grace is capable of perfecting sanctifying grace according to specific modalities of human sanctification and perfection in charity.

Beyond its incompatibility with the instrumentality of human nature, John of St. Thomas further suggests that the concept of actual grace is not compatible with perfective sacramental instrumentality. Because he sees the concept of actual grace as the direct action of God, it cannot be compatible with a perfective notion of sacramental instrumentality in which the sacraments "touch" (*attingere*) the final reality of sacramental grace as instruments.[95] There is a sense then in

---

operatur homo per illam gratiam secundum quod vivit vita christiana, et secundum communicationem peculiarem ex gratia Christi, hoc autem quod est habere in se vitam christianam secundum imitationem gratiae Christi, non est solus actualis concursus, sed aliquid permanens. Adde quod per gratiam sacramentalem operatur homo ad libitum, quando vult: ergo debet aliquid permanens esse in homine, quo operetur ut vult, et non solum aliquid per modum transeuntis, sicut prophetia, quae ideo non est in manu prophetae ut illa utatur quando voluerit, quia non per modum habitus, sed actualis concursus datur." John of St. Thomas, *De Sacramentis*, Disp. XXIV, Art. II., Dub. 1, sec. 14, t. 9 (Paris: Vivès, 1886), 287–88.

94. D. Spezzano shows the connections that exist in Aquinas' thought between the conjoined instrumentality of Christ's humanity and our participation in divine life, using the concept of instrumentality to illumine Aquinas' teaching on grace, charity and sacramentality. Spezzano, *The Glory of God's Grace*, 289–314.

95. "Denique, quia si gratia sacramentalis in solo actuali concursu consistit, non

which John of St. Thomas' conception of sacramental grace is an outgrowth of the shift towards perfective sacramental instrumentality as
he understands it and represents a deeper integration of sacramental
grace within Aquinas' mature understanding of grace as a supernatural reality deduced obedientially from the potencies of human nature.

Although John of St. Thomas seems convinced that actual grace
does not admit of instrumentality on the part of the sacraments or
the graced individual in the full sense, Cajetan himself clearly understands actual grace to be the product of perfective sacramental instrumentality.[96] Whether there is a broader understanding of actual
grace that admits of Cajetan's approach is beyond our present scope.
However, both theories are made possible by a perfective approach
to sacramental causality and the shift away from grace as created from
nothing. However, the approach of John of St. Thomas has a certain
appeal because it integrates sacramental grace within the context of
habitual grace as an elevation of created potency. John of St. Thomas'
theory of sacramental grace gained a certain following in the twentieth century because of its perceived ability to integrate sacramental
action, grace, and sign in a coherent unity.[97]

Aquinas' treatment of grace and causality in the context of the
sacraments not only frames the instrumentality of the sacraments
in perfective language but recasts the category of grace into the language of act and potency. In the next chapter, we will examine the
way in which this approach to grace is integrated with Aquinas' approach to merit and Christological instrumentality in the *Summa*, in
contrast with alternative approaches from the modern period.

As has been already shown, the value of the concept of obedien-

---

poterit effective procedere a sacramentis, quia concursus actualis est actio Dei, quae
non attingitur ab illo instrumento: ergo ut gratia sacramentalis sit effectus sacramenti,
oportet quod aliquid intrinsecum et permanens ponat in homine." John of St. Thomas,
Cursus Theologicus: De Sacramentis, Disp. XXIV, Art. II., Dub. 1, sec. 15, t. 9 (Paris: Vivès,
1886), 288.

96. For a more comprehensive treatment of Cajetan's position on actual grace in
the context of the sacraments, see Shea, "A Survey of the Theology," 106–7.

97. Colman O'Neill, "The Role of the Recipient and Sacramental Signification,"
(two parts) *The Thomist* 21 (1958): 257–301, 508–41, and "The Mysteries of Christ and
the Sacraments," *The Thomist* 25 (1962): 1–53. See also Charles Crowley, The Role of
Sacramental Grace in Christian Life," *The Thomist* 2 (1940): 519–45; Robert Masterson,
"Sacramental Graces: Modes of Sanctifying Grace," *The Thomist* 18 (1955): 311–72.

tial potency in the context of sacramental causality and grace begins with the Incarnation, where Aquinas himself uses the concept to describe the integral unity that exists between Christ's human and divine natures. Our own union with the person of Christ through the instrumentality of his human nature takes on a similar character in grace, as an expression of divine wisdom. Human nature could be simply elevated obedientially by God to participate in supernatural beatitude; but the fittingness of the Incarnation is further expressed by sacramental instrumentality and again by the elevation of the moral dimension of the human person in divinized human acts, facilitated by the infusion of virtue. The *ratio* of the final and formal cause is contained in the efficient and is visible at the outset. The Incarnation itself reveals the intention of divine wisdom to divinize the flesh to unite human nature with divinity. The sacramental economy, grace and all forms of instrumentality here implied, are expressions of the form of this wisdom. Grace as participation, infused through perfective sacramental causality, fits more closely with the ratio of the Incarnation than does the infusion of grace as created *ex nihilo*, which does not follow the obediential pattern of redemption which divinizes our flesh according to the exemplarity of the union of Christ's flesh with the Word.

This graced relationship with Christ is perpetuated and strengthened by our continual participation in the sacraments. As a person continues to receive sacraments (and therefore sacramental graces) long after his initial reception of sanctifying grace, the perfective approach to sacramental grace that is found in the later Thomistic commentators allows for a continued participation of the sacraments as instruments in the spiritual growth of the person that is, like grace itself, intrinsically directed towards the end of perfection in charity. In a similar way, we participate in the merits of Christ's humanity intrinsically because of the nature of grace itself.

4

Early Modern
Approaches to the Sacraments
Melchior Cano

Aquinas' theory of sacramental causality, the development of which has been examined in the preceding chapters, has been presented as an intrinsic approach to sacramental causality that stands in continuity with the inherited Augustinian tradition and the later decrees of Trent, presenting the causal dimension of the sacraments in a way that integrates systematically other important areas of Thomistic theology. In the first chapter, we examined some alternative approaches to sacramental causality from among Aquinas' contemporaries and the nominalists of the late scholastic period. Although many of these theories are worthy of further study, this present chapter will devote itself to Melchior Cano's theory of moral causality because of its historical importance for theology in the modern period. Moral causality quickly became popular in the sixteenth century and remained so into the twentieth, becoming integrated into many non-Thomistic modern theological systems. As a result, moral causality represents not only a counterpoint to Aquinas' teaching on sacramental causality but an alternative theological hermeneutic for the sacraments. For those interested in the contemporary retrieval of Aquinas' sacramental theology, Cano provides an historical counterpoint to Aquinas which draws out the significance of other theological topics in connection with the sacraments, such as grace, merit, and Christology. This not only highlights the significance of Aquinas' approach to sacramental causality in conjunction with these broader ideas but warns against the consequences of an alternative approach which does not allow perfective instrumental causality its full scope.

This chapter will begin with Melchior Cano's historical context, establishing his own roots in both the Iberian Thomistic revival and humanism, and offering both an explanation and a critique of his theory from this perspective. Because of the emphasis Cano places on merit, this will be followed by a critical comparison of Cano and Aquinas on the subject of Christological merit in relation to the sacraments. This chapter will conclude by examining the way in which these distinct features of Cano's approach to merit and sacramental causality were assimilated by non-Thomistic schools of thought after the *de Auxiliis* controversy.

HUMANISM AND SCHOLASTICISM

Although moral causality was later employed in many different contexts, it is important to understand the roots of this theory in Cano's own intellectual formation. Cano's theory of sacramental causality was articulated at a time in which Europe as a whole was consumed by the difficulties of the Protestant Reformation. While these external pressures were significant, Cano's thought was shaped internally by other factors that were making their way into the intellectual climate of the Spanish universities during his lifetime. In addition to his scholastic formation, Cano's exposure to Renaissance humanism strongly influenced his own theological hermeneutics, and traces of this influence are visible in his approach to sacramental causality as well.

During the fifteenth and sixteenth centuries, universities throughout Europe were changing in significant ways. This included not only a turn towards nominalism but the rise of humanism as well. At Paris, both of these movements had become strong influences by 1500.[1]

---

1. Vincente Muñoz Delgado, *La Logica Nominalista en la Universidad de Salamanca: 1510–1530* (Madrid: Publicaciones del Monasterio de Poyo, 1964), 73. Anthony Levi, *Renaissance and Reformation: The Intellectual Genesis* (New Haven, Conn.: Yale University Press, 2002), 61. Although the study of nominalism at Paris was banned by royal decree

During this time, however, Paris also saw under the Dominican Peter Crockaert at St. Jacques a small but determined revival of Thomism that would eventually exert wider influence as well.[2] The influence and prestige of the University of Paris served to promote nominalism and humanism (and to a lesser extent the Thomistic revival) elsewhere in northern Europe. Spain remained relatively isolated from these trends, however, and was comparatively slow to follow Paris' example. The University of Salamanca, Spain's oldest and most prestigious institution, had almost no nominalist presence until the beginning of the sixteenth century.[3] Even after this, Salamanca retained its traditional curriculum. With the foundation of the University of Alcalá at the beginning of the sixteenth century, things in Iberia began to change. Although some elements of the scholastic approach remained at Alcalá, the new university challenged the medieval scholastic synthesis that had been until this time preserved at Salamanca.[4]

---

in 1474, interest in the writings of Ockham and other nominalists only increased, and the decree was rescinded in 1481. E. J. Ashworth, *The Eclipse of Medieval Logic*, in *The Cambridge History of Later Medieval Philosophy*, ed. Norman Kretzmann, Anthony Kenny and Jan Pinborg (New York: Cambridge University Press, 1989), 789.

2. For a history of Thomism during this period, see Frederick Roensch, *Early Thomistic School* (Dubuque, Iowa: The Priory Press, 1964), 14–19. See also Andrew Newman, "*Jus Divinum* and the Sacrament of Penance in Two Tridentine Theologians: Melchior Cano and Ruard Tapper" (PhD diss., The Catholic University of America, 1969), 10n16. James Farge implies that Crockaert's movement may have had some indirect influence at the University of Cologne as well, where the Dominican Conrad Köllin fostered a similar revival of Thomism. James Farge, *Orthodoxy and Reform in Early Reformation France: the Faculty of Theology of Paris, 1500–1543*, Studies in Medieval and Reformation Thought, ed. Heiko Oberman, vol. 32 (Leiden: Brill, 1985), 246.

3. A Nominalist Chair was introduced at Salamanca in 1509. Delgado, *La Logica Nominalista*, 77–82.

4. Alcalá was founded as a university in approximately 1499. In addition to promoting various humanist disciplines, Ximénez also served as Primate and Grand Inquisitor of Spain during this time. The University of Alcalá came to be known for its emphasis on humanism and biblical studies, particularly after its production of a polyglot Bible. Ulrich Horst, *The Dominicans and the Pope: Papal Teaching Authority in the Medieval and Early Modern Thomist Tradition*, trans. James D. Mixson (Notre Dame, Ind.: University of Notre Dame Press, 2006), 43. Levi, *Renaissance and Reformation*, 210–29. CE s.v. "Francisco Ximénez de Cisneros." From the beginning Alcalá emphasized biblical languages, and by 1515 four chairs were established there in Greek and Hebrew. John Edwin Sandys, *A History of Classical Scholarship: From the Revival of Learning to the End of the Eighteenth Century in Italy, France, England and the Netherlands* (New York: Cambridge University Press, 2011), 180–81.

During the first half of the sixteenth century, humanism gradually gained influence in Spain either vicariously through the faculty at Alcalá or through the many Spanish scholars who had been sent to study in Paris and began to return, bringing with them the model of instruction used in the Paris arts faculty. Gradually, these newcomers began to bring the influence of the Paris method even to Salamanca itself.[5] These trends were not visible at Salamanca until the middle of the sixteenth century, however.[6]

Both of these universities would play important roles in the development of Spanish theology in the coming centuries, and each would play a central role in Melchior Cano's intellectual formation. Born at Tarancón in 1509, Cano entered the Dominican Order at Salamanca in 1523, where he completed his initial philosophical and theological studies. After his ordination to the priesthood in 1531, Cano taught at a number of faculties in Spain, including the University of Alcalá, where he was awarded the first chair in 1543.[7] In 1546 Cano returned to the University of Salamanca.[8] Although humanism was only just gaining a foothold at Salamanca when Cano arrived, his time at Alcalá had already exposed him to this movement.

The contrasting tenors of these two universities represents a crisis at work among Spanish intellectuals at this time. The different trends of humanism and scholasticism that were at work in Spanish universities during the sixteenth century each brought different—and sometimes incompatible—methodologies and approaches to the organization of knowledge. This crisis affected all intellectual disciplines within the University, and each scholar working within this environment had to come to grips with the implications of these contrasting ideas, deciding for himself how best to respond. As will be shown,

5. Delgado, *La Logica Nominalista*, 73, 77–82.

6. Bernhard Körner, *Melchior Cano: De Locis Theologicis. Ein Beitrag zur Theologischen Erkenntnislehre* (Graz: Verlag Ulrich Moser, 1994), 142.

7. After his ordination to the priesthood in 1531, Cano was assigned to the order's *Studium Generale* in Valladolid. After completing the degree of Lector, Cano began to teach philosophy in 1533. In 1536, he was appointed to the Second Chair of Theology at Valladolid. In 1542 he was made a Master of Sacred Theology, and in 1543 he moved to the University of Alcalá, where he was given the First Chair in Theology. Newman, *"Jus Divinum,"* 4–6.

8. *DTC* s. v. "Cano, Melchior."

Cano himself attempts to balance these trends in his own later work on theological methodology and the sacraments.

There is no doubt that Cano received a strong grounding in Thomistic principles during his early education. One of the earliest figures to influence Cano was the Thomist Francisco de Vitoria, who taught Cano during his initial formation for the priesthood at Salamanca. Vitoria was a leading figure of the Thomist revival in Spain, a movement which he had first encountered in Paris as a student of Crockaert.[9] One of the most influential pedagogical and methodological features of the Thomistic revival in both Paris and Salamanca was the practice of teaching directly from Aquinas' *Summa Theologiae* without the medium of Lombard's *Sentences*, the pedagogical dominance of which had lessened as the influence of scholasticism waned in the universities.[10] Paradoxically, this provided an opportunity for the *Summa* to come into its own, replacing the *Sentences* in many faculties as the primary text for theological instruction.[11] Vitoria would import this practice to Spain, helping to establish the *Summa* at Salamanca during his tenure there.[12] Cano was deeply influenced by this as a student and would lecture from the *Summa* even in the progressive environment of Alcalá.[13]

One of the key questions for any Thomist in a pluralistic intel-

9. See Richard Garcia Villoslada, *La universidad de Paris durante los estudios de Francisco de Vitoria* (Rome: Universitatis Gregorianae, 1938), 216–44. After his initial course in philosophy and theology at Burgos, Vitoria had been assigned to Paris for further studies in 1507, during which time he came into contact with the Thomist revival initiated by the Flemish Dominican Peter Crockaert, who was then living at St. Jacques. Crockaert was lecturing on the *Summa* at St. Jacques, and Vitoria attended these lectures. Vitoria studied philosophy and theology from 1507–12. Vitoria began to teach arts at St. Jacques from 1512–16, and from 1516–23 he was charged with teaching theology. Horst, *The Dominicans and the Pope*, 44. Newman, "*Jus Divinum*," 12. LThK[3] s. v. "Vitoria, Francisco de." *OD.C.C* s.v. "Vitoria, Francisco de."

10. These issues were discussed in chapter 1. See Juan Belda Plans, *La Escuella de Salamanca y la renovación de la teología en el siglo XVI* (Madrid: Biblioteca de Autores Cristianos, 2000), 320.

11. Cano himself would provide an alternative to the *Summa* in the modern period. See note 48.

12. Jean-Pierre Torrell, *Aquinas's Summa: Background, Structure and Reception*, trans. Benedict M. Guevin (Washington, D.C.: The Catholic University of America Press, 2005), 98.

13. Newman, "*Jus Divinum*," 6.

lectual environment is not so much knowledge of Aquinas in the strict sense (although that too can be an issue) but hermeneutical approach. What methodological approach should be adopted when dealing with the wider university? To what degree should Aquinas' own theological method be adopted when faced with new sources and contrasting methodologies? These are questions that faced Crockaert, Vitoria, and Cano and that continue to confront us today. During this time, Thomists such as Cajetan engaged the humanist question in theology by reinvesting in biblical commentary and the study of ancient languages. Similarly, Vitoria became acquainted with leading humanists of his day such as Erasmus and Vivés and cultivated an appreciation for ancient languages to such an extent that he was most likely able to work with the texts of Aristotle and Scripture in Greek.[14] Vitoria studied Cajetan closely and cited him frequently in his lectures.[15] He differed from Cajetan methodologically, however, focusing more on moral problems than speculative issues and eschewing metaphysical abstraction in favor of convincing rhetoric.[16] In Vitoria, and then more clearly in Cano, we see a decision not only to be in dialogue with humanism but to invest in humanist methodology itself.[17]

Like Vitoria, Cano tried to situate the Thomist tradition within the wider intellectual trends of his day, admitting a certain methodological eclecticism if necessary to preserve the broader whole. Coming a full generation after Vitoria, Cano became more deeply entangled with humanism on a methodological level, systematizing many of the hermeneutical intuitions of his teacher in his principle work, De Locis Theologicis. Although Cano remained cognizant of his debt

---

14. Carlos Noreña, *Studies in Spanish Renaissance Thought* (The Hague: Martinus Nijhoff, 1975), 39. For a study of the reaction against Erasmus in Spain, see Erika Rummel, *Biblical Humanism and Scholasticism in the Age of Erasmus* (Leiden: Brill, 2008), 73–92.

15. Noreña, *Studies,* 44.

16. Noreña, *Studies,* 69–72. Although he favored the *Summa* as a text of instruction, Vitoria devoted far more time to the *Secunda Secundae* than to any other text. Ibid., 59. He is said to have been dismissive at times of Cajetan's speculative approach in his lectures. Ibid., 70–71.

17. Noreña, *Studies,* 71–73. For a more detailed treatment of this issue, see Belda Plans, *La Escuela de Salamanca,* 322–33. *NCE*[1] s. v. "Vitoria, Francisco de." Torrell, *Aquinas's Summa,* 99.

to scholasticism and continued to use the *Summa* in the classroom, his sacramental doctrine bore little resemblance to that found in the *Tertia Pars*.

CANO AND RENAISSANCE HUMANISM

In contrast to late scholasticism, humanism brought a renewed emphasis on the person and human enterprise. As a cultural and intellectual movement, humanism built upon the emerging prosperity of the Renaissance and propounded a more naturalistic and secularized conception of human life and society. In the universities, Renaissance humanism proposed an educational model that was in direct competition with the scholastic approach.[18] During the Renaissance, the study of rhetoric was undergoing a major shift. Framing themselves in contradistinction to the scholastic tradition as they understood it, humanists tended to distance themselves from traditional speculative logic, placing their emphasis instead on rhetoric.[19] To this end, some humanist rhetoricians voiced opposition to the traditional distinction between practical rhetoric and speculative dialectic. Lorenzo Valla (d. 1457) and other humanists began to develop a new relationship between rhetoric and dialectic that could serve the emerging needs of Renaissance thought.[20] Valla's emphasis on classical grammar and rhetoric led him to significantly devalue the traditional understanding of dialectic, which functioned according to more strictly syllogistic patterns. For Valla, persuasion and probability counted for more than rational certainty.[21] Although some of these sentiments

---

18. CE, *NCE*[1] s.v. "Humanism."

19. Charles Schmitt, *Aristotle and the Renaissance* (Cambridge, Mass.: Harvard University Press, 1983), 16. Joseph A. Mazzeo, "Universal Analogy and the Culture of the Renaissance," *Journal of the History of Ideas* 15 (April 1954): 303.

20. Brian P. Copenhaver, "Translation, Terminology and Style in Philosophical Discourse," in *The Cambridge History of Renaissance Philosophy*, ed. Charles B. Schmitt and Quentin Skinner (New York: Cambridge University Press, 1988), 104.

21. "Valla's emphasis on *consuetudo* as the ultimate arbiter in the study of language led him to a drastic reassessment of the study of dialectic in the curriculum.... The major part of actual argumentation and controversy, Valla maintained, is concerned not with *certainty* (that area of ratiocination appropriately systematized in formal syllogistic as traditionally taught) but with persuasion and probability." Lisa Jardine, "Humanism

were shared by Vitoria, this shift in emphasis would affect Cano's general theological methodology a great deal, and its influence can be seen in his particular approach to sacramental causality as well.

Rudolf Agricola (d. 1485), an Italian-trained humanist originally from the Netherlands, would exercise the most direct influence on Melchior Cano's theological method.[22] Completed in 1479, Agricola's *De Inventione Dialectica* became extremely popular during the sixteenth century and was printed with unheard of frequency between 1515 and 1575, becoming the standard humanist textbook in dialectical method at many universities. Because of its wide distribution, *De Inventione* played a central role in the ascendancy of humanism in universities formerly dominated by scholasticism.[23] There is evidence that Erasmus himself was influenced by Agricola in his approach to dialectic.[24] Cano found himself in the middle of this transition, teaching at Alcalá and then Salamanca at the peak of Agricola's influence. In *De Inventione*, Agricola reformulates the disciplines of rhetoric and dialectic in relation to his own list of logical topics.[25]

---

and the Teaching of Logic," in *The Cambridge History of Later Medieval Philosophy*, ed. Norman Kretzmann, Anthony Kenny, and Jan Pinborg (New York: Cambridge University Press, 1989), 798.

22. Agricola was born in the Netherlands, completing his Bachelor of Arts at Erfurt in 1458 and a Masters in Arts from Louvain in 1465. Subsequently, however, he studied civil law at Pavia from 1468?–75, and the humanities at Ferrara from 1475–79, after which time he returned to the Netherlands. Fokke Akkerman, ed., *Rudolph Agricola: Six Lives and Erasmus's Testimonies*, Bibliotheca Latinitatis Novae (Van Gorcum, BV: Royal Van Gorcum, 2012), 3. *LThK*³ s.v. "Agricola, Rudolf."

23. Peter Mack, *A History of Renaissance Rhetoric: 1380–1620* (New York: Oxford University Press, 2011), 74. Charles Lohr, "Medieval Latin Aristotle Commentaries, Authors: Robertus-Wilgelmus," *Traditio* 29 (1973): 123–24. *LThK*³ s.v. "Agricola, Rudolf." *The Cambridge History of Renaissance Philosophy*, ed. Charles Schmitt and Quentin Skinner (New York: Cambridge University Press, 1988), 71, 104, 806. The popularity of Agricola's text may be attributed in part to the availability of the printing press, which came to the Netherlands in 1477–80. Akkerman, *Rudolph Agricola*, 4, 7.

24. Lisa Jardine argues that Erasmus' later introduction to the *Seneca* (a 1529 edition) shows the influence of Agricola so strongly that at times subsequent editions actually attributed this introduction to Agricola. Lisa Jardine, "Ghosting the Reform of Dialectic," in *Renaissance Rhetoric*, ed. Peter Mack (New York: St. Martin's Press, 1994), 38–40. P. Mack argues that Erasmus' *De copia* was strongly influenced by Agricola as well. Mack, *A History of Renaissance Rhetoric*, 70.

25. See Peter Mack's schema of Agricola's *Topics*: Mack, *A History of Renaissance Rhetoric*, 63.

Recalling the language of Aristotle and Boethius, Agricola objected to the way in which the concept of "loci" (or topics) had come to
be employed in formal logic and wanted these loci to function not
only in the realm of speculative logic but as a practical source for
discussion and argument as well.[26] Significantly, although his "topics" bear some resemblance to Aristotle's *Categories*, he will not use
the technical (and more abstract) language of predication, which allows logic to proceed analogically to conclusions about the nature of
things in themselves. Agricola seems to prefer more simplistic categories based on visual similarity or association—useful for rhetoric but
less so for speculative demonstration.[27]

Although Valla and others reacted against Aristotelianism and traditional logic, a new Aristotelianism did emerge within the humanist
movement.[28] Agricola was more favorable to Aristotle, citing him fre-

26. Jardine, "Humanism and the Teaching of Logic," 798n5; John Monfasani, "Lorenzo Valla and Rudolph Agricola," *Journal of the History of Philosophy* 28, no. 2 (1990): 190.

27. Walter Ong's observations on this point clarify the difference between the Aristotelian *Categories* and Cano's *Topics*. Walter Ong, *Ramus: Method and the Decay of Dialogue* (Cambridge, Mass.: Harvard University Press, 1983), 104–23. "The Aristotle whom
Agricola exploits is not the Aristotle of the *Categories* nor of the *Analytics* but the Aristotle of the *Topics*.... [Agricola aims] to free his dialectic from the concern with predication which forms a principle axis of Aristotle's own thought. The concern Agricola says
not only obtrudes in other parts of the *Organon* but beclouds the discussion in the very
Topics themselves.... [Agricola] does not care, he adds, *how* one thing applies to another, provided only that it apply and that the application be teachable. He wants a dialectic
purged of psychological and epistemological implications, built not out of an account
of the nature of human knowledge but out of a list of the topics as objects of common
knowledge on which discourse turns." Ong, *Ramus*, 106. In conjunction with this, Ong
cites *De Inventione* lib 1, c. 3. P. Mack has suggested that the meaning of the term "probable" for Agricola is quite broad, seeming to extend in some isolated cases to scientific
proof. Peter Mack, *Renaissance Argument: Valla and Agricola in the Traditions of Dialectic and Rhetoric*, Studies in Intellectual History, vol. 33 (Leiden: Brill, 1993), 171. However, Moss and Wallace convincingly argue that these references to certainty can be better
understood with reference to the effect of the argument on the audience, rather than
the structure of the argument itself. Jean Dietz Moss and William Wallace, *Rhetoric and
Dialectic in the Time of Galileo* (Washington, D.C.: The Catholic University of America
Press, 2003), 29.

28. Humanists tended to focus more on Aristotle's *Ethics, Politics,* and *Rhetoric* rather than his metaphysical works. Through the impetus of Leonardo Bruni and others, a
"humanistic Aristotelianism" began to emerge. Edward Mahoney, "Aristotle and Some
Late Medieval and Renaissance Philosophers," in *The Impact of Aristotelianism on Modern Philosophy*, ed. Riccardo Pozzo, Studies in Philosophy and the History of Philosophy, vol. 39 (Washington, D.C.: The Catholic University of America Press, 2004), 7.

quently. Agricola's approach to Aristotle was hardly that of scholasticism, however. Under the influence of nominalism, scholastic logic had drifted away from its moorings in experience; broadly speaking, the humanist movement manifested a desire for what could be called rhetorical realism—that is, a rhetoric unencumbered by the abstractions of scholastic dialectic and more closely connected with human experience. Agricola clearly shared this desire but was more inclined to see the humanist project as complementary to the work of Aristotle and Boethius.

Like other humanists, Agricola was deeply concerned with rhetoric and wished to give it special emphasis. Like Valla, Agricola focused more on probability and persuasion than on logical certainty and tended to view all knowledge in light of practical human application.[29] To this end, Agricola rejected the distinction between rhetoric and dialectic and sought a form of logical reasoning that was both practical and rhetorically effective.[30] For humanists more interested in classical literature than in scholastic abstractions, Agricola made the tradition of rhetoric relevant once more, engaging with Cicero, Boethius, and most especially Aristotle.[31]

Although rhetoric complemented dialectic for Aristotle, Agricola effectively subordinates dialectic to rhetoric, rather than to logic itself.[32] The humanist focus on rhetoric was intended to yield a kind of practical realism in speech and writing which could be termed "rhetorical realism." For Aristotle, however, there is a sense in which the primacy of logic preserves actual metaphysical realism: for Aristotle, demonstration—which yields true knowledge (*scientia*) of a nature through its cause—is an important dimension of realist epistemology. When this realism is lacking, epistemology is limited to probabili-

29. A. J. Vanderjagt, "Rudolph Agricola on ancient and medieval philosophy," in *Rudolphus Agricola Phrisius 1444–1485: Proceedings of the International Conference at the University of Groningen 28–30 October 1985*, ed. F. Akkerman and A. J. Vanderjagt (Leiden: Brill, 1988), 221–22.

30. Marc Van der Poel, "Rudolph Agricola's De Inventione Dialectica libri tres," *Vivarium* 32 (1994): 104.

31. F. Muller, "Le *De inventione dialectica* d'Agricola dans la tradition rhétorique d'Aristote à Port-Royal," in *Rudolphus Agricola Phrisius*, 282. See also C.G. Meerhoff, "Agricola et Ramus—dialectique et rhétorique," in *Rudolphus Agricola Phrisius*, 271.

32. F. Muller, "Le *De inventione dialectica* d'Agricola dans la tradition rhétorique d'Aristote à Port-Royal," 282.

ty. The failure to appreciate the value of scientific demonstration mirrors other metaphysical assumptions that undergird the thought of Valla, Agricola, and other humanist rhetoricians.

Although rhetorical realism was frequently intended to stand in contrast to the syllogistic abstractions of scholasticism, the transition from scholasticism to humanism was infrequently seamless, and many humanists remained subconsciously indebted to scholasticism and medieval thought to varying degrees.[33] Valla himself was not immune to the influence of late scholasticism. In an attempt to simplify the categories of logic to conform more directly to his understanding of descriptive language, Valla dramatically reduced the Aristotelian categories to only substance, quality, and action, ruling out relation and the other categories of being to create a worldview resembling nominalism.[34] On the subject of singulars and universals, Valla's support for the nominalist position was explicit.[35] In Valla's case, the tension between these metaphysical assumptions and his desire for realism in speech and writing is self-defeating: if logical and rhetorical connections cannot be related to causal connections between actually existing things, whatever realism is achieved in argument or in prose can only be rhetorical.

Agricola, by contrast, appears more moderate; unlike Valla, he argued for the extramental existence of universals.[36] Although Agricola's overtures of realism make him seemingly attractive, concerning the individuation of singulars Agricola aligned himself explicitly with Scotus. For Scotus, it is *haecceitas* which distinguishes between sin-

33. *NCE*[1] s.v. "Humanism."

34. Lodi Nauta, "Lorenzo Valla and the Rise of Humanist Dialectic," in *The Cambridge Companion to Renaissance Philosophy*, ed. James Hankins (New York: Cambridge University Press, 2007), 199. Nauta is clear, however, that significant differences between Valla and nominalism remain. Lodi Nauta, "Lorenzo Valla," in *The Stanford Encyclopedia of Philosophy* (Summer 2013), Edward N. Zalta, ed., http://plato.stanford.edu/archives/sum2013/entries/lorenzo-valla/.

35. Valla *Dialectica*, lib. 1 c. 3–4 of 2; as cited by Monfasani, "Lorenzo Valla and Rudolph Agricola," 190–91.

36. Agricola, *De Inventione* lib. 1 c. 6–7; as cited by Monfasani, "Lorenzo Valla and Rudolph Agricola," 190–91. While some have associated Agricola with either nominalism or realism without qualification, Nauta argues for a more nuanced view of Agricola's position on universals. Lodi Nauta, "From Universals to Topics: The Realism of Rudolph Agricola, with an edition of his Reply to a Critic," *Vivarium* 50 (2012): 192–93.

gulars, not the subsistent actuation of matter.[37] Although Agricola's project is not as radical as Valla's, there is clearly room in Agricola for non-Aristotelian approaches to causality, despite his interest in Aristotle's topics. If there is a form of realism at work here, therefore, it falls short of the metaphysical and ontological realism necessary to sustain Aristotelian hylomorphism.

Although the rise of humanism can in some ways be seen as a reaction to the disconnect between speculative logic and the real in nominalism, simply emphasizing the category of rhetoric will do little to address this problem. For Aristotle, rhetoric and dialectic are not distinguished by their degree of association with the real; both are rooted in the truth of reality. However, this connection with reality is dependent on an ontologically robust understanding of logical demonstration in which *scientia* is allowed unfettered access to natures in themselves. For Aristotle, demonstrative knowledge of natures and their causes is scientific and therefore certain. By contrast, both rhetoric and dialectic taken in themselves lack the certainty of logical demonstration.[38]

37. Scotus, *Quest. Metaph.* Lib. 7, q. 7 and qq. 8–16. Peter King, "Scotus on Singular Essences," *Medioevo* 30 (2005): 111. While the term *haecitas* is generally used to describe Scotus' theory of individuation, Scotus employs a number of terms to describe this concept. See King, "Scotus," 121n17. The question of individuation has been the subject of some recent debate among Scotists, much of which has been recently summarized by Richard Cross: "Duns Scotus—Some Recent Research," *Journal of the History of Philosophy* 49, no. 3 (July 2011): 275–79. J. Monfasani quotes Agricola's work on universals to show his implicit dependence on Scotus, although the term *Haecceitas* is not used: "In the insert *de universalibus* between chaps. 6 and 7 of Book. I of the *De inv. dial*... : 'Sed singularia in universali conveniunt, ut Socrates et Plato conveniunt quatenus uterque est homo. Differunt autem singulari quatenus hic est Socrates, ille vero Plato, uterque, scilicet, ab altero, notione vel proprietate addita humanitati, cuius simile non est in ullo alio inveniri [invenire *editio*]. Quam, qui Ioannis Scoti sectam tuentur, differentiam individualem vocant.' See also Book x, chap. 26: 'Scotus, omnium qui philosophiam tractaverunt disputator multorum consensu acerrimus.' Agricola also mentions Scotus at the end of Book 2, chap. 23." Monfasani, "Lorenzo Valla and Rudolph Agricola," 191n52. L. Nauta concurs: "[Agricola] seems to follow Scotist teaching in thinking that universals as common nature exist independent from the intellect but that 'community' is something that arises only because the mind notices and judges things as similar in a particular respect." Nauta, "From Universals to Topics," 204. See also H.A.G. Braakhuis, "Agricola's View on Universals," in *Rudolphus Agricola Phrisius*, 244–45. See also Allan Wolter, "John Duns Scotus," in *Individuation in Scholasticism: The Later Middle Ages and the Counter-Reformation, 1150–1650*, ed. Jorge Gracia (Albany, N.Y.: State University of New York Press, 1994), 271–98.

38. Aristotle, *Rhet.* I.1–2, 1354a–1357a. William Wallace, *The Elements of Philosophy:*

However, rhetoric and dialectic are still realist for Aristotle. They concern truths of reality, and in the hands of one who possesses demonstrative knowledge of the real, both rhetoric and dialectic can serve to advance the cause of truth. When a certain truth is accepted as demonstrable, dialectic can advance the conversation about possibilities and contingents among those who either already possess scientific knowledge of certain principles or are at least willing to accept them for the sake of argument. Furthermore, if something is known by demonstration, this knowledge can be communicated to a popular audience through rhetoric. Even in the case of contingent or probable truths, rhetoric can serve to promote the judgment of a wise man concerning a practical situation.

In order to escape the charge of sophistry, however, the objectivity of both rhetoric and dialectic require that they be grounded in metaphysical realism; that is, rhetoric and dialectic must remain accountable to scientific knowledge of natures in themselves through their causes. Although many humanists believed that a renewed emphasis on rhetoric could remedy the perceived deficiencies of speculative logic, for Aristotle and Aquinas the shift to rhetoric does not bring a heightened grasp of the real. When a realist approach to logical demonstration is lacking, simply emphasizing either rhetoric or dialectic can never rectify those underlying metaphysical assumptions which undermined realism in the first place.

In the end, however, although Agricola was interested in Aristotelian ideas, faithful exposition of Aristotle was not so much his aim. Agricola was primarily interested in creating a system of thought that could serve the needs of Renaissance humanism. For Agricola, the distinction between scientific demonstration and probable reasoning is not clearly maintained, and in the end Agricola favors a definition of dialectic which enables probable reasoning that produces conviction in its audience.[39] To this end, Agricola uses the topics as a source for dialectical and rhetorical argumentation, leaving little room for

---

A Compendium for Philosophers and Theologians (New York: Alba House, 2014), 35. Moss and Wallace, Rhetoric and Dialectic in the Time of Galileo, 13–17. See also Robin Smith, "Aristotle's Logic," The Stanford Encyclopedia of Philosophy (Spring 2014), Edward N. Zalta, ed., plato.stanford.edu/archives/spr2014/entries/aristotle-logic/.

39. Ong, Ramus, 101.

the more abstract concepts of demonstration and *scientia*. Agricola is concerned with building a system that can extend to all areas of study, enabling the student to draw arguments from a variety of disciplines.[40] By providing an updated list of "topics," Agricola hopes to provide a dialectical structure that can unite the emerging humanist disciplines into a coherent whole. For Agricola the topics provide a commonality in argumentation that advances the project of dialectical conversation among diverse disciplines, even if demonstrative *scientia* is not emphasized.

DE LOCIS

The influence of Agricola's approach to rhetoric and the organization of topics or "loci" can be seen clearly in Cano's larger work on theological method that he began during his time at Salamanca: *De Locis Theologicis*.[41] *De Locis* was Cano's principal work in dogmatic theology; unlike many of his contemporaries, Cano never published a commentary on the *Sentences* or the *Summa*.[42] *De Locis* attracted broad interest and is considered by many to be the founding document of modern fundamental theology.[43]

In *De Locis*, Cano proposes an original approach to the organization of theological study marked on a methodological level by the

40. Nauta, "Lorenzo Valla and the Rise of Humanist Dialectic," 205–7.

41. Although published posthumously in 1563, the project which eventually became *De Locis* was most likely begun by Cano as early as 1546, during his first year at Salamanca. Mandonnet, 1538. See *NCE*[2] s.v. "Cano, Melchior." Cano's *De Locis* (along with Cano's other works) can be found in Jacque-Hyacinth Serry's 1734 edition of his *Opera*. Subsequently, an edition of *De Locis* appeared in J. P. Migne, *Theologiae Cursus Completus*, vol. 1 (Paris: 1860), 58–715. Recently, Juan Belda Plans has also produced a Spanish edition of the text (Madrid: Biblioteca de Autores Cristianos, 2006). The Serry edition (cited here) contains the complete works of Cano, as well as a defense of his doctrines by Serry. See Melchior Cano, *Opera* (Facsimile Reprint of the Hyacinth Serry Edition, Padua: Typis Seminarii, 1734) (Kila, Mont.: Kessinger, 2011).

42. *LThK*[3] s. v. "Cano, Melchior."

43. Belda Plans argues that Agricola was the principal inspiration for *De Locis*. Belda Plans, *La Escuela de Salamanca*, 552. Many theological manuals from the nineteenth and twentieth century owed more to Cano's *De Locis* than to Aquinas' *Summa*. See Lang, *Die Loci Theologici des Melchior Cano und die Methode des Dogmatischen Beweises*; Jared Wicks, *A Note on* "Neo-scholastic" *Manuals of Theological Instruction, 1900–1960," Josephinum* 18n1 (2011): 242.

influence of Agricola's *De Inventione Dialectica*.[44] Agricola attempted to conform the *loci* of classical rhetoric to the needs of Renaissance humanism; in *De Locis*, Cano attempts to do the same for theology, articulating and synthesizing the sources (or *loci*) of theology in order to present a comprehensive model for pursuing theological study within an intellectual climate marked by the rising influence of the European Renaissance. To this end, Cano's presentation of the "loci" of theology allows the relative weight of various authorities and scholarly sources to be combined in a single methodological approach to theology that would prove useful in view of the ecclesiastical and social needs of his day. For Cano, these *loci* range from traditional theological sources such as Scripture and Tradition to more secular disciplines drawn from the emerging Renaissance, such as the humanist and natural sciences and the study of human history.[45] Because the humanist movement was generally more concerned with persuasive argument than with speculative proof, in *De Locis* Cano positions theology in such a way that it can function in a convinc-

---

44. Lang, *Melchior Cano*, 918. For a discussion of the role of Aristotle's *Topics* in *De Locis*, see Körner, *Melchior Cano: De Locis Theologicis*, 24–29, 142–46.

45. In *De Locis* Cano identifies ten sources for theology: (1) the writings of Scripture, (2) Apostolic (or oral) tradition, (3) the authority of the Catholic Church, (4) Councils, (5) the Church of Rome, (6) the Holy Fathers (such as saints and doctors of the Church), (7) scholastic theologians, (8) natural reason and humanist sciences, (9) philosophers, and (10) historical studies. See *De Locis Theologicis* in Melchior Cano, *Opera*, Serry edition, 1734. See also Mandonnet, 1539. Cano's interest in historical studies, human sciences, and a textual approach to Scripture (which he juxtaposes to "Tradition" and received modes of interpretation) point to the influence of humanism. Further, there is evidence of other contemporary political and ecclesiastical tensions here as well: the division of ecclesial authority between Church, councils and Roman authority reflects a set of social, political, and ecclesiological issues which no doubt stem from his own involvement in Spanish ecclesiastical and secular politics. Suffice to say, however, that the concern to balance these authorities indicates a decidedly modern hermeneutic, reflecting the debates over conciliarism, papal authority, and Scripture that marked the changing conceptions of ecclesiology in Spain and wider Europe during the sixteenth century. See Horst, *The Dominicans and the Pope*, 48–50. *De Locis* has also attracted the interest of modern scholars interested in ecclesiology and Church authority. See Ulrich Horst, *Unfehlbarkeit und Geschichte: Studien zur Unfehlbarkeitdiskussion von Melchior Cano bis zum I. Vatikanischen Konzil* (Mainz: Matthias-Grünewald-Verlag, 1982). Elmar Klinger, *Ekklesiologie der Neuzeit: Grundlegung bei Melchior Cano und Entwicklung bis zum 2. Vatikanischen Konzil* (Vienna: Herder, 1978). See also Lang, *Die Loci Theologici des Melchior Cano und die Methode des Dogmatischen Beweises*.

ing and relevant manner alongside other, newer intellectual trends.[46] Given the changing intellectual climate of the academy, Cano's principal concern in *De Locis* is to balance differing sources in such a way that the discipline of theology can continue within a cogent and commonly agreed upon framework. Because of this, Cano's humanism is most visible at the hermeneutical level, where questions of methodology and integration are driven by the eclecticism and intellectual pluralism of Renaissance intellectual culture. It may well be that Cano's direct engagement with humanism was an attempt to defend against its risks.[47] On apologetical grounds, common principles are essential for any rhetorically convincing defense of the faith. However, one is rarely able to accept an opponent's premises and method without ceding to some of his conclusions as well.

Whatever Cano's intentions in crafting *De Locis*, the text played a central role in the emerging struggles over curriculum in the arts and theology at Salamanca. *De Locis* was composed during a period in which the University of Salamanca was attempting to reconcile the new challenges of Renaissance humanism with the older scholastic traditions still present at the University. Traditionally, instruction in theology presumed that the student has completed a preparatory course in philosophy; humanism changed the way in which the arts curriculum was organized, however, and many found that Cano's *De Locis* provided a smoother interface between theology and the new educational landscape of the Renaissance. Because of its eclectic methodology and sympathy for humanism, for some Cano's *De Locis* came to represent a new alternative to scholastic methodology.[48]

Although not treated extensively in *De Locis*, Cano's sacramen-

---

46. Following along these same lines, Cano's concerns extend beyond the relationship between theology and Renaissance humanism. He also intends to provide his students with the tools to defend the faith amid the challenges to orthodoxy that were arising in the sixteenth century due to the Protestant Reformation. *De Locis* closes with a chapter on the use of these sources in theological disputations. There were two successive chapters planned that would have discussed the use of these sources in the exposition of Scripture and in debates with adversaries of the Catholic faith. However, these were left incomplete at the time of Cano's death. *NCE*[2] s.v. "Cano, Melchior."

47. See Horst, *The Dominicans and the Pope*, 50.

48. Although the *Summa* had replaced Lombard's *Sentences* as the basic text of theological instruction by the middle of the sixteenth century, not all applauded this shift. A formal attempt to reform the curriculum at Salamanca began in 1771. Significant

tal theology evidences the same humanist influences that shaped his hermeneutical approach to theology in *De Locis*, and the same historical currents which fuelled the popularity of *De Locis* would advance Cano's approach to sacramental causality as an attractive alternative to Thomism in the post-Tridentine period.

CANO ON THE SACRAMENTS:
MORAL CAUSALITY

From the beginning of his time at Salamanca, Cano was actively engaged with topics in sacramental theology, including sacramental causality. During the summer months it had been the practice of Vitoria to offer *relectiones* or disputations that dealt with current topics in theology. When he arrived at Salamanca, Cano continued this practice. In 1547, the topic of Cano's *relectio* was the nature of the sacraments and their efficacy.[49] Cano's work, *Relectio de Sacramentis in Genere*, is a direct outgrowth of this disputation and was first published in 1550.[50] Although it was published much later, a great deal of material that would eventually become part of *De Locis* was begun around this time as well.[51] Accordingly, many of the wider trends that affect Cano's methodological approach to theology proposed in *De Locis*, can be seen at work in a more specific sense in his treatment of sac-

---

portions of the arts faculty argued forcefully to replace St. Thomas' *Summa* with Cano's *De Locis* (whole or in part), although there was strong resistance from elements of the theological faculty. See George M. Addy, *The Enlightenment in the University of Salamanca* (Durham, N.C.: Duke University Press, 1966), 116–17, 189–202.

49. Newman, "*Jus Divinum*," 7.

50. Ibid., 18.

51. Cano had certainly begun this work when he returned to Salamanca in 1546. *LThK*² s. v. "Cano, Melchior." Belda Plans believes that it is very possible that Cano began this project as early as 1543, while still at Alcalá. Belda Plans, *La Escuella de Salamanca*, 553–54. The topic of his *relectio* for the summer of 1548 was the sacrament of Penance, and this was eventually published as *Relectio de Sacramento Poenitentiae*. Newman, "*Jus Divinum*," 7. In 1548 Cano began lecturing on the *Prima Pars* during the regular academic year, and the *relectiones* for the summers of 1548–49 may well have concerned theological sources related to Cano's study of the *Prima Pars*, the results of which were eventually incorporated into *De Locis* itself. Newman, 17–18. In making this claim, Newman relies primarily on the work of V. de Heredia. See Vincente Beltran de Heredia, "Melchior Cano en la Unversidad de Salamanca," *La Ciencia Thomistica*, 48 (1933): 189.

ramental causality. Cano's affinity for humanist hermeneutical methods, shown in the composition of *De Locis*, is present in his treatment of the sacraments as well. In this case, however, it would be the humanist emphasis on rhetoric that would exercise the most direct influence on Cano's presentation of the sacraments.

In his *Relectio de Sacramentis*, Cano argues that the sacraments are moral, rather than natural (or physical) causes of grace. This concept was not unique to Cano, who most likely inherited some version of this theory from Vitoria.[52] In *De Sacramentis*, Cano distinguishes between two species of efficient causality: "natural" causes and "moral" causes.[53] For Cano, a moral cause is that which induces the free will to act. Unlike a natural cause, which touches (*attingere*) the finality which it effects, a moral cause makes no such contact with the effected end. Rather, it convinces another agent to act in a physically causal manner.[54] A moral cause is a kind of convincing speech, which

52. It has been argued that Vitoria communicated this teaching to Melchior Cano and Martin Ledesma, both of whom were his students. Aloisius Ciappi, *De Sacramentis in Communi: Commentarius in Tertiam Partem S. Thomae (qq. LX–LXV)*, Pontificum Institutum Internationale Angelicum (Turin: R. Berruti, 1957), 71n7. Cano and Ledesma may have influenced each other , although Vásquez claims that Ledesma taught the concept before Cano. Vásquez, *In III*, disp. 132, a. 5. As in Michael Gierens, ed., *De Causalitate Sacramentorum seu de Modo Explicandi Efficientiam Sacramentorum Novae Legis: Textus scholasticorum Principaliorum*, in vol. a6 of Textus et Documenta, Series Theologica (Rome: Pontificia Universitas Gregoriana, 1935), 113. John F. Gallagher suggests that, although there are similarities between moral causality and the *sine qua non* tradition, moral causality may bear closer resemblance to the theories of fourteenth-century thinkers like Peter Aureol and John of Bassalis. Gallagher, *Significando Causant : A Study of Sacramental Efficiency*, Studia Fribugensia New Series 40 (Fribourg: The University Press, 1965), 154n1, 158.

53. "Sacramenta non sint gratiae causa finalis, aut materialis, aut formalis, colligimus, esse causas efficientes ... causas esse in duplici differentia, alteras naturales, alteras morales." *Relect. de Sacram.*, Pars IV, concl. 6, in Melchior Cano, *Opera*, 487–88. "Sacramenta esse causas efficientes instrumentales nostrae salutis, gratiae, & justitiae, loquendo de causa morali." *Relect. de Sacram.*, Pars IV, concl. 6, in Melchior Cano, *Opera*, 489. See also Antonio Belda Plans, "Estudio Historico-Sistematico de la Releccion 'De Sacramentis in Genere' de Melchior Cano" (PhD diss., Universidad de Navarra, 1985), 83.

54. "Causas esse in duplici differentia, alteras naturales, alteras morales. Morales autem appellamus causas liberas, quae scilicet libere movent: ut qui consulit, qui imperat, ejus rei causa est, quae per ejus aut imperium, aut consilium efficitur. Juxta quam distinctionem cum actio peccati dupliciter consideratur, & in ordine effectuum naturalium, & in ordine effectuum moralium, Deus quidem causa naturalis dicitur actionis, quae peccatum est: concurrit siquidem ad brachii motionem, qua hominem interficio,

induces another to action.[55] To illustrate this, Cano offers the example of a person who counsels another to commit murder: while the
natural cause of the murder may be a stick in the murderer's hand,
the one who counsels murder functions as a moral cause of the murder itself.[56] The natural cause "touches" (*attingere*) the end of murder
while the moral cause does not, and yet both effect this same end.

Although he makes no direct textual reference to Cajetan, it is
quite possible that Cano is aware of Cajetan's position: as has been
shown earlier, it was Cajetan who first argued that, in the *Summa*,
Aquinas describes the sacraments as perfective physical instrumental causes, "touching" (*attingere*) the finality of grace through their
instrumental motion guided by divine agency. On this subject, Cajetan's position eventually came to be taken as an expression of the
collective wisdom of the Thomistic school, which had steadily deepened its appreciation for Aquinas' teaching on instrumental causality over the centuries, particularly in the case of sacramental causality.

In *De Sacramentis*, Cano seems to be aware of Aquinas' mature
doctrine of natural instrumental causality, describing the sharpness
of the saw as "touching" (*attingere*) its final effect: the division of the
branch.[57] However, it seems that Cano does not appreciate the instrumental dimension of this action and takes the term *attingere* to mean

---

quemadmodum & coelum, motorque angelus simul etiam concurrit. At concursus hic
naturalis est: non tamen illius actionis Deus est causa moralis: neque enim aut consulit,
aut praecipit, quin potius prohibet. Inter has autem causas discrimen est. Nam naturales
suos effectus attingunt per vim a natura inditam, ut ignis calefacit per calorem. Morales
vero non attingunt actione physica effectus suos, nec influunt, aut producunt qualitates
aliquas. Neque enim oportet, ut qui consulit homicidium, actione aliqua physica & naturali quicquam efficiat, quemadmodum natura efficere consuevit." *Relect. de Sacram.*,
Pars IV, concl. 6, in Melchior Cano, *Opera*, 488.

55. "Causa morali, qualis oratio fuit." *Relect. de Sacram.*, Pars IV, concl. 6, in Melchi-
or Cano, *Opera*, 488.

56. Text as in note 54. In fairness to Cano, he does not compare sacramental activity
directly to murder. Rather, he knowingly invokes an example of bad moral behavior to
explain the nature of a moral cause. The reference to a stick in the hand may well be an
allusion to Aquinas' doctrine of sacramental causality. See *ST* III[a] Q. 62 a. 5 co.

57. "Sacramentum novae legis non attingit vi sua instrumentali & supernaturali
qualitatem, quae est gratia, vel fidem, aut charitatem, aut alios habitus infusos, ut serra attingit figuram rei artificiosae actione reali." *Relect. de Sacram.*, Pars IV, concl. 5, in
Melchior Cano, *Opera*, 487. For Aquinas' employment of this metaphor in the context
of the sacraments, see *ST* III[a] 62 a. 1 co.

only physical contact.[58] For Aquinas, the saw blade certainly "touches" the tree it cuts. However, it also "touches" (*attingere*) the finality towards which the sharpness of its blade has been directed by the artist who wields it (the stool, table or house, for example)—ends with which the blade itself makes no physical contact, except through the potency of its action as an instrumental efficient cause. To a large extent, what the instrument "touches' in this sense depends on the finality of the artist. It is this understanding of instrumental efficient causality that allows Aquinas to argue that the causal capacity of natural thing—the saw-blade or the water of Baptism—can be directed towards supernatural purposes by the divine artist, in which case even these same natural causes come to participate and "touch" (*attingere*) a supernatural end.[59] However, Cano does not follow Aquinas in this regard and argues that because of the insufficiency of natural causes, some other quality or power would need to be added to them to effect grace.[60] Cano's brevity and rhetorical style make it difficult to investigate his stance on this issue more thoroughly. Nonetheless, it seems that he has not fully appropriated the Thomistic tradition on this point. In particular, his approach seems to imply an incomplete grasp of the dynamic of act and potency.

Although Cano's approach is not identical to *sine qua non* causality, certain parallels do exist between Cano's account of moral causality and sacramental occasionalism. For Cano, no physical motion whatsoever is involved in the working of a moral cause. As a metaphysical system, occasionalism obscures the potency of secondary efficient causes in order to avoid compromising divine power and freedom. The sacramental implications of occasionalist metaphysics tend towards some version of the theory of pact, in which God institutes the sacraments in complete freedom by establishing juridical processes or occasions, the correct use of which he subsequently chooses to

58. There is a certain parallel here with Scotus' sacramental theory; Scotus questions the ability of words and syllables, which move the air through sound, to produce the supernatural end proper to the sacraments. Duns Scotus, *Op.Ox.* IV.1.4–5.5. Wadding (*Opera Omnia, 1639*), 8.82–83. See note 75.

59. This dimension of Aquinas' teaching is expounded in detail in chapter 3 of this book.

60. "Sine nova virtute addita sacramenta id efficere, quod ante non poterant." *Relect. de Sacram.*, Pars IV, concl. 5, in Melchior Cano, *Opera*, 487.

reward. No reference to natural potency is necessary; instead, meta-physical voluntarism is the sole operative category. For Cano, the physical things that make up sacramental signs (and thus constitute our point of contact with sacramental realities) are not instruments through which God operates in the Thomistic sense. Cano does imply that there is a physical or efficient cause at work that "touches" (*attingere*) the end of grace—the murderer with stick in hand—but it seemingly cannot be the sacraments themselves, which can be causally responsible only in the moral sense. Although Cano claims that the sacraments can still be considered efficient causes in the moral sense, Cano's rejection of the sacraments as natural or physical causes recalls the *sine qua non* tradition, which downplayed the role of natural or secondary causality and claimed that God alone was the only true efficient cause of grace. Cano lacks the technical approach of earlier occasionalists, and in this his approach is consistent with humanist methodology. However, although Cano's theory lacks the deeper metaphysical framework that sustained *sine qua non* causality in the thought of Auvergne and others, his treatment of natural causes bears a certain structural similarity to metaphysical occasionalism.

Although Cano's rejection of the sacraments as natural causes is in continuity with scholastic occasionalism, his description of the sacraments themselves as causes does seem to break with this tradition to some degree. As was mentioned in the first chapter, for Cano recent decrees of the Council of Trent made it necessary to distance his theory from strict occasionalism. Although the theory of moral causality may slightly predate Cano himself, Cano's treatment of moral causality is very much tied to the decrees of the Council. Cano's *relectio* on the sacraments *in genere* was given in the summer of 1547, directly after the promulgation in March of that same year of the seventh session of the Council, which dealt with the efficacy of sacraments.[61] In his *relectio*, Cano makes reference to the Council frequently and frames much of his teaching around the interpretation of canon six, which teaches that the sacraments contain (*continere*) the grace which they signify and confer (*confero*) this grace to those

61. Session 7 of the Council of Trent was promulgated on March 3, 1547. Norman Tanner, ed., *Decrees of the Ecumenical Councils*, vol. 2 (Washington, D.C.: Georgetown University Press, 1990), 684.

who are disposed to receive it, explicitly ruling out any reduction of
the sacraments to mere external signs.[62] Aquinas argued that *sine qua
non* causality reduced the sacraments to signs alone, and after Trent
many believed that sacramental occasionalism was not compatible
with the mind of the Council.[63] Because Trent insisted that the sacraments "contain" and "confer" grace, Cano must argue that there is
some power at work in the sacraments themselves. More than a mere
occasion for the reception of grace, Cano's moral cause seems to imply some power of persuasion (if not efficient motion) present in the
cause itself.

What then, is "contained" in the sacraments that can achieve
this moral effect? Cano argues that the power at work in the sacraments—the so-called moral cause—is the blood of Jesus Christ.
Consequently, Cano asserts that the sacraments function not in the
realm of physical or natural effect but in the order of merit.[64] Clear-

---

62. Cano cites the Council: "Hanc eandem sententiam Concilium Tridentium
modo probavit sessione septima de sacramentis in communi, canone sexto, cujus verba ejusmodi sunt: Si quis dixerit, sacramenta novae legis non continere gratiam, quam
significant, aut gratiam ipsam non ponentibus obicam non conferre, quasi signa tantum
externa sint acceptae per fidem gratiae vel iustitiae...a. s." *Relect. de Sacram.*, Pars IV,
concl. 6, in Melchior Cano, *Opera*, 485. See Conc. Trid. Sess. 7 decl. 1 c. 6.

63. See *ST* III^a Q. 62, a. 1, co. Despite their other theological differences, both Suarez and Vasquez agree that occasionalism no longer offers a viable explanation of sacramental causality. Suarez, *In IIIa*, q. 62 a. 4, disp. 9. Vasquez, *In IIIa*, q. 62, a. 4, disp. 132.
P. Pourrat, *Theology of the Sacraments: A Study in Positive Theology*, 4th ed. (St. Louis:
Herder), 185.

64. "Deinde magnopere considerandum, omnia quae de Sacramentis novae legis
asseruntur, eadem & de sanguine Christi in sacris literis affirmari–1. Joan. I. Sanguis Jesu
Christi emundat nos ab omni peccato. Apoc. I. Lavit nos a peccatis nostris in sanguine
suo. & c. 12. Vicerunt eum propter sanguinem agni: & ad Rom. 3. quem proposuit Deus
propitiationem in sanguine ipsius. Eodem ergo sensu Sacramenta dici poterunt lavare,
mundare, causae esse nostrae victoria ac remissionis peccatorum, quo sanguis Christi
lavat, mundat, peccataque remittit." *Relect. de Sacram.*, Pars IV, concl. 6, in Cano, *Opera*, 488. Cano's reference to Romans 3:25 requires some qualification: "Iustificati gratis
per gratiam ipsius, per redemptionem, quae est in Christo Iesu, quem proposuit Deus
propitiationem per fidem in sanguine ipsius, ad ostensionem iustitiae suae propter remissionem praecedentium delictorum in sustentatione Dei, ad ostensionem iustitiae
eius in hoc tempore: ut sit ipse iustus, et iustificans eum, qui est ex fide Iesu Christi."
Rom. 3:24–26. *Biblia Sacra iuxta Vulgatam Clementiam novo editio*, eds. Alberto Colun-
ga and Laurentio Turrado, 12th ed. (Madrid: Biblioteca de Autores Cristianos, 2005).
This text, taken from the Clementine Vulgate, reads *"per fidem in sanguine ipsius,"* where
Cano's citation omits the phrase *"per fidem."* While this omission may very well be the

ly a theology of redemptive merit has broad scriptural warrant, and
Cano uses texts from Paul, 1st John, and Revelation to support this
claim.[65] To describe the meritorious quality of Christ's blood as a
form of moral causality, Cano uses the example of a Christian prisoner held captive by the Turks: in order to gain his freedom, a ransom
must be paid to the captor. According to Cano, a ransom paid in this
sense is a true instrumental cause of the redemption of the prisoner
but in the moral rather than the physical sense.[66] Although different
from Cano's example of murderous counsel, his metaphor of Turk-
ish captivity retains the essential dimension of persuasion: a moral
cause is an act of persuasion which convinces another party to act in
a physically causal manner. However, the offering of money for the
release of a prisoner strikes a more legalistic tone and recalls a classic
example from the *sine qua non* tradition: the leaden coin, of no value in itself but rendered an acceptable ransom in the eyes of the king
by divine decree. However, the subject of Cano's monetary analogy
is not entirely congruent with previous formulations: where earlier
proponents of the *sine qua non* tradition tended to use the coin to refer to the human performance of sacramental rites—clearly of no value taken apart from divine action—Cano's reference is to the action
of God alone. For Cano, the monetary sum contained in the sacraments—the blood of Christ—is of inherent value. No divine command or pact is necessary to render an otherwise worthless human
action valuable; it is the merit of Christ's passion itself which holds
the power to persuade.

---

result of textual variants, the larger context of faith in Christ in which this passage occurs renders it a less obvious reference to the blood of Christ as a form of efficient sacramental causality. However, Cano also cites I Jn. 1:7, where the image of washing from
sins has more discernible baptismal overtones. Cano further references I Cor. 1, where
the connection between Christian Baptism and the crucifixion is clearly drawn.

65. Although Cano's assertion that the sacraments contain the price of our redemption may tempt us to recall Hugh of St. Victor's claim that the sacraments contain grace
as medicine in a vial, Cano's emphasis on merit and volition belie later theological influences, of which the Victorines were unaware.

66. "Sacramenta esse causas efficientes instrumentales nostrae salutis, gratiae, &
justitiae, loquendo de causa morali.... Quemadmodum, si ego essem apud Turcas cap-
tivus, & eum qui daret pecunias redemptionis, videlicet pretium, & manum qua pecunias porrigeret, & pecunias etiam ipsas, quae sunt instrumenta ad redimendum, redemptionis causas esse, non naturales quidem, sed morales, nemo sanae mentis ibit
inficias." *Relect. de Sacram.*, Pars IV, concl. 6, in Melchior Cano, *Opera*, 489.

Cano's influences are broad and frequently difficult to quantify, but the influence of Renaissance humanism can certainly be seen in his approach to the sacraments. Although the structural influence of Agricola's *De Inventione* is far more visible in *De Locis*, the humanist emphasis on rhetoric can be detected in Cano's *Relectio de Sacramentis* as well, not only in the style of composition but in Cano's concept of moral causality itself. A moral cause is effective because it persuades. Early in his treatise, Cano gives the example of a written note, the contents of which can be called a cause with regard to subsequent effects.[67] Cano describes the moral cause as a form of persuasion or counsel rather than a natural cause. It is possible to employ dialectic to persuade, arguing that a certain conclusion is either necessary or probable. Cano's examples seem to fall outside the structure of logical syllogism, however. A note, or murderous counsel, seems rather to be examples of rhetoric, which, when effective, convinces the listener to accept the conclusion proposed. Clearly, a strict application of rhetorical persuasion in the common sense of the term could not be applied to the sacraments, especially after Trent, which taught that the sacraments confer grace by their own intrinsic power. Although Aristotle allows that counsel can be a form of efficient causality when it initiates movement towards an end, rhetoric does not bind the hearer by logical necessity: at times counsel may be accepted, at other times not.[68] Unlike a sermon which might possibly move the hearer to an act of faith, the sacraments give grace by the working of the sacramental rite itself, *ex opere operato*.[69] In order for the sacraments to function in this manner, they must be not only morally convincing but causally necessary. It is most likely for this reason that

67. "Consequentia videtur esse nota, quoniam id vocamus causam, qua applicata sequitur effectus." *Relectio de Sacramentis*, pars IV, in Melchior Cano, *Opera*, 483.

68. *Metaphysics*, bk. 5, c. 2, 1013a24–1013b16.

69. "Si quis dixerit, per ipsa novae legis sacramenta ex opere operato non conferri gratiam, sed solam fidem divinae promissionis ad gratiam consequendam sufficere: a.s." Conc. Trid. Sess. 7 decl. 1 c. 8. See Dominic Rover, "The Sacramental Efficacy of the Act of Preaching," *Proceedings of the CTSA* (1962): 241–47. B. Bernard Leeming also uses the example of a sermon to show the difference between the sacraments as causes *ex opere operato* and other elements of the Church's life which can also give grace, *ex opere operantis*. Leeming, *Principles of Sacramental Theology* (Westminster, Md.: Newman, 1963), 5–10.

Cano defines moral causality as a species of efficient causality. Although he does not accept the idea of the sacraments as instrumental causes in the Thomistic sense, because of the then recent decrees of Trent he must clearly avoid any appearance of occasionalism. However, one wonders if Cano has overextended the category of rhetoric in this case. While convincing speech might have the power to move another to act, it is not clear that the category of rhetoric is sufficient to describe the causal necessity of the sacraments, which cause their effects by the very working of the rite itself. That is, the sacraments, when correctly performed and worthily received, always effect the end for which they are intended. The same cannot be said of rhetorical speech.[70]

After the Council of Trent, moral causality became very popular in certain theological circles. Because radical occasionalism was no longer acceptable after Trent, most theologians felt the need to strengthen their sacramental theories to appear more objective and intrinsically efficacious. It needed to be made clear that there was real power at work in the sacraments themselves. Cano's system of moral causality offers this, by claiming that the power at work in the sacraments is the redemptive merit of Jesus Christ.[71] Cano's theory resonates immediately with the biblical text and conforms to the language of Trent itself: the sacraments function as true "moral" causes because they contain (*continere*) the blood of Jesus Christ as the price of our redemption. The merit of this blood then moves God to confer grace. For Cano, this saving effect is "contained" in the sacraments as causes, not in the manner that an effect is contained in a physical efficient cause but in the moral sense. As the price of ransom is contained in a purse and then dispensed in payment, so too is the price of our redemption contained in the sacraments.[72] For Cano, the sac-

---

70. Suarez argues a distinction between physical and moral causes on the grounds of necessity: while physical causes effect a thing *per se*, moral causes do not, although an effect may be imputed to it, as in the case of advice given or interference withheld, the imputation of moral responsibility can be said to have a causal quality to it, although this is clearly distinct from a physical cause which actually caused the effect *per se*. Suarez, *Metaphysical Disputations*, Disp. 17.6. See Francisco Suarez, *On Efficient Causality: Metaphysical Disputations 17, 18, and 19*, trans. Alfred Freddoso (New Haven, Conn.: Yale University Press, 1994), 16–17.

71. Pourrat, *Theology of the Sacraments*, 181–84.

72. "Sacramenta ... continere (in quam) non ut causa naturalis continet suum effec-

raments are no longer simply occasions that God chooses to bless; they actively accomplish what they signify.

If the category of rhetoric alone is insufficient, however, what then can describe the causal necessity, *ex opere operato*, of the sacraments themselves? Cano has already ruled out the instrumental involvement of physical things, leaving God alone as physical efficient cause. The category of rhetoric simply does not carry the necessary causal force, and it seems that for Cano, nothing is left in physics or metaphysics to sustain the functionality of the sacraments except divine decree. Despite Cano's efforts to the contrary, it seems that something resembling the theory of pact is implicitly necessary to maintain the sacraments as causes *ex opere operato*. Cano is careful to distance himself from the tradition of Auvergne, Bonaventure, and the nominalists by explicitly rejecting the theory of *sine qua non* causality.[73] In the end, however, he does not require his adherents to adopt metaphysical assumptions at variance with this same tradition.

Allowing for certain humanist conventions, the committed deontologist finds himself at home with Cano's theory: as a moral cause, the blood of Christ contained in the sacraments is rhetorically persuasive before the divine *imperium*. Seventeenth-century Scotists such as Bartolomeo Mastri (d. 1673) adopted the category of moral causality to defend the Scotist position after Trent.[74] Although Cano's theory is different in its form of expression and its context of origin, even its rhetorical emphasis would not be entirely unfamiliar to Scotus, who relies in part on an analysis of language to support his theory of sacramental efficacy.[75]

---

tum, sed ut causa moralis. Crumena siquidem continere dicitur captivi redemptionem, quoniam pecuniam continet: & Sacramenta, quae continent sanguinem Christi, continere dicuntur gratiam, & remissionem peccatorum: & sicut crumena pecuniam administrans redemptionem conferre; ita Sacramentorum virtus, quae adeo multorum ingenia torsit. Virtus enim redemptionis in marsupio est, in quo pretium redemptionis servatur; & virtus Sacramentorum sanguinis Christi est, qui in Sacramentis adhibetur." *Relect. de Sacram.*, Pars IV, concl. 6, in Melchior Cano, *Opera*, 489.

73. Cano explicitly distances himself from sacramental occasionalism by denying that the sacraments can be causes *sine qua non*. "Sacramentum novae legis non est causa sine qua non, sive per accidens." *Relect. de Sacram.*, Pars IV, concl. 4, in Melchior Cano, *Opera*, 486.

74. *In IV Sent.*, disp. I, q. 4, aa. 1–3. Bartolomaei Mastri de Meldula, *Disputationes Theologicae in Quartum Librum Sententiarum* (Venetiis, 1719), 24–34.

75. It is not entirely surprising that post-Tridentine Scotists took so readily to

Beyond this, there is a crucial ambiguity in Cano's application of the category of moral causality to the case of the sacraments: does the category of moral cause apply to the sacraments themselves, or to what they contain? Here the mode in which the sacraments are said to "contain" becomes important. For Aquinas, the sacraments are instruments because they contain grace, as an effect is contained in the efficient cause. This makes the sacramental elements instrumental participants in the end that is effected by their instrumental motion, which is grace. Cano does say that the sacraments are causes of grace, and Trent insists that the sacraments "contain the grace which they signify."[76] Although Cano positions his theory as an interpretation of this canon,[77] he does not say that the sacraments contain grace but rather the meritorious blood of Jesus Christ. If this seems semantical, consider the implications of claiming that a created thing—such as the water of Baptism—participates as an instrumental cause in the merit of Jesus Christ. Although Aquinas clearly speaks of the meritorious causality of Christ's passion and of his humanity, the sacraments participate instrumentally in the conferral of grace, not in the meritorious action of Christ himself.

Despite the fact that Cano says that the sacraments are causes of grace, it is clear that the merits of the blood of Christ are the persuasive "moral cause" operative in his theory. Cano argues that this merit is "contained" in the sacraments like the price of ransom in a purse.[78]

Cano's theory. Beyond the external motivations found in the Tridentine decrees, there are elements within Scotus' theory of sacramental causality that dispose towards a rhetorical approach. Duns Scotus, in responding to the theory of physical instrumental causality, shows a certain obsession with words: Scotus asks whether instrumentality should be attributed to each syllable of the prayer (such as the Eucharistic prayer) in order that the prayer might have an immediate instrumental effect. Scotus asks whether the first, last, or middle syllable of a word or even a phrase is responsible instrumentally for causing. In this, he seems to rely on a certain understanding of motion: it is the formation of the syllable that moves the air locally as a kind of physical cause of its effect; even this, Scotus comments, is not instantaneous. Duns Scotus, *Op.Ox.* IV.1.4–5.5. Wadding, 8.82–83. Scotus will rely instead on his theory of divine pact with the Church to render these words and phrases causal.

76. "Sacramenta novae legis sunt causa gratiae, & vere salutem animae conferunt." *Relect. de Sacram.*, Pars IV, concl. 1, in Melchior Cano, *Opera*, 483. "Si quis dixerit, sacramenta novae legis non continere gratiam, quam significant … a.s." Conc. Trid. Sess. 7 decr. 1 c. 6.

77. See note 62.

78. Although Cano does not cite him, Augustine makes a similar reference in at

Although he does not discuss the way in which this merit is contained in the sacraments with any greater specificity, it would seem that it must be causally univocal, because any causal participation in the meritorious persuasion at work in the blood of Christ by a creaturely instrument would be unacceptable theologically. It is therefore not the sacramental signs and actions *per se* but what they are said to contain, that is the persuasive moral "cause." Can the purse be said to persuade of itself, or does it only signify the price which it contains? If then the purse—which for Cano represents the sacraments—does not participate causally in the persuasive act of the money it contains, it would seem that the sacraments themselves are thus reduced to signs and occasions, in which the univocal merit of Christ's blood is at work, convincing God to cause grace. In the end, it seems that Cano's theory is closer to the occasionalist leaden coin than originally supposed.

This poses difficulties vis-à-vis Trent, which clearly says that "grace is ... conferred by the sacraments of the New Law *ex opere operato.*"[79] Here, the phrase *ex opere operato* indicates more than even the causal necessity of logical demonstration in contrast to rhetoric. It means that grace is conferred through the sacramental action itself. If the persuasive "moral cause" is the merit of Christ's blood contained by the purse of the sacraments, how then is grace conferred through the action of the sacraments? Even allowing that the sacraments somehow contain the merit of Christ's blood, it would seem that they are still neither containers nor causes of the grace effected within the human soul.

And yet even if they do "contain" merit, Cano has not shown how this is possible. In what sense are the sacraments "containers"? For many during the scholastic period, from Hugh of St. Victor to Aqui-

---

least three places. In sermon 329, in Psalm 146, and Tract. 28 on John, Augustine refers to the purse containing the price of our redemption being opened on the cross by the soldier's lance. *Sermo* 329, 1–2 *PL* 38, 1454–55, *In Psalm.* 146.4 CCL 40: 2124, *Jo. Ev. Tr.* 28.2 CCL 36.278. In each of these three instances Augustine's imagery is explicitly incarnational and cruciform. Unlike Cano, Augustine's reference here is to Christ's act of redemption itself and not the sacramental mediation thereof. Although Cano may be ostensibly in accord with Augustine on the topic of justification, he is at odds with Augustine's sacramental realism, which contextualizes this doctrine of justification.

79. "Si quis dixerit, per ipsa novae legis sacramenta ex opere operato non conferri gratiam, sed solam fidem divinae promissionis ad gratiam consequendam sufficere: a.s." Conc. Trid. Sess. 7 decr. 1 c. 8.

nas, this was an important question which necessitated a discussion of natural potency in relation to divine ends. Roland of Cremona's use of efficient causality was accepted by many. By contrast, sacramental occasionalists such as Auvergne, Bonaventure, and Scotus were comparatively unconcerned with describing the sacraments as "containers" of grace. Instead, they were content to let the burden of efficient causality fall univocally on God. In eschewing Cremona's answer to this question, however, they reduced the sacramental rite to a mere occasion on which grace can be directly conferred by God. Although this may have been acceptable in the thirteenth century, Trent of course insists, in continuity with Augustine and the best of the scholastic tradition, that grace is conferred through the rite. We have already noted the seeming difference between the example of the leaden coin and moral causality: when the sacraments are considered as leaden coins they are understood as inherently worthless elements, rendered economically viable with respect to our redemption only by decree of the king. Although the merits of Christ's passion may be intrinsically valuable, Cano's theory does not extend this value to the sacraments themselves. Although Cano may have satisfied the letter of Trent, a closer study of his proposals reveals that the structural outline of sacramental occasionalism is still very much present beneath a fresh rhetorical veneer.

BAÑEZ

Domingo Bañez (d. 1604) was the first to respond to Cano's theory of moral causality from within the Thomist tradition. Bañez was a student at Salamanca when he entered the Dominican novitiate in 1546; during his time as a student at the University he studied with Melchior Cano and was most likely present for Cano's 1547 *Relectio* on the sacraments *in genera*.[80] Bañez strongly opposed Cano's theory of moral causality in his lectures, favoring instead the approach of Cajetan.[81]

---

80. Heredia, "Introduccion," in Bañez, *Comentarios Ineditos a la Tercera Parte de Santo Tomas*, vol. 2, *De Sacramentis: QQ. 60–90*, 6. NCE[1] s.v. "Báñez and Bañezianism."

81. See Bañez *in* III, q. 62, a. 1. Bañez, *Comentarios Ineditos a la Tercera Parte de Santo Tomas*, vol. 2, *De Sacramentis: QQ. 60–90*, 43–51. Although his commentaries on earlier

In his commentary on the *Tertia Pars*, Bañez argues that Cano's theory of moral causality is insufficient to describe the sacraments as causes. To illustrate his point, Bañez uses one of Cano's own examples against him: Cano had distinguished between a stick in the hand of the murderer (natural cause) and the one who counsels the murder (moral cause). Bañez readily agrees that the blood of Christ functions as a meritorious cause, but he insists that merit alone is not sufficient to describe the sacraments as causes of grace. He offers the example of an archer who aims an arrow and the one who counsels him to do so. The offering of counsel alone does not fully account for the release of the bow or the flight of the arrow.[82] Unlike Aquinas' theory of instrumental causality, in which the power of the principle agent to effect the intended end is conveyed through the instrument, Cano's moral cause is insufficient in itself to explain the attainment of the effect which it recommends. Cano himself makes this clear by distinguishing between a moral cause, which does not "touch" (attingere) the finality it counsels, and a natural cause, which does.

As was shown previously, Bañez argues that, while Christ's passion is certainly the meritorious cause of our redemption, this assertion must be accompanied by a discussion of the role of the sacramental elements themselves as physical instruments in the conferral of grace.[83] Bañez refocuses the conversation on core principles of Ar-

---

parts of Aquinas' *Summa* were published in the sixteenth century (Sections of the *Prima Pars* and the *Secunda Secundae* were published at Salamanca in 1584; the *Prima Pars* [q. 65 usque in finem] in 1588; the *Secunda Secundae* [q. 57–68 in 1594]), Bañez' comments on the *Tertia Pars* were not published until de Heredia's edition in the mid-twentieth century. Banez's commentary on the *Tertia Pars* was assembled in critical edition by V. B. de Heredia from various manuscripts that date from throughout his teaching career. Although Banez would permanently return to Salamanca in 1577 and take the first chair in theology in 1580, he spent the academic year of 1572–73 at Salamanca, during which time he lectured on the sacraments *in genere* (qq. 60–66). De Heredia's critical edition of his commentary on the *Tertia Pars* (qq. 60–62 a. 1) is taken from this period, which indicates that Bañez was teaching against moral causality by 1572, if not earlier. De Heredia, "Introduccion," in *Comentarios Ineditos a la Tercera Parte*, vol. 2, *De Sacramentis: QQ. 60–90*, 9, 19.

82. "Instrumentum causae moralis quod caret libero arbitrio non potest habere rationem efficientiae, nisi physice aliquam actionem habeat propriam. V gr., quando quis sagitta voluntarie occidit hominum, sagitta est instrumentum occisionis, habet tamen propriam actionem." Bañez, *in* III, q. 62 a. 1, concl. 5. See Bañez, *Comentarios Ineditos a la Tercera Parte*, vol. 2, 47.

83. This topic was discussed in chapter 3. See pp. 138–43.

istotelian physics such as motion, act and potency—principles which, for Aquinas, made it possible to describe the sacraments as "containing" grace, as an effect is contained in its efficient cause. Bañez claims that with respect to the causation of grace, moral and *sine qua non* causality are not so dissimilar. Bañez points out that the leaden coin approach to sacramental causality and the redemptive merit of Cano's moral causality both need some form of physical instrumentality to explain the actual accomplishment of the sacramental action itself.[84] Aquinas argued that the example of the leaden coin reduced the sacraments to mere signs. Similarly, Bañez argues that Cano's so-called "moral cause" is only a sign of the intention of the speaker.[85] In chapter 3, it was shown that Bañez argues that merit alone is not enough to describe the sacraments as causes of grace in the person: a discussion of perfective physical instrumentality, which actuates the passive obediential potency of the soul to respond to God in grace, is also necessary.[86]

Bañez' quarrel with Cano extends beyond these concerns to the nature of merit itself: although Cano speaks of the merit of Christ's blood, for Bañez even the meritorious dimension of Christ's passion cannot be described in exclusively moral terms. Because Aquinas saw the humanity of Christ as a conjoined instrumental efficient cause, the meritorious suffering of this same sacred humanity is more than morally persuasive. It is a proper efficient cause of our redemption in the physical sense, as an instrument conjoined to the word and operative in the sacraments as separated instruments.[87] Bañez argues

---

84. See Bañez, *in* III, q. 62, a. 1. Bañez, *Comentarios Ineditos a la Tercera Parte de Santo Tomas*, vol. 2, *De Sacramentis: QQ. 60–90*, 47–48.

85. "At vero epistola v. gr., quam dedid David ad occidendum Uriam, ita dicitur instrumentum morale quod non excedit rationem signi voluntatis regis, ut etiam denarius plumbeus, de quo dicit divus Thomas quod non excedit rationem signi voluntatis regis et ordinationis." Bañez, *in* III, q. 62 a. 1, concl. 5. See Bañez, *Comentarios Ineditos a la Tercera Parte*, vol. 2, 47. We have already noted that Aristotle allows for counsel to be considered an efficient cause when it results in efficient motion (see note 68). Although it seems that there may be exceptions to Bañez's reduction of rhetoric to sign, it is certainly true that it lacks the force of causal necessity. Further, the natural example of counsel as efficient cause fails when applied to God; Aristotle argued that counsel could be defined as an efficient cause when it directly led to some kind of physical movement, and no amount of counsel can induce movement in God of any kind.

86. See pp. 150ff.

87. "Nam divus Thomas 3 p., q. 48, docet passionem Christi causam fuisse nostrae

that a solely moral cause is not able to function as a principal efficient cause in relation to subordinate instruments.[88] Building on this, deeper challenges emerge in the area of Christology. Bañez implicitly shows that, when the value of the blood of Christ is reduced to merit alone, the absence of physical efficient instrumentality strips Christology of its instrumental efficacy. For Aquinas, the merit of Christ's passion is rooted in the *ratio* of the Incarnation itself, which is by nature instrumental and ordered not only towards the payment of ransom but to the divination of the person in grace. Bañez argues that Christ's passion cannot be understood as only juridically meritorious. It is physically efficacious as the principle from which the sacraments, as separated instruments, draw their strength.[89] In this Bañez reveals the importance of the sacraments as a point of contact with the potency of the Incarnation itself.

As Bañez correctly argues, when physical instrumentality is denied to the sacraments, the supposed advantages of moral causality over the *sine qua non* approach begin to evaporate. While moral causality does place more emphasis on what Aquinas would call the meritorious causality of Christ's passion than do many previous forms of sacramental occasionalism, grace cannot be effected by the sacra-

---

salutis per modum meriti et satisfactionis et per modum sacrificii, per modum redemptionis et per modum efficientiae; ubi divus Thomas distinguit istos modos, quorum ultimus non est moralis, alias non esset distinctus ab aliis moralibus. Praeterea divus Thomas in art. 5 hujus quaest. ait sacramenta habere virtutem ex passione Christi, quae per modum meriti et efficientiae operata est nostram salutem et quod operantur sacramenta ut instrumenta separata. Praeterea ratio divi Thomae in hoc art. non procedit de causa morali, sed de causa efficienti ad modum causae artificialis, sicut serra efficit scamnum." Bañez, *in* III, q. 62 a. 1, concl. 5. See Bañez, *Comentarios Ineditos a la Tercera Parte,* vol. 2, 47–8.

88. "*Secundo* arguitur. Sacramenta novae legis non possunt habere majorem efficientiam quam humanitas Christi, quae est instrumentum conjunctum. Sed ipsa humanitas causat gratiam modo de facto solum ut causa moralis. Ergo sacramenta non sunt nisi instrumenta in genere causae moralis. Ad hoc respondetur primo negando consequentiam, ex eo quod potest instrumentum causae moralis habere aliam rationem efficientiae quam ipsa principalis causa. V. gr., judex est causa moralis ut suspendatur aliquis per suam sententiam; minister vero qui exequitur sententiam aliam rationem habet efficiendi, qui est instrumentum causae moralis. Secundo respondetur quod etiam ipsa humanitas Christi est principium efficiens non solum ut causa moralis, sed etiam est principium efficax instar causa naturalis vel artificialis." Bañez, *in* III, q. 62 a. 1, concl. 5. See Bañez, *Comentarios Ineditos a la Tercera Parte,* vol. 2, 49.

89. Ibid.

ments if they contain only Christ's merit and not the physical potency of the very humanity—conjoined to the Godhead—that suffered,
died, and rose, and abides now in the economy of the Church as a
source of eternal life.

MERIT

Although Cano's use of humanist rhetoric does little to improve upon
the limitations of sacramental occasionalism, his appeal to moral persuasion as an explanation of sacramental efficacy has both Christological and anthropological implications for the doctrine of merit because of the central importance that Cano places on the redemptive
merit of Christ's blood in the context of the sacraments themselves.

Both Cano and Aquinas make reference to Christology in the
context of sacramental causality. Aquinas' understanding of Christic
instrumentality is rooted in the instrumentality of the Incarnation itself: when considered in reference to human sanctification, the implications of the hypostatic union unfold, displaying the unified instrumental motion of Christ's humanity and by extension the sacraments,
working towards the finality of grace as instrumental causes under
the principal agency of divine causality. By contrast, Cano makes no
direct reference to the hypostatic union in the context of sacramental
causality; rather than incorporating a sense of instrumentality drawn
from this union into his sacramental doctrine, Cano insists on opposing the merits of Christ to physical causality.[90] Although Cano intends to account for the limitations of natural potency with respect to
grace, he effectively implies that merit functions in a sphere distinct
from physical efficient causality. This is explicit in the case of the sacraments and may have implications for Christology as well.

For Aquinas, the doctrine of instrumental causality allows for a
deeper and more seamless integration between natural and divine
causality in the case of Christology, the sacraments, and meritorious
action in Christ and the just. In the *Tertia Pars*, Aquinas describes the
potency of Christ's human nature as functioning in an instrumental

---

90. Although not completely analogous, Cano's concept of "physical" or "natural"
causality is roughly equivalent to Aristotle's category of efficient causality.

relationship with his divinity because of the hypostatic union. For Aquinas, natural creation itself enjoys a kind of instrumental relationship with its creator, in which God works through the potency of created natures to achieve the goodness and order which he has ordained for creation in wisdom.[91] In the enfleshment of the Word, however, natural potency—and in particular the potency of human nature—is caught up in a further instrumentality, this time ordained to a supernatural end by the wisdom of God's redemptive intent for fallen humanity. Certain features of Aquinas' mature doctrine of instrumental causality—visible also in his approach to sacramental causality—enable Aquinas to describe the humanity of Christ as a true instrumental cause, avoiding the extremes of univocity and equivocity. Even in the case of natural instrumentality—a saw cutting—an instrumental cause functions not according to the power of its own form but according to the power of the principal cause. This means that, while the instrument is truly in motion, the efficient causality at work is not solely attributable to the form of the instrument. This enables Aquinas to speak of perfective causality in the sacraments and authentic participation in grace without lapsing into Pelagianism or causal univocity.

As has been shown, this represents a development from his early work, where Aquinas was more inclined to conflate the natural form of the instrument with its natural instrumental end.[92] All effi-

91. "Causalitas autem Dei, qui est primum agens, se extendit usque ad omnia entia, non solum quantum ad principia speciei, sed etiam quantum ad individualia principia, non solum incorruptibilium, sed etiam corruptibilium. Unde necesse est omnia quae habent quocumque modo esse, ordinata esse a Deo in finem, secundum illud apostoli, ad Rom. XIII, *quae a Deo sunt, ordinata sunt*. Cum ergo nihil aliud sit Dei providentia quam ratio ordinis rerum in finem, ut dictum est, necesse est omnia, inquantum participant esse, intantum subdi divinae providentiae. Similiter etiam supra ostensum est quod Deus omnia cognoscit, et universalia et particularia. Et cum cognitio eius comparetur ad res sicut cognitio artis ad artificiata, ut supra dictum est, necesse est quod omnia supponantur suo ordini, sicut omnia artificiata subduntur ordini artis." *ST* Iª Q. 22, a. 2, co.

92. This is noticeable when Aquinas' teaching on sacramental causality in the *Sentences* is compared with his mature teaching in the *Summa*. See *Super Sent*. lib. 4 dist. 1 q. 1 a. 4, solutio I and *ST* IIIª Q. 62 a. 1 ad 2. While in the *Sentences*, Aquinas seems to describe the natural instrumental end of the axe (the stool) as determined to a certain extent by the axe's natural form, in the *Summa* Aquinas is more clear, limiting the natural form of the axe to its sharpness, the stool itself being a properly instrumental end deter-

cient causality is rendered intelligible by its formal and final causes. In the case of an instrumental cause, however, its own form cannot supply this. Reference to the intent of the architect must be made to understand the purpose and teleology of the motion of the instrument. This is not to say, however, that the form of the instrument is meaningless. A tool may retain its own operation—such as the saw's cutting by the form of its sharpness—and still be moved by a power and intentionality greater than itself. Further, the operation proper to the form of some natural tools fits them in a particular sense for certain instrumental ends. The sharpness of the saw is selected by a builder who holds the form of the stool in his mind and directs the motion of the saw towards the achievement of that end. Although the operation of the tool is distinct from its power in this sense, there can exist a deep connaturality between the nature of the tool and its instrumental end, and because the power at work is dictated by the form of the principal cause, the formal limitations of the tool's nature do not make it unsuited to the task to which it is put. Its potency is actuated according to its natural operation under the impulse of the artist's power.[93] Although the power of the principal cause is responsible for the actuation of the tool's potency, its motion towards the end still has the quality of an authentic efficient cause, albeit in an instrumental sense.

Even in the case of ends ordained by divine power, outside the power of created being entirely—such as miracles, the forgiveness of sins, justification, and deification in grace—the same principles of instrumentality apply, making those natural tools which God employs causes in the full instrumental sense. In the *Summa*, Aquinas applies these ideas in the case of the sacraments, describing the sacramental elements—the operation of which is already fitted to their purpose in the order of sign—as causes of grace in the instrumental sense.[94]

---

mined by the form of the principal agent. See "Cajetan's Harp: Sacraments and the Life of Grace in Light of Perfective Instrumentality," *The Thomist* 78 (2014): 94-100.

93. "Ad secundum dicendum, quod instrumentum habet duas actiones: unam instrumentalem, secundum quam operatur non in virtute propria, sed in virtute principalis agentis; aliam autem habet actionem propriam, quae competit sibi secundum propriam formam; sicut securi competit scindere ratione suae acuitatis, facere autem lectum inquantum est instrumentum artis. Non autem perficit actionem instrumentalem nisi exercendo actionem propriam; scindendo enim facit lectum." *ST* III^a Q. 62 a. 1 ad 2.

94. "Et similiter sacramenta corporalia per propriam operationem quam exercent

In the case of Christology, however, this same understanding of instrumentality is operative. In the unity of the Incarnation, the divinity and humanity of Christ both retain the operations proper to their nature. Concerning the humanity of Christ, it retains its operations and the potency natural to its form. However, when functioning as an instrumental cause in relation to the divine nature, it is moved, not by its proper form but according to the power of its principal cause. Aquinas again uses the example of a tool in the hands of an artisan to illustrate this.[95]

This has particular implications for Aquinas' doctrine of merit. Does Christ merit in his human nature, and if so, how? Because the humanity of Christ functions as an instrumental cause, there is no risk of ascribing the end of salvation to the power of a natural form. And yet the operations of Christ's humanity are fitted proportionally to the ends of beatitude and union with divinity—not by their natural power but as a tool to its instrumental end. An instrumental action cannot be distinguished from the action of the principal agent.[96]

---

circa corpus, quod tangunt, efficiunt operationem instrumentalem ex virtute divina circa animam: sicut aqua baptismi, abluendo corpus secundum propriam virtutem, abluit animam inquantum est instrumentum virtutis divinae; nam ex anima et corpore unum fit. Et hoc est quod Augustinus dicit, quod corpus tangit et cor abluit." *ST* III^a Q. 62 a. 1 ad 2.

95. "Respondeo dicendum quod, sicut supra dictum est, haeretici qui posuerunt in Christo unam voluntatem, posuerunt etiam in ipso unam operationem.... Quia actio eius quod movetur ab altero, est duplex, una quidem quam habet secundum propriam formam; alia autem quam habet secundum quod movetur ab alio. Sicut securis operatio secundum propriam formam est incisio, secundum autem quod movetur ab artifice, operatio eius est facere scamnum.... Et ideo, ubicumque movens et motum habent diversas formas seu virtutes operativas, ibi oportet quod sit alia propria operatio moventis, et alia propria operatio moti, licet motum participet operationem moventis, et movens utatur operatione moti, et sic utrumque agit cum communione alterius. Sic igitur in Christo humana natura habet propriam formam et virtutem per quam operatur et similiter divina. Unde et humana natura habet propriam operationem distinctam ab operatione divina, et e converso. Et tamen divina natura utitur operatione naturae humanae sicut operatione sui instrumenti, et similiter humana natura participat operationem divinae naturae, sicut instrumentum participat operationem principalis agentis." *ST* III^a Q. 19, a. 1 co. Cajetan interprets this Christological passage, which clearly establishes an instrumental relationship between the operations of Christ's two natures united in one person, with reference to the instrumental end of sanctification. Cajetan, Commentary on *ST* III^a Q. 19, a. 1, nn. I, II (Leonine ed. 11:241–42).

96. *ST* III^a Q. 19, a. 1, ad 2.

For this reason, Christ's merit is an intrinsic principle that emerges from the operation of his human nature acting in union with his divinity. Because the motion of these operations is an authentic form of efficient causality, the activity of Christ in his human nature can be meritorious because of its union with the principal efficient causality of Christ's divine nature. By the operation of his human nature according to its natural form, Christ is able to merit in the same manner as any other man, according to the goodness of nature.[97] As head of the Church, however, Christ is united with all of the baptized and is able to merit for them because of this union.[98] The operation of Christ's human nature is a real human act, elevated by divine power. The merits which Christ applies to the baptized united with him in the communion of the Church are not those proportioned only to his human nature, however. As an instrument of the Word, Christ's human nature is graced by its union with divinity and made capable of the sacrifice of his passion, which as a free offering in charity manifests the priestly identity of Christ that is made possible by the hypostatic union: Christ offers the flesh of his nature and ours to the Father in one single, perfect act of divine worship.[99]

Because instrumental efficient causality is so essential for Aquinas' understanding not only of the sacraments but of the humanity of Christ itself, Bañez is right to criticize Cano for characterizing Christ's passion as a purely "moral" or meritorious cause. It is true that in Aquinas' Christology a broad causal spectrum is at play: in question 48 of the *Tertia Pars*, Aquinas argues that the passion of Christ is the cause of our salvation by way of merit and satisfaction by way of sacrifice and redemption and through efficient causality.[100] Although there is a sense in which Christic merit itself is a cause of our salvation, Bañez is quick to point out that, when considering the relationship between the instrumental operations of Christ's humanity

97. *ST* III^a Q. 19, a. 3, co. 98. *ST* III^a Q. 19, a. 4, co.
99. *ST* III^a Q. 48, a. 3, co.
100. "Deinde considerandum est de effectu passionis Christi. Et primo, de modo efficiendi; secundo, de ipso effectu. Circa primum quaeruntur sex. Primo, utrum passio Christi causaverit nostram salutem per modum meriti. Secundo, utrum per modum satisfactionis. Tertio, utrum per modum sacrificii. Quarto, utrum per modum redemptionis. Quinto, utrum esse redemptorem sit proprium Christi. Sexto, utrum causaverit effectum nostrae salutis per modum efficientiae." *ST* III^a Q. 48, Prooemium.

(such as the passion itself) and the sacraments as instruments, physical efficient causality plays an essential role.[101] In article 5 of question 62, Aquinas argues that the sacraments have their power from the passion of Christ, by way of merit and the operation of efficient causality, which operates for our salvation through the sacraments functioning as separated instruments. For this reason, Bañez notes that Aquinas' argument for the causality of the sacraments is not framed in terms of meritorious causality but efficient instrumental causality under the mode of artistry—as a saw's shaping a stool under the directive impulse of the artist himself.[102] This in turn focuses our attention on the instrumental character of Christ's humanity, which highlights the role of merit in the context of the hypostatic union. For Aquinas, there is an inherent connection between instrumental causality and Christic merit, such that it is not possible to describe the hypostatic union, and therefore the meritorious quality of Christ's passion, without reference to natural potency, considered in its instrumental mode. Because of this, Bañez is able to argue that the sacraments themselves cannot be considered as purely meritorious causes; physical potency must be considered. Even prescinding from Aquinas, however, it is essential that physical acts of Christ—such as his passion, death, and resurrection—be understood as causally efficacious.

Although Cano does not deny the importance of these central Christological truths, Cano's separation of merit and physical causality cannot hold here. The implications of Bañez' argument are well taken: if Cano were to oppose Christ's merit to physical causality in an absolute sense, the implications of his theory could raise questions about the integrity of the hypostatic union itself, the merit of which depends on the physical instrumentality of Christ's body. Even if his aims are less systematic, his ambiguity on this point is evidence of a lack of integration on the subject of instrumental causality, which could affect the doctrine of merit directly with respect to the potency of Christ's humanity and ours.

Previous Thomistic commentators such as Cajetan had raised the issue of merit in the baptized in this same Christological context,

---

101. Bañez, in ST IIIª Q. 62, a. 1. Concl. 5 (*Comentarios Ineditos a la Tercera Parte*, vol. 2:47–48).

102. Ibid.

highlighting the connection between anthropology and Aquinas' approach to Christology. When describing the possibility of merit for the faithful, Aquinas again employs the categories of instrumentality: creatures have both a proper motion and operation according to their nature and an operation by means of divine power according to a divinely ordained end.[103] Grace, as the ontological reality which makes this kind of instrumental operation possible, bears fruit in supernatural charity, which animates the soul through the enjoyment of God as goodness himself.[104] Despite the disproportion between our own will and beatitude, under the influx of the Holy Spirit, charity produces actual condign merit, which is proportioned to eternal life.[105] Because of this, the Thomist school argued that the merits of Christ's humanity were intrinsically efficacious.

By extension, concerning this same question Cajetan observed that the language of instrumental causality enables an authentically intrinsic doctrine of merit. Cajetan contrasted this approach with that of Scotus, who sees no intrinsic merit in this action; God simply decides to accept the actions of those who have previously received grace as meritorious.[106] Scotus' extrinsic and univocal approach ac-

---

103. "Manifestum est autem quod inter Deum et hominem est maxima inaequalitas, in infinitum enim distant, et totum quod est hominis bonum, est a Deo. Unde non potest hominis ad Deum esse iustitia secundum absolutam aequalitatem, sed secundum proportionem quandam, inquantum scilicet uterque operatur secundum modum suum. Modus autem et mensura humanae virtutis homini est a Deo. *Et ideo meritum hominis apud Deum esse non potest nisi secundum praesuppositionem divinae ordinationis, ita scilicet ut id homo consequatur a Deo per suam operationem quasi mercedem, ad quod Deus ei virtutem operandi deputavit. Sicut etiam res naturales hoc consequuntur per proprios motus et operationes, ad quod a Deo sunt ordinatae.* Differenter tamen, quia creatura rationalis seipsam movet ad agendum per liberum arbitrium, unde sua actio habet rationem meriti; quod non est in aliis creaturis" (emphasis mine). *ST* I^aII^ae Q. 114, a. 1 co.

104. *ST* I^aII^ae Q. 114, a. 4, co.

105. *ST* I^aII^ae Q. 114, a. 3, co. See also Joseph Wawrykow, *God's Grace and Human Action: Merit in the Theology of Thomas Aquinas* (Notre Dame, Ind: University of Notre Dame Press, 1995), 157–255. Elsewhere Wawrykow notes that in his mature teaching on grace and merit, Aquinas has been influenced to a certain extent by Augustine. Ibid., 266–76. See also Joseph Wawrykow, "Grace," in *The Theology of Theology of Thomas Aquinas*, ed. Rik Van Nieuwenhove and Joseph Wawrykow (Notre Dame, Ind.: University of Notre Dame Press, 2005), 209.

106. "Scilicet motio Spiritus Sancti et gratia, non sunt duae disperatae causae meriti, sed sunt causae subordinatae: motio quidem Spiritus Sancti ut actio causae primae, et gratia ut causa secunda operis inquantum meritori. Movet enim Spiritus Sanctus homi-

tually effects the primacy of charity in relation to merit. For Scotus, grace does not fundamentally change the act of natural love but only raises it by degree.[107] For Aquinas, the act of charity is uniquely possible to the state of grace and meritorious in itself because of the new instrumental relationship established between God and the human person in divine sonship.[108] By contrast, while Scotus establishes an uncomfortable proportionality between charity and the natural will, he fails to establish a meaningful proportionality between the infused theological life and beatitude. Therefore while merit is possible for Scotus, his extrincisist anthropology of grace makes it difficult to speak of the divinization of the person in meaningful terms.

By contrast, Aquinas is able to argue that the merits of the just are intrinsic because Christ's merit is intrinsic, therefore building an anthropology of grace around a more robust understanding of the hypostatic union itself. In this we find a definitive hallmark of the Thomistic school, which views merit as essentially analogical, rather than univocal.[109] By pointing to the importance of physical causality

---

nem ad merendum mediante gratia…. Contra … occurrit Scotus, in I *Sent.*, dist. XVII, qu. I, tenens quod actus elicitus a gratia non est meritorious simpliciter vitae aeternae; sed oportet quod, ultra hoc quod sit informatus gratia, sit acceptus Deo, idest ordinatus a Deo ad consequendam vitam aeternam." Cajetan, in *ST* I^{a}II^{ae} Q. 114, a. 3, nn. II, III (Leonine ed. 7:348). See Scotus, in I *Sent.*, d. XVII, q. 1, a. 1. Concerning the relationship between merit and reward, however, Cajetan differs slightly from de Soto and Bañez. See Cajetan, in *ST* III^a Q. 62, a. 1, n. V (Leonine ed. 12:21). Bañez, in *ST* III^a Q. 62, a. 1, concl. 5 (*Comentarios Ineditos a la Tercera Parte*, vol. 2:48).

107. Scotus, *Ord.* 1, d. 17, q. 3 nn. 179–82 (Vat., 5.224–26); Idem, *Ord.* 3, d. 27, q. un., n. 63 (Vat., 10.77); Idem, *Lect.* 1, d. 17, n. 79–81 (Vat., 17.206–7); Idem, *Lect.* 3, d. 23, q. un., n. 48 (Vat., 21.115–16). As cited by Thomas Osborne, *Human Action in Thomas Aquinas, John Duns Scotus and William of Ockham* (Washington, D.C.: The Catholic University of America Press, 2014), 212n81.

108. "For Thomas, grace and charity are necessary for a meritorious act if there is going to be some intrinsic way in which the agent and his acts are proportioned to charity. God could save someone without such an intrinsic proportion, but this proportion itself does not depend on God's free decision. By their very nature, grace and charity cause merit. In contrast, Scotus does not argue for the necessity of merit by considering any intrinsic features of grace or charity, such as their ability to raise the agent to a supernatural level, or the way in which charity enables the agent to perform a specifically distinct kind of act. Scotus thinks that the connection between morality, grace, and charity is extrinsic and established by God's free decree." Osborne, *Human Action*, 212–13.

109. Reginald Garrigou-Lagrange, *Reality: A Synthesis of Thomistic Thought*, trans. Patrick Cummins (St. Louis: Herder, 1950), 265–66.

in the context of Christological merit, Bañez speaks from within this tradition and calls our attention to the conceptual connection that unites Christology, sacramentology, and grace.[110]

Since at least the time of *De Auxiliis*, the Thomist school has placed great importance on the doctrine of grace, insisting on its intrinsic and divinizing effects on the person, who is caught up and transfigured in his natural powers by union with divinity. This incarnational analogy animates Thomistic virtue theory, in which the theological life enriches, perfects, and elevates the pursuit of happiness according to natural virtue. This vision, most recently championed by the late Servais Pinckaers, OP, has always been opposed to the extrinsicism and deontological legalism first of nominalism and, by extension, Molinism and casuistry.[111] For Cano, however, grace is not clearly distinguished from merit; although Trent taught that grace was contained in the sacraments, Cano argues that the sacraments contain the merits of the blood of Christ. The fact that Cano sees this as unproblematic indicates that he does not sufficiently distinguish between grace and merit in the person who receives the sacraments; further, the distinction between the merits of Christ himself and the meritorious acts of the baptized person is seemingly absent. This stark univocity leaves little room for the perfection and divinization of the person in supernatural charity, which the Thomist tradition understood to be an analogical outgrowth of the baptized person's contact with the sacred humanity of Christ. The implications of moral causality for the doctrine of grace were not lost outside of the Thomistic world, however.

Bañez' critique of the implications of moral causality highlights

---

110. For Bañez, Aquinas' mature teaching on the sacraments as instrumental causes is enabled by the concept of obediential potency. "Gratia creatur a Deo; sed ad creationem solus Deus concurrit et nullo modo creatura neque instrumentaliter quidem: ergo sacramenta non possunt concurrere ad gratiam. Ad hoc respondeo negatur major, quia creatio simpliciter est ex dicatur quod sequitur quod anima rationalis non creatur a Deo quia etiam producitur in materia a Deo, et videtur educi de potentia obedientiali ipsius subjecti: respondetur negando partatem rationis, nam anima rationalis ita producitur a Deo, quod non dependet a subjecto in fieri et conservari. At vero gratia, quae est quaedam qualitas et accidens supernaturalis, ita producitur in subjecto, quod dependet ab illo in fieri et conservari." Bañez, in *ST* IIIª Q. 62, a. 1, arg. 3 (*Comentarios Ineditos a la Tercera Parte*, vol. 2:50).

111. Servais Pinckaers, *The Sources of Christian Ethics*, 3rd ed., trans. Sr. Mary Thomas Noble, OP (Washington, D.C.: The Catholic University of America Press, 1995), 191–298.

an important dimension of the Thomistic synthesis, in which Christology, the sacraments, and moral theology are interconnected not only by piety or by common purpose but speculatively through the concept of instrumental efficient causality. Bañez' challenge to Cano on this point names a critical juncture of speculative theology that is overlooked when moral theology, sacramentology, and Christology are viewed independently. When the broader implications of this doctrine are accepted, however, a synthetic integration between grace, the moral life, and sacramental-Christological participation begins to flourish. For Thomists, the doctrine of instrumental causality not only allows the sacraments to function as true efficient instrumental causes but enables the baptized person to participate analogically in divine life as one whose graced human activity has been united to the merit of Christ himself.

DE AUXILIIS AND MODERN THEOLOGY

Despite the objections of Bañez and other Thomists, moral causality rose to become one of the most popular explanations of sacramental causality in the modern period. This began at the close of the sixteenth century, when moral causality began to find support among certain theologians of the Society of Jesus. Emerging at the University of Paris in the 1530s, the Jesuits were steeped in the humanist movement that was making inroads in many universities at that time. In particular, the Jesuits established an early presence at Alcalá and drew many of their Spanish vocations from among the student body there.[112] It is therefore not surprising that by the late sixteenth century, some Jesuit theologians found a natural affinity between Cano's sacramental theology and the broader intellectual tenure of the Society.[113]

This pique of interest in Cano's sacramental theology parallels a broader trend at the University of Salamanca, where, after 1570, the Renaissance began to take deeper root in certain quarters.[114] During

112. John O'Malley, *The First Jesuits* (Harvard, Mass.: Harvard University Press, 1993), 27–28, 54–55, 202.

113. There is a certain irony here because of Cano's own opposition to the early Jesuits. See John McManamon, *The Text and Contexts of Ignatius of Loyola's "Autobiography"* (Fordham, N.Y.: Fordham University Press, 2013), 1–2, 68–69.

114. Körner, *Melchior Cano*, 142.

the later half of the sixteenth century, Melchior Cano's sacramental theology was championed by Gabriel Vásquez (d. 1604), a Jesuit theologian who was educated at Alcalá and taught there until his death.[115] During his initial formation at Alcalá, Vásquez studied both philosophy and theology under Bañez, although it seems that other aspects of the intellectual culture at Alcalá left a deeper impression.[116] Not all members of the Jesuit school defended Cano's position, however. Broadly speaking, the appeal of Cano's theory among Jesuits can be seen to rise as their objections to Molinism decrease. The Spanish scholastic revival did find a measure of support in the Society: Suárez, who opposed a pure Molinism, argued against moral causality and believed that the sacraments were physical efficient causes of grace.[117]

The controversy *de Auxiliis*, which concerned the relationship between grace and human freedom, reached its height with the publication of Luis de Molina's tract on grace and the freedom of the will in 1588. Domingo Bañez, who then held the Dominican Chair at Salamanca at the time, became involved in the controversy almost immediately.[118] Molina's interpretation of Aquinas was characteristic of larger trends at work in the Society of Jesus. Although the early Jesuits valued Aquinas highly, their approach to the study of his works was frequently eclectic. Although he studied the texts of Aquinas and debated with Bañez, Molina's understanding of grace and free will owed as much to his Jesuit formation and the surrounding humanist environment as it did to the Angelic Doctor.[119]

115. Pourrat, *Theology of the Sacraments*, 184, 191. *CE* s.v. "Gabriel Vasquez." "At licet sacramentis nostris tribuamus idem genus efficacitatis moralis, quod sanguini et meritis Christi, nihilominus non dicimus, sacramenta operari nostram salutem per modum meriti." Vásquez, *in* III, disp. 132, a. 5. As in Gierens, *De Causalitate Sacramentorum*, 113–14.

116. John Doyle, "Hispanic Scholastic Philosophy," in *The Cambridge Companion to Renaissance Philosophy*, ed. James Hankins (New York: Cambridge University Press, 2007), 262. Although never a student there, Bañez taught at Alcalá from 1567–1572. *NCE*[1] s.v. "Báñez and Bañezianism."

117. *In* III, q. 62 a. 4, disp. 9 sec. II n. 10, 18–23. As has been noted, Suárez's theory of potency is at odds with that of the Thomistic school.

118. Although Molina's work was published in 1588, previous conflicts had erupted at Louvain in 1581. *CE* s.v. "De Auxiliis." The conflict would last until the eve of the seventeenth century, however, and although a special Roman congregation was created to resolve it, no definitive conclusions were reached. Although the *de Auxiliis* controversy was not formally resolved, its effects lingered in Western theology for several centuries.

119. Romanus Cessario, "Molina and Aquinas," in *Companion to Luis de Molina*,

Despite the strenuous objections of Bañez and many other Thomists, *de Auxiliis* was never satisfactorily resolved, and as a result Molinism had a strong effect on many theological schools in the post-Tridentine period. In addition to Vásquez, Cano's theory was embraced by later Jesuits sympathetic to Molinism, such as de Lugo (d. 1660) and Franzelin (d. 1886).[120] Their support propelled the theory of moral causality well beyond the scope of Cano's own influence. Although committed Thomists continued to object, moral causality had found itself at home in the manualist tradition that dominated Catholic theology in the modern period.

The historical connection between moral causality and *de Auxiliis* gestures towards deeper ties that would associate moral causality within the structures of systems of moral theology developing in the modern period. There is a sense in which one's approach to broader theological topics predetermines one's view of the sacraments. A comprehensive theology of grace is clearly essential for any speculative discussion of the sacraments, and as a result sacramental theory cannot be effectively disentangled from larger hermeneutical approaches to grace and the questions which surround it.

For Aquinas, grace is about the divinization of the human person, infused with virtues and the gifts of the Spirit, remade in the image of Christ as a participant in divine life. Because of this anthropological orientation, the theology of grace cannot be fully understood if it is reduced, as an abstract consideration, to the final end of inanimate sacramental signs. Therefore, the way in which the relationship between divine agency and human freedom is characterized does much to shape our understanding of the moral dimension of the human person. For the Thomist school, grace is considered under moral theology, which deals with human action. In this regard, a virtue-based approach presumes a functional understanding of efficient causality wherein the person has the scope, within the limits of secondary causality, to function as a moral agent.

---

vol. 50 of *Companions to the Christian Tradition*, ed. Mathias Kaufman and Aichele Alexander (Leiden: Brill, 2013), 291–309.

120. Johann Auer and Joseph Ratzinger, eds., *Dogmatic Theology*, vol. 6, *A General Doctrine of the Sacraments and the Mystery of the Eucharist*, by Johann Auer, trans. Erasmo Leiva-Merikakis, trans. and ed. Hugh M. Riley (Washington, D.C.: The Catholic University of America Press, 1995), 79.

While the occasionalists of the scholastic period essentially eviscerated secondary causality to make room for divine agency and freedom, some humanists and enlightenment thinkers emphasized human radical volitional autonomy, in some cases substantially reducing the involvement of divine providence in the created order. Although these positions are opposed on a metaphysical level, there are also certain conceptual links between nominalism and some humanisms: whether the potency of secondary causality is radically reduced or exaggerated, a conflict of agency is presumed between human volition and divine power that is not satisfactorily resolved. As a result, true instrumental causality remains an impossibility both metaphysically and anthropologically. The results of this outlook can be seen in moral theology, where the dynamic of act and potency—as constitutive of human nature—is not available to describe the growth of the human person in the life of grace with the language of virtue. Instead, metaphysical reductionism produces an impoverished anthropology.

During the modern period, deontological moral theology emphasized legalism. The Thomist approach, by contrast, emphasized virtue and grace.[121] Although sacramental theology has not always been recognized as an important dimension of the de Auxiliis controversy, it does have larger implications for the theology of grace and therefore moral theology. The association between moral causality and Molinism is more than simple coincidence. In the end, sacramental theology shows the effects of more fundamental stances taken in metaphysics, natural philosophy, and anthropology, which dictate the possibilities for speculative descriptions of sacramental action within a given system. For the Thomists, who effectively resolved the problem of divine and created causality by developing the theory of natural act and potency within the context of secondary and instrumental causality, a robust sacramental realism integrated within an anthropology of virtue and grace is possible; for others, however, the possibilities became more limited.

Because grace is anthropological, it implies an elevated sense of moral activity. The elements of sacramental activity are causally efficacious because they have been elevated to participate in divine power. Grace allows for a new understanding of moral action, elevated along

---

121. Pinckaers, *The Sources of Christian Ethics*, 191–298.

the same lines. The graced human person is actuated through the infused virtues and gifts, as nature itself is perfected and drawn into a supernatural participation in Trinitarian life, where the perfection of the new man, recreated in Christ, shows himself in a charity which reflects ever more deeply the Divine image. This sense of graced human action imparts an understanding of moral theology that cannot be reduced to law and merit. For the Thomist mind, the question of sacramental efficacy must always be linked not only to larger metaphysical questions such as occasionalism but to the specifically anthropological questions of the modern period as well. Thomistic moral and sacramental theology relies on an active appreciation of the potency of secondary causes—either in the case of sacramental instruments or the virtues of the human person (natural and theological)—which Cano's theory of moral causality is ill-suited to support.

Although it might not be impossible to wed Cano's sacramental system to a virtue-based approach to moral theology, this was infrequently done, and Cano's theory retained its popularity almost exclusively among those committed to a deontological approach to grace and the moral life. His theory of moral causality remained quite popular until the early twentieth century, and his emphasis on the power and redemptive merit contained in Christ's passion fit well with the devotional piety of the modern period. Cano's largely metaphorical description of the causal process of the sacraments provided a series of vivid metaphors which did much to make this system more appealing but did little to address its underlying problems. Cano's rhetorical realism also appealed squarely to devotional piety, which rightly associates the sacraments with the blood of Christ.

Anthony Levi has noted that, during the modern period, the nominalist emphasis on merit and reward was sometimes accompanied at the cultural level by more pronounced artistic expressions of the physical suffering of Jesus; this in turn was associated with a rise in devotion to Christ's heart, blood, and wounds.[122] These devotional

---

122. Levi, *Renaissance and Reformation*, 59. These trends, which began in the fourteenth century, fit well with the devotional and theological tenure of Cano's sacramental theology. Anthony Levi associates the rise of these devotional movements with the rise in nominalism, particularly that of Ockham, and the corresponding breakdown of scholasticism. See Levi, *Renaissance and Reformation*, 56–61. It goes without saying that the devotional practices mentioned above are not wrong or necessarily detrimental to the

practices are of course laudable in themselves, and only grave meta-physical decontextualization could render them otherwise. However, even the best of devotional piety can be robbed of its rightful mean-ing if accompanied by legal reductionism in the moral and liturgi-cal realm. Such imagery and practices could only become unhelpful if employed as a kind of window dressing of devotional sentiment, shielding the metaphysical nudity of occasionalism from the public eye. In the end what makes this kind of rhetorical realism dangerous is not only its failure to address occasionalism but its active conceal-ment of the core speculative and structural elements of the nominal-ist problem, which by their nature do not allow metaphysical real-ism to flourish on a sacramental or anthropological level. Although it seemed to provide a refuge from high scholastic nominalism for thinkers like Valla, in the end a realism that was only rhetorical did lit-tle to rid these same thinkers of the harmful first principles which led to the very errors they argued so strenuously against.

Although there is a great deal of commonality between moral causality and occasionalism, Cano's approach was popular because it spoke of the sacraments in a mode compelling to his intellectual contemporaries. This became a danger again in the twentieth centu-ry, when many theologians objected to the perceived legalism and ab-struse speculation at work in the school positions on topics within sacramental theology, seeking to replace these outmoded structures with new, more rhetorically compelling models that seemed to reso-nate more directly with liturgical experience and modern culture.

The lesson of historical experience is this: unless core metaphys-ical questions which concern the sacraments, grace, and anthropol-ogy are addressed directly, new rhetorical modalities, be they drawn from Patristics, the Bible, or contemporary philosophy, can do little to improve upon the perceived deficiencies of previous models. By contrast, the Thomistic approach to sacramental realism offers not only a nuanced response to metaphysical occasionalism but a sapien-tial synthesis of theological doctrine, and it is the task of the Thomis-tic school to articulate that synthesis in our own time.

---

sacramental economy. When such an emphasis on mercy emerges as a popular response to legalism in sacramental theology, however, it cannot be considered as a sign of spiri-tual or liturgical health.

Conclusion

In the preceding pages we have examined the teaching of St. Thomas Aquinas on sacramental causality, studying the development of his thought from his early work in the *Sentences* to his mature teaching in the *Summa Theologiae*. A preliminary attempt has also been made to situate this development within its history, describing important elements of the environment in which Aquinas' teaching emerged and the context in which it was received by subsequent generations. We have seen that Aquinas' position on sacramental causality evolves from dispositive to perfective physical causality and that this later theory of sacramental instrumentality is closely tied to the instrumentality of the sacred humanity of Christ operative in the sacraments as a conjoined instrument that moves the human person united to him towards Christian perfection and ultimately beatitude. For Aquinas, Augustine's "cleansing of the heart" implies both a sacramental and a moral realism in which the instrumentality of the sacraments prepare the graced person for beatitude through an intrinsic renewal of the person after the heart of Christ in the divine friendship of charity.

The first chapter situated Aquinas' thought within the broader tradition, clarifying that the question of sacramental efficacy has a long history in Western theology that has undergone significant development and refinement, such that the conceptual details of the way in which the efficacy of the sacraments is presented can have wide-ranging theological implications. This chapter shows the organic connection that exists between Aquinas' approach to sacramental causality and that of earlier figures in the theological tradition such as Augustine, the Victorines, and Aquinas' scholastic predecessors. Although Aquinas' position stands out amidst this field, his continuity with the broader tradition is palpable, and his contribution here is a response to questions that have emerged from the broad flow of the Church's tradition rather than its margins.

The second chapter of this book began our engagement with the texts of Aquinas by studying his early thought in the *Commentary on the Sentences*. Too frequently, modern interpreters of Aquinas on sacramental causality have focused all but exclusively on his mature works, referencing his early work primarily through secondary sources. We have seen that by focusing more attention on the *Sentences*, we were better able to see Aquinas' theory as part of a developing conversation within the thirteenth century that is concerned with new scholastic questions such as the theological value of the concept of efficient causality and the doctrine of creation. This chapter shows the manner in which, even in his early thought, Aquinas begins to respond to these issues in a way that preserves the intrinsic nature of the sacraments as true instrumental causes in a manner consistent with the received Augustinian tradition. Although Augustine's prose tends to defy systemization, even in the *Sentences* Aquinas offers a cogent interpretation of Augustine's sacramental language that is more robust than that of many of his scholastic contemporaries. The strength of Aquinas' theory of instrumentality is that it preserves the intrinsic nature of divine power working through material signs, leaving this central component of Augustine's sacramental theology unscarred by metaphysical reductionism. This is an insight that is retained in Aquinas' mature thought, which despite advances in the theory of instrumentality continues to show a manifest debt to the Augustinian doctrine of sign.

The third chapter shows how Aquinas' unique ability to surmount speculative challenges concerning grace and creation allowed him to preserve an intrincisist approach to sacramental causality. To this end, this book also indicates the importance of the doctrine of grace in conjunction with sacramental causality, showing that developments within Aquinas' thought on sacramental cause are deeply related to developments in his theory of grace. The long-term fruit of this bears itself out in the Thomistic tradition, which, through its own sustained contemplative reflection on these questions, is able to continue to express this intrincisist approach to grace and instrumentality in the context of *de Auxiliis* and other new challenges during the early modern period; in all this, an intrinsic approach to grace not only preserves sacramental realism but couples this to a metaphysically rich approach to the moral life of the graced human person.

The fourth chapter presents the issue of sacramental efficacy from a very different perspective. Beyond questions of historical context, this chapter questions the cogency of moral causality as an explanation of the way in which the sacraments cause grace in the recipient. Because of its fundamental connection with the nature and purpose of the Church, the question of sacramental efficacy can be posed within different theological hermeneutics; Renaissance humanism is not, therefore, a per se impediment to answering this question adequately. However, as a critical engagement with Melchior Cano, this chapter shows the impact that methodological choices and intellectual context can have on theology. It is clear that humanism shaped not only the internal form of moral causality as a theory but constituted part of the wider theological environment in which this theory came to be contextualized during and after *de Auxiliis*. One might argue that a revival of this theory in the present day seems unlikely. However, in a post-Kantian world where metaphysically realist solutions to questions of causality continue to be undesirable for some, the temptation to a merely rhetorical realism remains, even if it is voiced in new forms.

At the end of this work we are left with a variety of avenues for further research. At root, this book is primarily concerned with sacramental causality as a topic in speculative theology. The historical dimension of this study was intended to contextualize the question of sacramental causality, situating Aquinas' thought within the broader tradition of thought on this subject. If successful in this much, it no doubt also raises many new questions that could bear fruit under further study. The early patristic period and biblical roots of this issue could be investigated; similarly, the approach of the Eastern Church to the theological question of sacramental efficacy is worthy of study. Concerning scholasticism, a more detailed study of the concept of dispositive causality in the mid-thirteenth century would be valuable. In addition, a study of Reformation authors in dialogue with their Catholic contemporaries would be desirable.[1] There are no doubt

1. Ueli Zahnd begins this important work in his *Wirksame Zeichen?* Spätmittelalter, Humanismus, Reformation 80 (Tübingen: Mohr Siebeck, 2014).

many more avenues of historical research that would prove enriching, although they fall outside the immediate scope of this present study.

Concerning systematic theology more broadly, many of the points of interest for historical scholarship are of relevance to systematic theology as well. Textually speaking, this study shows the historical development that takes place across Aquinas' work. However, correctly understanding Aquinas will always require a sapiential approach that moves beyond the technical scrutiny of isolated texts. This book not only shows the textual development of Aquinas on sacramental causality, but the way in which the theological question of sacramental causality itself is intertwined with larger speculative and historical concerns. Aquinas' theory is uniquely valuable because it integrates sacramental realism within the context of broader theological concerns that range from the doctrine of merit to Christology, moral theology, and theological anthropology. Many connections between these important theological topics and the question of sacramental causality are discussed here, and far more await further research.

Second to causality itself, one of the central areas of systematic theology indicated here is the doctrine of grace. This book shows that developments within Aquinas' thought on sacramental cause are deeply related to developments in his theory of grace, highlighting the importance of the relationship between nature and grace in this context. For Aquinas the question of supernatural ends both in the context of sacramental causality and in the doctrine of grace itself relies on a nuanced approach to natural potency in relation to divine motion. Grace, nature, and the supernatural have been controversial in twentieth century theology, but the larger implications of these issues–particularly in the area of sacramental theology—are infrequently discussed. Aquinas shows the rich connections that exist between grace, the supernatural, and the sacramental economy. In this, a unique degree of speculative integration between seemingly disparate theological topics can be seen in the synthesis of Thomistic thought, where the classical Thomistic tradition provides a theological hermeneutic which is sensitive to this conceptual interdependence.

Beyond the controversy over nature and grace in itself, there has been a palpable desire in the twentieth century to develop a sacramental theory of the Church in the world that could build upon the connaturality that exists between the sign value of sacraments and human nature and culture (the works of Edward Schillebeeckx and to a certain extent, Odo Casel, are notable here). Although some may feel that distinctions between nature and the supernatural are un-helpful for this project, Aquinas' sacramental theory offers a differ-ent approach in which the sacraments, in their signate connaturality with human nature and experience, are a participatory bridge link-ing us with the supernatural reality of grace. Because of the relation that exists between the doctrines of sacramental instrumentality and obediential potency, the sacraments unite nature and the supernat-ural without conflation or compartmentalization. While they serve a manifestly supernatural end in grace, the very nature of the sacra-ments as instrumental causes—as tools taken from the natural world and put to divine purposes—ensures that sacramentality is not cor-doned off as a purely supernatural reality, disconnected from the nat-ural world and human experience. We know from our own encounter with sacraments that it is quite the opposite, and the Thomistic theo-ries of instrumentality and obediential potency can enable us to pre-serve this natural intuition even in the world of speculative theology. To the extent that contemporary approaches to liturgiology and the history of the sacraments have become isolated from conversations in other areas of theology, a renewed appreciation for the importance of sacramental causality from a Thomistic perspective could provide a point of dialogue between systematic theology and these fields.

Because of their essential role in the economy of salvation, the sacraments stand at the heart of the Christian mystery. As not only signs but causes, the sacraments effect what they signify and for those who live in the communion of the Church form the ordinary means of contact with the risen humanity of Christ which animates the members of his body with divine life. Because of the importance of their effects, the efficacy of the sacraments will always be of central relevance and should never be marginalized or forgotten in theologi-cal discourse.

Selected Bibliography

Addy, George M. *The Enlightenment in the University of Salamanca*. Durham, N.C.: Duke University Press, 1966.

Akkerman, Fokke, ed. *Rudolph Agricola: Six Lives and Erasmus's Testimonies*. Bibliotheca Latinitatis Novae. Assen, Netherlands: Van Gorcum, 2012.

Akkerman, Fokke, and A. J. Vanderjagt, eds. *Rudolphus Agricola Phrisius 1444–1485: Proceedings of the International Conference at the University of Groningen 28–30 October 1985*. Leiden: Brill, 1988.

Albert the Great. *Alberti Magni Opera Omnia*. Edited by Augusti Borgnet. Paris: Vivès, 1890–99.

Alexander of Hales. *Glossa in Quatuor Libros Sententiarum Petri Lombardi*. Bibliotheca Franciscana Scholastica Medii Aevi 15. Quaracchi, 1957.

————. *Summa Theologica*. Edited by Bernard Klumper. (Rome: ad Claras Aquas, 1924).

Aquinas, Thomas. *On Love and Charity: Readings from the Commentary on the Sentences of Peter Lombard*. Translated by Peter A. Kwasniewski, Thomas Bolin, and Joseph Bolin. Washington, D.C.: The Catholic University of America Press, 2008.

————. *Opera Omnia*. Edited by Petri Fiaccadori Parmae. 1852–1873. Second printing with a new introduction by Vernon Bourke. New York: Mesurgia Publishers, 1948.

————. *Opera Omnia iussu impensaque Leonis XIII P.M. edita*. Rome: Ex Typographia Polyglotta S.C. De Propaganda Fide, 1882–.

————. *Quaestiones Disputatae et Quaestiones Duodecim Quodlibetales*. Turin: Marietti, 1931.

————. *Scriptum Super Libros Sententiarum Magistri Petri Lombardi Episcopi Parisiensis*. Edited by Pierre Mandonnet and Fabien Moos. 4 vols. Paris: Letheilleux, 1929–47.

————. *Summa Theologiae*. Editiones Paulinae. Turin: Comerciale Edizioni Paoline s.r.l., 1988.

————. *Super Evangelium s. Ioannis lectura, c. 1, lect. 1*. Edited by R. Cai. Turin: Marietti, 1952.

Aristotle. *Opera*. Edited by Immanuel Bekker. Berlin: Georgium Reimerum, 1831–1870.

Auer, Johann. *A General Doctrine of the Sacraments and the Mystery of the Eucharist*. Translated by Erasmo Leiva-Merikakis. Vol. 6 of *Dogmatic Theology*. Edited by Johann Auer and Joseph Ratzinger. Washington, D.C.: The Catholic University of America Press, 1995.

Backes, Ignaz. *Die Christologie des hl. Thomas v. Aquin und die griechischen Kirchenväter*. Paderborn: Schöningh, 1931.

Bañez, Domingo. *Comentarios Ineditos a la Tercera Parte de Santo Tomas*. Vol. 2, *De Sacramentis: QQ. 60–90*. Edited by Vincente Beltran de Heredia. Biblioteca de Teologos Españoles 19. Salamanca: 1953.

———. *The Primacy of Existence in Thomas Aquinas: A Commentary in Thomistic Metaphysics*. Translated with introduction and notes by Benjamin S. Llamzon. Chicago: Henry Regnery, 1966.

Barnes, Corey. "Christological Composition in Thirteenth Century Debates," *The Thomist* 75 (2011): 173–206.

———. *Christ's Two Wills in Scholastic Thought: The Christology of Aquinas and Its Historical Contexts*. Toronto: Pontifical Institute of Mediaeval Studies, 2012.

———. "Thomas Aquinas's Chalcedonian Christology and Its Influence on Later Scholastics." *The Thomist* 78 (2014): 189–217.

Barron, Roger. "Hughes de Saint-Victor: Contribution à un Nouvel Examen de son Oeuvre." *Traditio* 15 (1959): 223–97.

Bedouelle, Guy, Romanus Cessario, and Kevin White. *Jean Capreolus en son temps (1380–1444)*. Mémoire Dominicaine, no. 1. Paris: Les Éditions du Cerf, 1997.

Belda Plans, Antonio. "Estudio Historico-Sistematico de la Releccion 'De Sacramentis in Genere' de Melchior Cano." Doct. diss., Universidad de Navarra, 1985.

Belda Plans, Juan. *La Escuella de Salamanca y la renovación de la teología en el siglo XVI*. Madrid: Biblioteca de Autores Cristianos, 2000.

Bernard of Clairvaux. *Sermones II*. Vol. 5 of *Sancti Bernardi, Opera*. Edited by Jean Leclercq and H. Rochais. Rome: Editiones Cistercienses, 1968.

Blankenhorn, Bernhard. "The Instrumental Causality of the Sacraments: Thomas Aquinas and Louis-Marie Chauvet." *Nova et Vetera* (English) 4 (2006): 255–94.

———. "The Place of Romans 6 in Aquinas' Doctrine of Sacramental Causality: a Balance of History and Metaphysics." In *Resourcement Thomism: Sacred Doctrine, the Sacraments, and the Moral Life,* edited by Reinhard Hütter and Matthew Levering, 136–49. Washington, D.C.: The Catholic University of America Press, 2010.

Bonaventure. *Opera Omnia*. Edited by A. C. Peltier. Paris: Vivés, 1866.

Borgman, Erik. *Edward Schillebeeckx: A Theologian in His History*. Vol. 1, *A Cath-*

olic Theology of Culture (1914–1965). Translated by John Bowden. New York: Continuum, 2003.

Bouëssé, Humbert. "La causalité efficiente instrumentale de l'Humanité du Christ et des Sacraments chrétiens," *Revue Thomiste* 39 n. 83 (1934): 256–98.

Bouëssé, Humbert, and Jean-Jacques Latour, eds. *Problémes actuels de christologie*. Paris: Desclée de Brouwer, 1965.

Cano, Melchior. *Opera. Edited by Hyacinth Serry. Padua: Typis Seminarii, 1734.*

Capreolus, John. *Defensiones Theologiae Divi Thomae Aquinatis*. Vol. 6. Edited by Ceslai Paban and Thomae Pègues. Turin: Alfred Cattier, 1906.

Casel, Odo. *Die Liturgie als Mysterienfeier*. Vol 9, *Ecclesia Orans: Zur Einführung in den Geist der Liturgie*. Freiburg im Breisgau: Herder, 1923.

———. *The Mystery of Christian Worship and Other Writings*. Edited by Burkhard Neunheuser. Westminster, Md.: Newman. 1962.

The Catholic Encyclopedia. New York: Robert Appleton, 1913.

Cessario, Romanus. "Molina and Aquinas." In *Companion to Luis de Molina*. Edited by Mathias Kaufman and Aichele Alexander. Companions to the Christian Tradition 50. Leiden: Brill, 2013.

Chenu, Marie-Dominique. *Toward Understanding Saint Thomas*. Translated by A.-M. Landry and D. Hughes. Chicago: Henry Regnery, 1964.

Ciappi, Aloisius M. *Capita Doctrinae pro Examine ad Licentiam: ex IIIa Parte Summae S. Thomae (Summarium pro Auditoribus)*. Pontificum Athenaeum Internationale Angelicum. Rome: 1955.

———. *De Sacramentis in Communi: Commentarius in Tertiam Partem S. Thomae (qq. LX–LXV)*. Pontificum Institutum Internationale Angelicum. Turin: R. Berruti, 1957.

Connolly, Grahame. *Sacramental Character in Five Famous Medievals: A Study of the Teachings of Peter Lombard, Alexander of Hales, St. Albert the Great, St. Bonaventure and St. Thomas Aquinas*. Pontificium Athenaeum Angelicum. Rome: 1961.

Coolman, Boyd Taylor. *The Theology of Hugh of St. Victor: An Interpretation*. New York: Cambridge University Press, 2010.

Copleston, Frederick. *A History of Medieval Philosophy*. New York: Harper and Row, 1972.

Corpus Christianorum, Series Latina. Turnholt: Brepols, 1953–.

Corpus Scriptorum Ecclesiasticorum Latinorum. Vienna: Tempsky, 1865–.

Courtenay, William. "The King and the Leaden Coin: The Economic Background of 'sine qua non' Causality." *Traditio* 28 (1972): 185–209.

———. "Sacrament, Symbol and Causality in Bernard of Clairvaux." In *Bernard of Clairvaux: Studies Presented to Dom Jean Leclercq*, edited by Basil Pennington, 111–22. Cistercian Studies Series 23. Kalamazoo: Cistercian Publications, 1973. (Republished in William J. Courtenay, *Covenant and Causality in Medieval Thought: Studies in Philosophy, Theology, and Economic Practice*, 111–22. London: Variorum Reprints, 1984.)

Crisogono de Jesus. *The Life of St. John of the Cross.* Translated by Kathleen Pond. New York: Harper and Brothers, 1958.

Cross, F. L., and E. A. Livingstone, eds. *Oxford Dictionary of the Christian Church.* 3rd rev. ed. Oxford: 2005.

Cross, Richard. *The Physics of Duns Scotus: The Scientific Context of a Theological Vision.* Oxford: Clarendon, 1998.

———. *Duns Scotus.* New York: Oxford University Press, 1999.

———. *Duns Scotus on God.* Burlington, Vt.: Ashgate, 2005.

———. "Duns Scotus: Some Recent Research." *Journal of the History of Philosophy* 49 n. 3 (July 2011): 271–95.

Crowley, Charles B. "The Role of Sacramental Grace in the Christian Life." *The Thomist* 2 (1940): 519–45.

Crowley, Paul. "Instrumentum Divinitatis in Thomas Aquinas: Recovering the Divinity of Christ." *Theological Studies* 52, no. 3 (September 1991): 451–75.

Cullen, Christopher. *Bonaventure.* New York: Oxford University Press, 2006.

Dauphinais, Michael, Barry David, and Matthew Levering, eds. *Aquinas the Augustinian.* Washington, D.C.: The Catholic University of America Press, 2007.

de la Soujeole, Benoît-Dominique. "The Importance of the Definition of Sacraments as Signs." In *Resourcement Thomism: Sacred Doctrine, the Sacraments, and the Moral Life,* edited by Reinhard Hütter and Matthew Levering, 127–35. Washington, D.C.: The Catholic University of America Press, 2010.

Delgado, Vincente Muñoz. *La Logica Nominalista en la Universidad de Salamanca: 1510–1530.* Madrid: Publicaciones del Monasterio de Poyo, 1964.

Denzinger, Henricus and Adolfus Schönmetzer, eds. *Enchridion Symbolarum Definitionum et Declarationum de Rebus Fidei et Morum.* 36th ed. Barcelona: Herder, 1965.

Dictionnaire de Théologie Catholique. Paris: Letouzey et Ané, 1902–50.

Diekamp, Franciscus. *Theologiae Dogmaticae Manuale: quod Secundum Principia S. Thomae Aquinatis Extravit.* Edited by Adolphus Hoffmann. 4 vols. Paris: Desclée, 1946.

Donahue, Matthew J. "Sacramental Character: The State of the Question." *The Thomist* 31 (1967): 445–64.

Dondaine, H.-D. "A propos d'Avicenne et de S. Thomas de la causalité dispositive." *Review Thomiste* 51 (1951): 441–53.

Doolan, Gregory T. *Aquinas on the Divine Ideas as Exemplar Causes.* Washington, D.C.: The Catholic University of America Press, 2008.

Duns Scotus, John. *Opera Omnia.* Facimile reprint of Wadding (1639). Edited by Georg Olms. Hildesheim: Verlagsbuchhandlung, 1968.

———. *Opera Omnia.* Civitas Vaticana: Typis Polyglottis Vaticanis, 1950–2013.

Evans, G. R., ed. *Mediaeval Commentaries on the Sentences of Peter Lombard: Current Research.* Vol. 1. Boston: Brill, 2002.

Farge, James. *Orthodoxy and Reform in Early Reformation France: the Faculty of*

Theology of Paris, 1500–1543. Edited by Heiko Oberman. Studies in Medieval and Reformation Thought 32. Leiden: Brill, 1985.

Feingold, Lawrence. *The Natural Desire to See God according to St. Thomas Aquinas and His Interpreters.* 2nd ed. Faith and Reason: Studies in Catholic Theology and Philosophy Series. Naples, Fla: Sapientia, 2010.

Feliziani, Alfonso. "La Causalita Dei Sacramenti in Domenico Soto." *Angelicum* 16 (1939): 148–94.

Felmberg, Bernhard Alfred R. *Die Ablaßtheologie Kardinal Cajetans (1469–1534).* Leiden: Brill, 1998.

Filthaut, Ephrem. *Roland von Cremona, OP, und die Anfänge der Scholastic im Predigerorden: Ein Beitrag zur Geistesgeschichte der älteren Dominikaner.* Vechta i. O.: Albertus-Magnus-Verlag der Dominikaner, 1936.

Finn, Thomas. "The Sacramental World in the *Sentences* of Peter Lombard." *Theological Studies* 69 (2008): 557–82.

Fitzgerald, Allan D., ed. *Augustine through the Ages.* Grand Rapids, Mich.: Eerdmans Publishing Company, 1999.

Freddoso, Alfred, trans. *Francisco Suarez on Efficient Causality: Metaphysical Disputations 17, 18, and 19.* New Haven, Conn.: Yale University Press, 1994.

Gallagher, John F. *Significando Causant: A Study of Sacramental Efficiency.* Studia Fribugensia New Series 40. Fribourg: The University Press, 1965.

Galot, Jean. *La Nature du Charactére Sacramentel: Étude de Théologie Médiévale.* Museum Lessianum: Desclée de Brouwer, 1956.

Garrigou-Lagrange, Réginald. *Grace: Commentary on the Summa Theologica of St. Thomas, Ia IIae, Q. 109–114.* Translated by the Dominican Nuns of Corpus Christi Monastery, Menlo Park California. St. Louis: Herder, 1952.

——. *De Revelatione per Ecclesiam Catholicam Proposita.* 5th ed. 2 vols. Rome: F. Ferrari, 1950.

——. *Reality: A Synthesis of Thomistic Thought.* Translated by Patrick Cummins. St. Louis: Herder, 1950.

Gierens, Michael. "Zur Lehre des hl. Thomas uber die Kausalitat der Sacramente." *Scholastik* 9 (1934): 321–45.

——, ed. *De Causalitate Sacramentorum seu de Modo Explicandi Efficientiam Sacramentorum Novae Legis: Textus Scholasticorum Principaliorum.* Textus et Documenta, Series Theologica 16. Rome: Pontificia Universitas Gregoriana, 1935.

Gilson, Étienne. *History of Christian Philosophy in the Middle Ages.* New York: Random House, 1955.

——. *The Christian Philosophy of St. Bonaventure.* Translated by Illtyd Trethowan and Frank Sheed. St. Anthony Guild Press, 1965

Gracia, Jorge, ed. *Individuation in Scholasticism: The Later Middle Ages and the Counter-Reformation, 1150–1650.* Albany: State University of New York Press, 1994.

Gredt, Josephus. *Elementa Philosophiae Aristotelico-Thomisticae.* Edited by Euchario Zenzen. 13th ed. 2 vols. Rome: Herder, 1961.

Haring, Nicholas M. "Berengar's Definitions of Sacramentum and Their Influence on Mediaeval Sacramentology." *Mediaeval Studies* 10 (1948): 109–47.

———. "The Character and Range of the Influence of St. Cyril of Alexandria on Latin Theology, (430–1260)." *Mediaeval Studies* 12 (1950): 1–19.

———. "A Brief Historical Comment on St. Thomas, *Summa Theol.* III qu. 67, a. 5: *Utrum non baptizatus possit sacramentum baptismi conferre.*" *Mediaeval Studies* 14 (1952): 153–59.

———. "St. Augustine's Use of the Word Character." *Mediaeval Studies* 14 (1952): 79–97.

———. "A Study of the Sacramentology of Alger of Liege." *Mediaeval Studies* 20 (1958): 41–78.

Hochschild, Joshua. *The Semantics of Analogy: Rereading Cajetan's De Nominum Analogia.* Notre Dame, Ind.: University of Notre Dame Press, 2010.

Hoenen, Maarten. "Being and Thinking in the 'Correctium fratris Thomae' and the 'Correctorium corruptorii Quare': Schools of Thought and Philosophical Methodology." In *Nach der Verurteilung von 1277: Philosophie und Theologie an der Universität von Paris im letzten Viertel des 13. Jahrhunderts*, edited by Jan Aersten, Kent Emery Jr., and Andreas Speer, 417–35. Miscellanea Mediaevalia 28. New York: de Gruyter, 2001.

Horst, Ulrich. *Unfehlbarkeit und Geschichte: Studien zur Unfehlbarkeitdiskussion von Melchior Cano bis zum I. Vatikanischen Konzil.* Mainz: Matthias-Grünewald-Verlag, 1982.

———. *The Dominicans and the Pope: Papal Teaching Authority in the Medieval and Early Modern Thomist Tradition.* Translated by James D. Mixson. Notre Dame, Ind.: University of Notre Dame Press, 2006.

Hugh of St. Victor. *Hugonis de Sancto Victore De sacramentis Christiane fidei.* Vol. 1 of *Corpus Victorinum.* Edited by Rainer Berndt. Münster: Aschendorff, 2008.

Hugon, Edouard. "La causalité instrumentale de l'humanité sainte de Jésus." *Revue Thomiste* 13 (1905): 44–68.

———. *La Causalité instrumentale dans l'ordre surnaturel.* 3rd ed. Paris: Pierre Téqui, 1924.

Hünermann, Peter, Helmut Hoping, Rober L. Fastiggi, et al. *Compendium of Creeds, Definitions, and Declarations on Matters of Faith and Morals.* 43rd ed. San Francisco: Ignatius Press, 2012.

Indices Commentaria Thomae de Vio Caietani et Francisci de Sylvestris Ferrariensis. Editio Leonina Manualis. Rome: Apud Sedem Commissionis Leoninae, 1948.

John Capreolus. *On the Virtues.* Translated with introduction and notes by Romanus Cessario and Kevin White. Washington, D.C.: The Catholic University of America Press, 2001.

Kennedy, Philip. *Schillebeeckx.* Outstanding Christian Thinkers Series. Collegeville, Minn.: Liturgical Press, 1993.

King, Peter. "Scotus on Singular Essences." *Medioevo* 30 (2005): 111–37.

King, Ronald F. "The Origin and Evolution of a Sacramental Formula: Sacramentum Tantum, Res et Sacramentum, Res Tantum." *The Thomist* 31 (1967): 21–82.

Klinger, Elmar. *Ekklesiologie der Neuzeit: Grundlegung bei Melchior Cano und Entwicklung bis zum 2. Vatikanischen Konzil.* Vienna: Herder, 1978.

Kluge, Eike-Henner. "Scotus on Accidental and Essential Causes." *Franciscan Studies* 66 (2008): 233–46.

Körner, Bernhard. *Melchior Cano: De Locis Theologicis. Ein Beitrag zur Theologischen Erkenntnislehre.* Graz, Austria: Verlag Ulrich Moser, 1994.

Kretzmann, Norman, Anthony Kenny, and Jan Pinborg, eds. *The Cambridge History of Later Medieval Philosophy.* New York: Cambridge University Press, 1989.

Lampen, Willibrord, ed. *De Causalitate Sacramentorum iuxta Scholam Franciscanam.* Florilegium Patristicum tam veteris quam medii aevi auctores complectens 26. Bonn: Peter Hanstein, 1931.

LaNave, Gregory. "Bonaventure's Theological Method." In *A Companion to Bonaventure,* edited by Jay Hammond and Wayne Hellmann, 81–120. Leiden: Brill, 2014.

Lang, Albert. *Die Loci Theologici des Melchior Cano und die Methode des Dogmatischen Beweises: Ein Beitrag zur theologischen Methodologie und ihrer Geschichte.* Müchener Studien zur Historischen Theologie 6. Munich: Kösel and Pustet, 1925.

Laumakis, John. "The Voluntarism of William of Auvergne and Some Evidence to the Contrary." *Modern Schoolman* 76 (1999): 303–12.

Lavaud, M.-Benoît. "Saint Thomas et la Causalité Physique Instrumentale de la sainte humanité et des sacrements." *Revue Thomiste* 32 (1927): 292–316.

Leclercq, Jean. *The Love of Learning and the Desire for God: A Study in Monastic Culture.* Translated by Catherine Misrahi. New York: Fordham University Press, 1974.

Lécuyer, Joseph. "La causalité efficiente des mystères du Christ selon saint Thomas." *Doctor comunis* 6 (1953): 91–120.

Leeming, Bernard. "Recent Trends in Sacramental Theology." *The Irish Theological Quarterly* 23 (1956): 195–217.

———. *Principles of Sacramental Theology.* Westminster, Md.: Newman, 1963.

Lennerz, H. *De Sacramentis Novae Legis in Genere.* Editio secunda. Rome: Typis Pontificiae Universitatis Gregorianae, 1939.

Levi, Anthony. *Renaissance and Reformation: The Intellectual Genesis.* New Haven, Conn.: Yale University Press, 2002.

Lewis, Charlton, and Charles Short, eds. *A New Latin Dictionary.* New York: 1981.

Lexikon für Theologie und Kirche. 2nd ed. Edited by Karl Rahner and Josef Höfer. Freiburg: Heerder, 1957–68.

Lexikon für Theologie und Kirche. 3rd ed. Edited by Walter Kasper. Freiburg: Herder, 1993–2001.

Liddell, Henry George, and Robert Scott, eds. *A Greek-English Lexicon*. 9th ed. with revised supplement. Oxford: Clarendon, 1996.

Lohr, Charles. "Medieval Latin Aristotle Commentaries, Authors: Robertus-Wilgelmus." *Traditio* 29 (1973): 93–198.

Lombard, Peter. *Sententiae in IV libris distinctae*. 3rd ed. 4 vols. Rome: ad Claras Aquas, 1971–81.

Long, Steven A. "Obediential Potency, Human Knowledge, and the Natural Desire for God." *International Philosophical Quarterly* 37, no. 1, issue 145 (1997): 45–63.

———. "On the Possibility of a Purely Natural End for Man." *The Thomist* 64 (2000): 211–37.

———. *Natura Pura: On the Recovery of Nature in the Doctrine of Grace*. New York: Fordham University Press, 2010.

Lynch, Killian. "The Quaestio de Sacramentis in Genere Attributed to Alexander of Hales." *Franciscan Studies* 11 (1951): 74–95.

———. "Texts Illustrating the Causality of the Sacraments from William of Melitona, *Assisi Bibl. Comm.* 182, and *Brussels Bibl. Royale* 1542." *Franciscan Studies* 17 (1957): 238–72.

Lynch, Reginald. "Domingo Bañez on Moral and Physical Causality: Christic Merit and Sacramental Realism." *Angelicum* 91, no. 1 (2014): 105–26.

———. "Cajetan's Harp: Sacraments and the Life of Grace in Light of Perfective Instrumentality," *The Thomist* 78, no. 1 (2014): 65–106.

———. "The Sacraments as Causes of Sanctification." *Nova et Vetera* (English) 12, no. 3 (Summer 2014): 791–836.

MacDonald, Allan J. *Berengar and the Reform of Sacramental Doctrine*. Merrick, N.Y.: Richwood, 1977.

Mack, Peter. *Renaissance Argument: Valla and Agricola in the Traditions of Rhetoric and Dialectic*. Leiden: Brill, 1993

———, ed. *Renaissance Rhetoric*. New York: St. Martin's, 1994.

———. *A History of Renaissance Rhetoric: 1380–1620*. New York: Oxford University Press, 2011.

Maltha, A. H. "De Causalitate intentionali Sacramentorum animadversiones quaedam." *Angelicum* 15 (1938): 337–66.

Mandonnet, Pierre. "Cano, Melchior." In *Dictionnaire de Théologie Catholique*, vol. 2. Paris: Librairie Letouzey et Ané, 1932.

Martos, Joseph. *Doors to the Sacred: A Historical Introduction to Sacraments in the Catholic Church*. Garden City, N.Y.: Doubleday, 1982.

Masterson, Robert R. "Sacramental Graces: Modes of Sanctifying Grace." *The Thomist* 18 (1955): 311–72.

Mazzeo, Joseph A. "Universal Analogy and the Culture of the Renaissance." *Journal of the History of Ideas* 15 (April, 1954): 299–304

McAuliffe, Clarence. *Sacramental Theology: a Textbook for Advanced Students*. St. Louis: Herder, 1958.

———. *De Sacramentis in Genere*. St. Louis: Herder, 1960.

McCord Adams, Marilyn. "Powerless Causes: The Case of Sacramental Causality." In *Thinking about Causes: From Greek Philosophy to Modern Physics*, edited by Peter Machamer and Gereon Wolters, 47–76. Pittsburgh: University of Pittsburgh Press, 2007.

———. "Essential Orders and Sacramental Causality." In *Proceedings of the Quadruple Congress on John Duns Scotus*, edited by Mary Beth Ingham and Oleg Bychov, Part 1: 191–205. St. Bonaventure, N.Y.: Franciscan Institute Publications, 2010.

McManamon, John. *The Text and Contexts of Ignatius of Loyola's "Autobiography."* New York: Fordham University Press, 2013.

McShane, Philip. "On the Causality of the Sacraments." *Theological Studies* 24 (1963): 423–36.

Meehan, Francis. *Efficient Causality in Aristotle and St. Thomas*. Washington, D.C.: The Catholic University of America Press, 1940.

Migne, J.-P., ed. *Patrologia Latina*. Paris: 1844–64.

Miyakawa, Toshiyuki. "The Ecclesial Meaning of the Res et Sacramentum: the Sevenfold Cultic Status in the Visible Church as the Effect of the Sacraments." *The Thomist* 31 (1967): 381–444.

Monfasani, John. "Lorenzo Valla and Rudolph Agricola." *Journal of the History of Philosophy* 28, no. 2 (1990): 181–200.

Moss, Jean Dietz, and William Wallace. *Rhetoric and Dialectic in the Time of Galileo*. Washington, D.C.: The Catholic University of America Press, 2003.

Murray, Campion. "The Composition of the Sacraments according to the 'Summa De Sacramentis' and the 'Commentarium in IV Sententiarium' of St. Albert the Great." *Franciscan Studies* 16, no. 3 (1956): 177–201.

Nauta, Lodi. "From Universals to Topics: The Realism of Rudolph Agricola, with an Edition of His Reply to a Critic." *Vivarium* 50 (2012): 190–224.

New American Bible. Rev. ed.. Charlotte, N.C.: St. Benedict Press, 2011.

New Catholic Encyclopedia. 1st ed. Washington, D.C.: The Catholic University of America, 1960–67.

New Catholic Encyclopedia. 2nd ed. Edited by Thomas Carson. Washington, D.C., 2002.

Newman, Andrew. "Jus Divinum and the Sacrament of Penance in Two Tridentine Theologians: Melchior Cano and Ruard Tapper." Doct. diss., The Catholic University of America, 1969.

The New Oxford Annotated Bible with Apocrypha. 3rd ed. New York: Oxford University Press, 2001.

Nielsen, Lauge Olaf. "Signification, Likeness and Causality: The Sacraments as Signs by Divine Imposition in John Duns Scotus, Durand of St. Pourcain, and Peter Auriol." In *Vestigia, Imagines, Verba: Semiotics and Logic in Medieval Theological Texts (XIIth–XIVth Century)*, edited by Constantino Marmo, 223–53. Turnhout: Brepols, 1997.

Noone, Timothy. "The Originality of St. Thomas's Position on the Philosophers and Creation." *The Thomist* 60, no. 2 (1996): 275–300.

Noreña, Carlos. *Studies in Spanish Renaissance Thought.* The Hague: Martinus Nijhoff, 1975.

Nutt, Roger. "On Analogy, the Incarnation, and the Sacraments of the Church: Consideration from the *Tertia pars of the Summa theologiae.*" *Nova et Vetera* (English) 12, no. 3 (2014): 1000–1004.

O'Callaghan, Denis, ed. *Sacraments: the Gestures of Christ.* New York: Sheed and Ward, 1964.

O'Malley, John. *The First Jesuits.* Cambridge, Mass.: Harvard University Press, 1993.

O'Neill, Coleman. "The Instrumentality of the Sacramental Character: An Interpretation of *Summa Theologiae,* III, q. 63, a. 2." *Irish Theological Quarterly* 25 (1958): 262–68.

———. "The Role of the Recipient and Sacramental Signification." *The Thomist* 21 (1958): 257–301, 508–41.

———. "The Mysteries of Christ and the Sacraments." *The Thomist* 25 (1962): 1–53.

———. *Meeting Christ in the Sacraments.* Rev. ed. New York: Alba House, 1991.

———. *Sacramental Realism: A General Theory of the Sacraments.* Princeton, N.J.: Scepter Publishers, 1998.

Ong, Walter. *Ramus: Method and the Decay of Dialogue.* Cambridge, Mass.: Harvard University Press, 1983.

Osborne, Thomas. *Human Action in Thomas Aquinas, John Duns Scotus and William of Ockham.* Washington, D.C.: The Catholic University of America Press, 2014.

Ott, Ludwig. *Fundamentals of Catholic Dogma.* Edited by James Canon Bastible. Translated by Patrick Lynch. Cork, Ireland: Mercier, 1958.

Pinckaers, Servais. *The Sources of Christian Ethics.* 3rd ed. Tranlated by Sr. Mary Thomas Noble, OP. Washington, D.C.: The Catholic University of America Press, 1995.

Plato. *Timaeus.* Translated by Donald J. Zeyl. In *Plato: Complete Works,* edited by John M. Cooper and D. S. Hutchinson. Indianapolis: Hackett, 1997.

Pourrat, P. *Theology of the Sacraments: A Study in Positive Theology.* Authorized translation from the French edition. 4th ed. St. Louis: Herder, 1930.

Pozzo, Riccardo, ed. *The Impact of Aristotelianism on Modern Philosophy.* Studies in Philosophy and the History of Philosophy 39. Washington, D.C.: The Catholic University of America Press, 2004.

Principe, Walter. *Hugh of Saint-Cher's Theology of the Hypostatic Union.* The Theology of the Hypostatic Union in the Early Thirteenth Century Series 3. Toronto: Pontifical Institute of Mediaeval Studies, 1970.

Ratzinger, Joseph. *The Theology of History in St. Bonaventure.* Translated by Zachary Hayes. Chicago: Franciscan Herald Press, 1989.

Redmond, R. P. *Berengar and the Development of Eucharistic Doctrine: Extract from a Thesis Presented for the Doctorate in the Faculty of Theology at the Pontifical Gregorian University, Rome.* Newcastle: Heber Tower, 1934.

Reynolds, Philip L. "Efficient Causality and Instrumentality in Thomas Aquinas' Theology of the Sacraments." In *Essays in Medieval Philosophy and Theology in Memory of Walter H. Principe, O.S.B.,* edited by James R. Ginther and Carl N. Still, 67–84. Burlington, Vt.: Ashgate, 2005.

Riches, Aaron. "Christology and duplex hominis beatitudo-Resketching the Supernatural Again." *International Journal of Systematic Theology* 14 (January 2012): 44–69.

Roensch, Frederick. *Early Thomistic School.* Dubuque, Iowa: Priory, 1964.

Rogers, Elizabeth Frances. "Peter Lombard and the Sacramental System." PhD. Diss., Columbia University, 1917.

Rosemann, Philipp W. *Peter Lombard.* New York: Oxford University Press, 2004.

―――. *The Story of a Great Medieval Book: Peter Lombard's Sentences.* Rethinking the Middle Ages 2. Edited by Paul Edward Dutton and John Shinners. Ontario: Broadview, 2007.

Rosier-Catach, Irène. *La Parole Efficace: Signe, Rituel, Sacré.* Paris: Éditions du seuil, 2004.

―――. "Signes sacramentels et signes magiques: Guillaume d'Auvergne et la théorie du pacte." In *Autour de Guillaume d'Auvergne (1249),* edited by Nicole Bériou and Franco, 93–116. Morenzoni. Turnhout, Belgium: Brepols, 2005.

Rover, Dominic. "The Sacramental Efficacy of the Act of Preaching." *Proceedings of the Catholic Theological Society of America (CTSA)* (1962): 241–47.

Rummel, Erika. *Biblical Humanism and Scholasticism in the Age of Erasmus.* Leiden: Brill, 2008.

Sandys, John Edwin. *A History of Classical Scholarship: From the Revival of Learning to the End of the Eighteenth Century in Italy, France, England and the Netherlands.* New York: Cambridge University Press, 2011.

Schenk, Richard. ed. *Robert Kilwardby, Questiones in Librum Quartum Sententiarum.* Bayerische Akademie der Wissenschaften 17. Munich: C. H. Beck, 1993.

―――. *Verum Sacrificium as the Fullness and Limit of Eucharistic Sacrifice in the Sacramental Theology of Thomas Aquinas: Historical Context and Current Significance.* In *Resourcement Thomism: Sacred Doctrine, the Sacraments, and the Moral Life,* edited by Reinhard Hütter and Matthew Levering, 136–49. Washington, D.C.: The Catholic University of America Press, 2010.

Schillebeeckx, Edward. *De Sacramentele Heilseconomie: Theologische Bezinning op S. Thomas' Sacramentenleer in het Light van de Traditie en van de Hedendaagse Sacramentsproblematiek.* Antwerp: H. Nelissen Bilthoven, 1952.

―――. *The Eucharist.* Translated by N. D. Smith. New York: Sheed and Ward, 1968.

————, ed. *The Sacraments in General: A New Perspective.* Vol. 31 of *Concilium: Theology in an Age of Renewal.* Edited by Edward Schillebeeckx and Boniface Willems. New York: Paulist Press, 1968.

————. *Christ the Sacrament of the Encounter with God.* Translated by Paul Barrett. Franklin, Wis.: Sheed and Ward, 1999.

————. *L'économie Sacramentelle du Salut.* Edited by Benoît-Dominique de la Soujeole and Benedikt Mohelnik. Translated by Yvon van der Have. Studia Friburgensia 95. Fribourg, Switzerland: Academic Press Fribourg, 2004.

Schleck, Charles A. "St. Thomas on the Nature of Sacramental Grace." *The Thomist* 18 (1955): 1–30, 242–78.

Schmitt, Charles. *Aristotle and the Renaissance.* Cambridge, Mass.: Harvard University Press, 1983.

Schmitt, Charles B., and Quentin Skinner, eds. *The Cambridge History of Renaissance Philosophy.* New York: Cambridge University Press, 1988.

Shea, George. "A Survey of the Theology of Sacramental Grace," *Proceedings of the CTSA* (1953): 81–130.

Smalley, Beryl. *The Study of the Bible in the Middle Ages.* 3rd ed. Notre Dame, Ind.: University of Notre Dame Press, 1978.

Sources chrétiennes. Paris: Éditions du Cerf, 1942–.

Spezzano, Daria. *The Glory of God's Grace: Deification according to St. Thomas Aquinas.* Ave Maria, Fla.: Sapientia Press, 2015.

Suarez, Francisco. *Opera Omnia, Commentaria ac Disputationes in Tertiam Partem D. Thomae, de Sacramentis in Genere, de Baptismo, de Confirmatione, de Eucharistia usque ad Quaestionem LXXIV.* Edited by M. André, and Charles Berton. Paris: Vivés, 1877.

Sylwanowicz, Michael. *Contingent Causality and the Foundations of Duns Scotus' Metaphysics.* New York: Brill, 1996.

Tappeiner, Daniel A. "Sacramental Causality in Aquinas and Rahner: Some Critical Thoughts." *Scottish Journal of Theology* 28 (1975): 243–57.

Teske, Roland. *Studies in the Philosophy of William of Auvergne.* Marquette Studies in Philosophy 51. Milwaukee, Wis.: Marquette University Press, 2006.

Torrell, Jean-Pierre. "La causalité salvifique de la résurrection du Christ selon saint Thomas." *Revue Thomiste* 96 (1996): 179–208.

————. *Saint Thomas Aquinas.* Vol. 1, *The Person and His Work.* Translated by Robert Royal. Washington, D.C.: The Catholic University of America Press, 1996.

————. *Saint Thomas Aquinas.* Vol. 2, *Spiritual Master.* Translated by Robert Royal. Vol. 2 Washington, D.C.: The Catholic University of America Press, 2003.

Tschipke, Theophil. *Die Menschheit Christi als Heilsorgan der Gottheit: Unter Besonderer Berücksichtigung der Lehre des Heiligen Thomas von Aquin.* Freiburger Theologische Studien 55. Freiburg im Breisgau: Herder, 1940.

Tuyaerts, M. M. "Utrum S. Thomas Causalitatem Sacramentorum Respectu Gratiae Mere Dispositivam Umquam Docuerit." *Angelicum 8* (1931): 149–86.

Van Den Eynde, Damien. "Stephen Langton and Hugh of St. Cher on the Causality of the Sacraments." *Franciscan Studies* 11 (1951): 141–55.

Van Nieuwenhove, Rik, and Joseph Wawrykow, eds. *The Theology of Thomas Aquinas.* Notre Dame, Ind: University of Notre Dame Press, 2005.

Van Steenberghen, Fernand. *Aristotle in the West: The Origins of Latin Aristotelianism.* 2nd ed. Translated by Leonard Johnston. Louvain: Nauwelaerts, 1970.

Vatican Council II. *Lumen Gentium.* November 21, 1964.

Vorgrimler, Herbert. *Sacramental Theology.* Translated by Linda M. Maloney. Collegeville, Minn.: Liturgical Press, 1992.

Wallace, William. *The Elements of Philosophy: A Compendium for Philosophers and Theologians.* New York: Alba House, 2014.

Wawrykow, Joseph. *God's Grace and Human Action: Merit in the Theology of Thomas Aquinas.* Notre Dame, Ind.: University of Notre Dame Press, 1995.

Weinandy, Thomas G. *The Human Acts of Christ and the Acts that are the Sacraments.* In *Resourcement Thomism: Sacred Doctrine, the Sacraments, and the Moral Life,* edited by. Reinhard Hütter and Matthew Levering, 150–68. Washington, D.C.: The Catholic University of America Press, 2010.

Weisweiler, Heinrich. *Die Wirksamkeit der Sacramente nach Hugo von St. Viktor.* Freiburg: Herder, 1932.

Wicks, Jared. "A Note on 'Neo-Scholastic' Manuals of Theological Instruction, 1900–1960." *Josephinum* 18, no. 1 (2011): 240–46.

William of Auvergne. *De Trinitate: An Edition of the Latin Text.* Edited, with an introduction, by Bruno Switalski. Studies and Texts Series 34. Toronto: Pontifical Institute of Mediaeval Studies, 1976.

———. *The Trinity, or The First Principle.* Introduction by Roland Teske. Translated by Roland Teske and Francis Wade. Milwaukee, Wis.: Marquette University Press, 1989.

William of Auxerre. *Summa Aurea.* Edited by Jean Ribaillier. Spicilegium Bonaventurianum XIX. Rome: ad Claras Aquas, 1985.

Zahnd, Ueli. *Wirksame Zeichen? Sakramentenlehre und Semiotik in der Scholastik des ausgehenden Mittelalters.* Tübingen: Mohr Siebeck, 2014.

Index